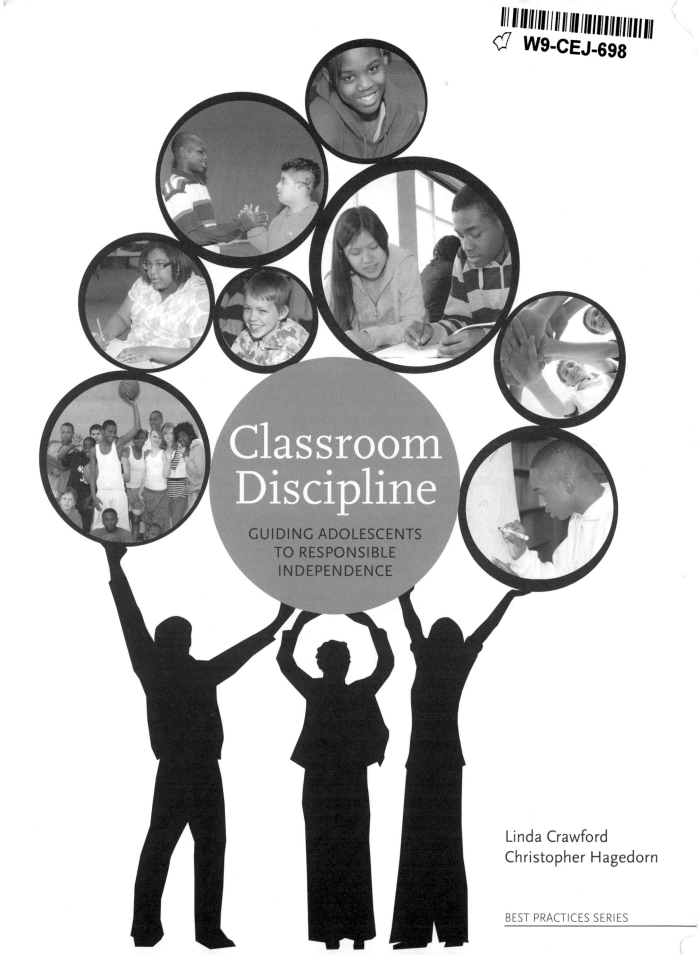

Classroom Discipline

GUIDING ADOLESCENTS TO RESPONSIBLE INDEPENDENCE

Linda Crawford
Christopher Hagedorn

BEST PRACTICES SERIES

ISBN 978-0-938541-13-4
Library of Congress Control Number 2009908960

Cover and book design by Heidi Neilson
Photographs by Jennifer Bush, with contributions from Scott Tyink and Jo Devlin

All net proceeds from the sale of *Classroom Discipline: Guiding Adolescents to Responsible Independence* support the work of The Origins Program, a nonprofit educational organization whose mission is to promote an equitable and humane multicultural society through quality education for all.

The stories in this book are all based on real events in classrooms. Names and many identifying characteristics of students and situations have been changed to protect the privacy of students.

Worldwide Web sites mentioned as citations and/or sources for further information may have changed or terminated since this book was published.

ORIGINS
DEVELOPMENTAL DESIGNS®
The Origins Program
3805 Grand Avenue South
Minneapolis, Minnesota 55409 USA

800-543-8715
www.originsonline.org

19 18 17 16 15   7 6 5 4 3

ACKNOWLEDGMENTS

We are grateful to the educators and students who provided invaluable support, including contributing classroom stories, reviewing early manuscripts, and inviting us in with our cameras. Your insights and collaboration bring eloquence, credibility, and the strong spirit of adolescence to the book.

Anne Andersen, St. Paul MN

Nick Bacigalupi, Cambridge MA

Mark Carbone, Richmond VT

Cathy Ann Chapman, Greenfield MA

Matthew Christen, LaCrosse WI

Keith Edmonds, Harrisburg PA

Jennifer Erickson, Tabernacle NJ

Sharon Greaves, Minneapolis MN

Steve Hasti, Minneapolis MN

Ana Knapp, Minneapolis MN

Kristen Konop, St. Paul MN

Donna Largent, Hanover NH

Kandace Logan, St. Paul MN

Janet Nelson, Red Lake MN

Diana O'Donnell, Wheeling IL

Jill Romans, St. Paul MN

Allison Rubin, Minneapolis MN

Pete Sampson, Minneapolis MN

Sydney Smith, St. Louis Park MN

Kenyon Tobias, New York NY

Dexter Yee Yick, Minneapolis MN

7th grade teaching team, Bemidji MN: Paula Maki, Doug Johnson, Matt Menne, Mark Studer

Origins thanks our team of educators and editors who make quality and clarity possible in our books:

Elizabeth Crawford, for her amazing capacity to hold the entire book in her head through myriad revisions

Terrance Kwame-Ross, for his on-the-spot capacity for depth and care when called on to true content to research and classroom experience

Brian Greening, for his dogged pursuit of accurate references, valuable perspective as a manuscript reader, and willingness to support the book in any way needed

Jo Devlin, for rigorously minding the details of language and the core ideas of our work

Scott Tyink, for introducing us to teachers far and wide and gathering their stories, and for sharing his knowledge of educational practice

Heidi Neilson, for her patience and inventive design which brought energy and order to our unruly manuscripts.

Additional Acknowledgments

I thank the staffs of Annunciation School, Greenfield Hebrew Academy of Atlanta, Kenneth Olsen Middle School, The Paul Cuffey School, Red Lake High School, and many others, for the privilege of serving you as a consultant, and the staffs of Lincoln Middle School, Colegio Americano, and Clara Barton Open School for the privilege of teaching with you for 16 years. And I thank my family, Sarah, Greta, Harry, Vivian, and Grace, for everything.

—Christopher Hagedorn

I acknowledge the perseverance of the educators who work every day to help adolescents learn. I'm especially grateful to my Origins colleagues who tirelessly work to true up our words to our lived lives in the classroom.

—Linda Crawford

TABLE OF CONTENTS

Introducing Responsible Independence

In my second year of teaching, I had two boys who were well-behaved in my class when I was teaching, but when I had a substitute, they made big trouble. They couldn't seem to control themselves with a guest teacher. I decided that the next time I needed a substitute I would arrange for them to attend class in a colleague's room during the time they were supposed to be in my class. That worked, and I got a good report from my colleague and from the substitute when I returned to school. I planned to do the same thing the next time I had to miss a day.

In a conversation with my mother, I told her about how I had solved the problem I'd been having with these two boys. "Well," she said, "I think before you send them off again you should ask yourself: Where are you headed with these children?" I thought about her question, and I realized that what I really wanted was not just to avoid a problem for me, but for them to grow in social skills so they could follow our agreements and use their self-controls every day, no matter who the teacher was.

The next day, I began to prepare them for a good day every day, including the ones when I wasn't there. I expressed my belief that they could be successful on their own, and promised I would show them how.

The next time I needed a substitute, I gave them the chance to stay in my room and manage themselves, and they handled it just fine. Ever since, the question, "Where am I headed with this student?" has become a touchstone for me. The answer always leads to growth for my students and for me.

—Middle level teacher, St. Paul MN

Where Are We Headed? Responsible Independence

This book is about student growth. It describes how to build a classroom climate in which students become responsibly independent because adults guide them incrementally toward the emotional, social, and academic skills necessary for successful self-management.

Being both independent and responsible benefits students and everyone around them. Independence means they are able to learn without constant assistance and to work productively without prodding. Responsibility means they take learning seriously and interact with others in ways that support learning. Nobody makes it alone in school. Misbehavior disrupts everyone, and a friendly, safe classroom empowers everyone. The time we invest in teaching adolescents the social/emotional skills of self-management pays off in a healthy school climate, the best possible setting for academic excellence.

What motivates students to follow the rules?

Adolescents may be motivated to behave in a consistently responsible way for a variety of reasons. In our approach, within the goal of responsible independence lies a deeper aim: building in our students the capacity to relate their behavior to the good of all, to become aware that everyone wins when everyone behaves responsibly. Many middle level students, even some who behave well, have yet to develop the desire to follow their school rules *because they want to support the community*. Getting to that level takes time and a great deal of guidance from adults determined that the adolescents in their care will develop responsible behavior that is increasingly motivated by their desire that others, not just they, do well.

Many theorists have addressed the issue of motivation. John Dewey, the 20th-century philosopher, psychologist, and educator, saw learning how to effectively participate in a democracy as the chief purpose of schooling. Without guidance, he said, young people would operate entirely out of convenience. Leaders dedicated to the common good would not emerge, and the electorate would not be wise enough to make good choices for society. Dewey insisted that we must teach our youth to think well and with a social spirit for our country to thrive.

In so far as the school represents, in its own spirit, a genuine community life; in so far as what are called school discipline, government, order, etc., are the expressions of this inherent social spirit... the school is organized on an ethical basis. (Dewey 1909, 43-44)

According to Lawrence Kohlberg's Six Stages of Moral Development, to operate out of universal principles of conscience, a commitment to others that supersedes even our own self-interest, requires the highest level of moral development.

Kohlberg's work on moral thinking in children up to age 16 resulted in a theory of stages of moral development. The six stages show a movement toward altruism:

Stage 1. Obedience and Punishment (Can I get away with it?)
Stage 2. Self-interest (What's best for me?)
Stage 3. Interpersonal Relationships (I wouldn't do that to my friend or my mother)
Stage 4. Maintaining the Social Order (It's against the law)
Stage 5. Maintaining Individual Rights (Everyone has inalienable rights)
Stage 6. Universal Principles (It's the right and just thing to do) (Kohlberg 1981)

In studying the means by which young people in a democracy develop social consciousness, Sheldon Berman synthesizes the research in fields such as moral and social development, political socialization, and citizenship education. He posits a theoretical framework for educators using social consciousness and social responsibility as its central organizing constructs.

This new framework treats the development of one's relationship with the political and social world and one's personal investment in the well-being of others and the planet as a central concern. (Berman 1997, 9)

The goal of making choices in the context of social responsibility is a moving target for both youth and adults. We move toward it throughout our lives. Effective behavior management is rife with opportunities to initiate and facilitate the journey.

Restorative Justice

Conversely, autocratic, punitive, or chaotic behavior management can slow or damage the process.

We do not expect that adolescent students in our care will become entirely altruistic! Our intention is to be an <u>influence in the direction of consideration for others</u> as well as themselves. We seek to engage students in an ongoing conversation about creating and living by rules, a conversation designed to benefit everyone.

Michelle did well in school and had lots of friends. Because she was especially good at helping other kids settle arguments, she became one of our best peer mediators. But when Michelle herself broke a rule or got into a disagreement with someone, she frequently told the story of what happened in a confusing way that didn't fit the facts. People gave her the benefit of the doubt because she was such a nice kid and came from a large family that supported school projects and events enthusiastically.

One day Michelle had taken school equipment outside when she was told not to. She kept insisting that nobody had told her, even though she and I knew that wasn't true. Finally I said to her, "Michelle, you are lying." Her face crumpled. "I know. I couldn't help it—it just came out." Through tears she asked, "What's the matter with me? I don't know why I lie. I can't stop! I do it at home, too. I'm the only one in my family who does it—my brothers get into trouble, but they admit what they did."

Michelle and I had a conversation about habits and conscious choices, and about the kind of person she wanted to be. Together, we made a plan for her to break her bad habit. We practiced, and I promised to check in with her now and then. By the end of the year, Michelle was doing well. Occasionally she would slip into a lie, but she soon repaired the damage by admitting the truth. Most of the time she told the truth in the first place.

—Principal, Northfield MN

Michelle was operating at a <u>level of social consciousness lower than her own standards</u> for being a good person. That's what the tears were about, and that's why she worked so hard to transform her bad habit. She moved from lying because she could get away with it to telling the truth because her family was honest and she didn't want to be the one who lied. She didn't want her brothers and her parents to think badly of her, or others to think badly of her family because of her behavior. Kohlberg would describe her growth as a move from Stage 1 to Stage 3. Dewey might say that she had begun to make decisions based on other than temporary convenience, moving from thinking only of herself to considering the effect of her behavior upon others. Educator-author Ruth Charney would say that she was developing "the capacity to care for oneself, for others, and for the world." (Charney 2002, 15)

What does it mean to be independent?

To be independent is to feel the power of freedom, to feel that you can navigate through life without others constantly propping you up or directing you. Adolescents, on the cusp of adulthood, crave that freedom. They've had enough of childhood dependency, and they have muscles to flex!

We need them to be able to stand alone in order to learn well. They have assignments to monitor, research to do, deadlines to meet, homework, test preparation, and projects to make to show what they know. The trick is to give them enough freedom to expand and develop, but not so much that they fail. Piece by piece, we need to share our power with them. Eventually, they will stand on their own in life, and the best way to help them get there is to have them take their early steps under the supervision of caring adults who can help them use their power wisely.

What does it mean to be responsible?

Responsible students show their capacity to handle independence with self-control, good judgment, reasoning, and focus. We give them projects to work on independently, and they have more opportunities to make decisions and explore because we know they can handle them. Becoming a responsible person has great value to our students. It provides them:

> The capacity to think long-term, beyond the impulse of the moment, so they can achieve their goals: *I can delay gratification for a long-term, more important benefit.*

> The ability to consider what is good for the group as well as for themselves: *I can learn better in an orderly setting with others learning all around me.*

Responsible independence requires us to go beyond compliance to social competence

There are basically two ways to build in young people behavior that respects the rules of a group. One is to demand compliance—make clear rules, and then enforce them with punishments for those who break them and rewards for those who comply. But students who follow rules out of fear of punishment can hardly be trusted with a lot of independence if their rule-abiding behavior occurs only when they think they might be watched and reported. If we want students to think for themselves and act for the good of all, then we can't settle for mere compliance with the rules.

[R]esearch revealed that not only tangible rewards but also threats, deadlines, directives, pressured evaluations, and imposed goals diminish intrinsic motivation because, like tangible rewards, they conduce toward an external perceived locus of causality. In contrast, choice, acknowledgment of feelings, and opportunities for self-direction were found to enhance intrinsic motivation because they allow people a greater feeling of autonomy. (Ryan and Deci 2000, 70)

The other way to foster respectful behavior is through mentorship, guiding students step by wobbly step to develop the habit of caring for others as well as themselves, the internally-based motivation to do so, and the thinking skills to figure out how. The result is approval not only from adults, but from themselves.

The establishment of self-approval is the strongest form of control. When thought of in this manner, discipline ceases to be a restriction. As teachers, we should no longer think of discipline in terms of an authority figure who rules with an iron fist. We need to think of discipline in terms of a leader who permits freedom within certain limits. (Dreikurs 1998, 81)

If we train our children to take orders, to do things simply because they are told to, and fail to give them confidence to act and think for themselves, we are putting an almost insurmountable obstacle in the way of ... establishing the truth of democratic ideals. (Dewey 1909, 304)

Responsibility and independence are interwoven in this behavior management approach, so that each nudges the other forward gradually, with the robust and consistent support of the teacher. Most important, the approach provides the tools necessary to guide students toward self-management and to maintain order in a classroom sustained by healthy relationships and fun. We are the bow, they are the arrows; fulfillment is in their successful flight.

How Will We Get There? By Meeting Adolescent Needs

One way or another, adolescents will meet their needs. Our job is to help them do so in ways that support their growth and learning. What are their basic needs? Several psychologists have made lists of them. In this approach, we draw from Rudolf Dreikurs, Abraham Maslow, William Glasser, SEL (social-emotional learning) research, and the work of psychologists Edward Deci and Richard Ryan to create our list of the needs that appear to be especially dominant in adolescents: *relationship, autonomy, competence,* and *fun.*

[I] believe we are genetically programmed to try to satisfy four psychological needs: love and belonging, power, freedom, and fun. All our behavior is always our best choice, at the time we make the choice, to satisfy one or more of these needs. (Glasser 1998, 28)

Ryan and Deci's research examined social conditions that enhance versus undermine intrinsic motivation, self-regulation, and well-being: "The findings have led to the postulate of three innate psychological needs—competence, autonomy, and relatedness—which when satisfied yield enhanced self-motivation and mental health and when thwarted lead to diminished motivation and well-being." (Ryan and Deci 2000, 68)

Adolescents express these four needs in particularly intense ways. Sometimes they know what they're looking for and how to find it: they seek appropriate friendships, have fun, find positive ways of being in control, and are on the lookout for opportunities to share their abilities and talents with their peers. This is partly why teaching them can be a joy.

At other times, though, adolescents are ill-equipped, clumsy, and dangerous to themselves and/or others. Their needs are strong, sometimes confusing, and they struggle to find their way. Theirs can be a meandering, perilous journey, often without destination. This is part of why teaching them can be quite a challenge!

Developmental science shows that there is more impulse than control in the adolescent brain. "The parts of the brain responsible for things like sensation-seeking are getting turned on in big ways around the time of puberty," says Temple University psychologist Laurence Steinberg. "But the parts for exercising judgment are still maturing throughout the course of adolescence. So you've got this time gap between when things impel kids toward taking risks early in adolescence, and when things that allow people to think before they act come online. It's like turning on the engine of a car without a skilled driver at the wheel." (Wallis 2004, 61)

See Appendix A for more research-based information about adolescent social, intellectual, and physical development.

Helping Adolescents Meet their Needs Constructively

Both before things go wrong and after rules are broken, our job is to work with students so their needs are met in such a way that they can achieve sustained, incremental growth toward responsible independence. We promote and support peer community, develop positive mentor-apprentice relationships, explicitly cultivate social skills, teach about behavior limitations, give choices, and build success upon success, one action at a time. In these ways, we guide young people to find ways to satisfy their basic needs constructively.

Citing studies conducted between 1998 and 2001, the Collaborative for Academic, Social, and Emotional Learning (CASEL) reports that learning is possible only when students' social, emotional, and physical needs are met. When those needs are met, students are more likely to succeed in school. (CASEL 2003, 7)

Relationship

As children enter adolescence, peer relationships become more and more the focus of their interest and concern. At their best, these relationships foster a sense of connection and belonging and can inspire students to grow. But in the process of seeking relationship, some may feel terribly lonely because of a lack of social skills. Cliques develop in middle level grades and segment the student body. Students who lack social capital may become loners, and some may seek out destructive relationships.

Meeting the need

We can't address all the causes of adolescent relationship angst, but we can structure into daily teaching the capacity to develop self-knowledge, healthy peer connections, and meaningful teacher-student relationships. We can invite students to become known by sharing about themselves; we can orchestrate gatherings with relationship-building in mind; we can engage in individual and group conversations, and teach with activities that help everyone get to know one another, and we can build opportunities into learning for positive social interaction and fun.

We can prepare students to understand and follow the rules, and when rules are broken, we can maintain positive relationships through redirections that are fair and consistent, and grant dignity to all, even when they break rules. When a young person begins to feel the power of being able to repair damage without the sting of punishment or rejection, she can continue to trust that the relationship behind the redirection is positive. Students perform at their best socially and academically in an atmosphere of trust. (See Chapter 3 for more on the importance of building trust in relationships.)

In the area of social-emotional development, young adolescents

- Have a strong need to belong to a group, with approval of peers becoming as important as adult approval, and on some matters even more important.
- In their search for group membership, may experience significant embarrassment, ridicule, or rejection from those in other cliques from which they are excluded. (NMSA 2003, 49)

Autonomy

When students seek autonomy, their need for control can manifest itself in power struggles. They are dependent on parents and other adults, but they want to make their own decisions. (NMSA 2003, 49) Their growing ability to think abstractly can spur a determination to understand and participate in decision-making. They may assert their independence in ways that put them at risk when they lack the maturity to guide themselves safely. At worst, they separate into disconnected rebels, or start competing against teachers or each other for supremacy.

Meeting the need

At its best, the urge for autonomy channels into independent accomplishment and peer leadership. We can watch for opportunities to put students in charge of themselves, and sometimes others, so they get their need for autonomy met appropriately. We can give them opportunities to lead, and we can teach them how to manage their own behavior, including being responsible to fix problems. We can make our redirections constructive, and use them to advance self-control and minimize future rule-breaking. We can teach students to reflect on their behavior and talk with them about the ways we will support them so they grow toward following the rules for reasons that are increasingly their own.

We must steadily work toward increased student autonomy. If we rule our classrooms as autocrats who are the deciders and enforcers of everything, doling out punishments and rewards using standards that we alone decide, at best we will get short-term, fear-based compliance from students who are intimidated, angry, or biding their time to seek revenge, depending upon their personalities.

Many students under autocratic teacher rule fail to develop a belief in their capacity to control their own behavior. Deci's research found that teachers most effectively supported student autonomy when they shared their authority and allowed students to play a role in meaningful decision-making. (Deci 1995, 144) They certainly don't get any training in it if we hold onto the reins tightly at all times. And, as with any workers, they are unlikely to produce creative, highest quality work in an atmosphere that suggests they are powerless.

On the other hand, if we give away too much power too fast, the classroom can become dominated by disruptive peers. Students don't feel safe in an unpredictable environment, and little work of quality is accomplished.

The ideal is an approach in which power is shared incrementally, and students are given as much responsibility as they can handle. What to allow shifts and changes as students develop their social and academic competencies in the two-steps-forward-one-step-back manner characteristic of young adolescents testing and experimenting.

Competence

Young adolescents observe the strengths of adults. They frequently evaluate their own competencies, and are prone to self-criticize. Compared to adults or peers, they may perceive themselves as inadequate physically, socially, and/or intellectually, and prematurely close doors to exploring interests. (NMSA 2003, 46) Discouragement can feed a sense of helplessness or distaste for the school environment in which they keep coming up short. When they have talents, they may choose to share them at the wrong time, pounding rhythms on their desks while others try to concentrate, or making long passes down the hallway. They may also show their competencies constructively through peer-to-peer help or by leading parts of a class meeting or teaching a skill or game.

Meeting the need

What can we do to build the skills and confidence we wish our students to have? Make sure they experience successes so they feel and become more and more competent. Assume nothing, and continually show them examples of the right way to behave. Provide opportunities to practice routines and procedures. Keep paying attention— there are no teacher vacations inside a middle level classroom! Every unaddressed act of rule-breaking, no matter how small, is likely to escalate.

Give students daily, frequent opportunities to think about what and how they have done, what they have said, and how they might have affected others. Teach them to reflect, so they can learn from their actions. Create personal and larger world connections to what they are learning to satisfy their growing intellectual curiosity about their place in the world. Help them develop the powerful cognitive skill of taking on the perspective of another, through interesting conversations that provide opportunities to think from more than one point of view.

In his review of the research, Sheldon Berman identifies providing students with opportunities to consider the needs, thoughts, feelings, and motivations of others as important to the development of social responsibility: "Perspective-taking and perspective-taking dialogue are the linchpins in social, moral, and political development. They are also vital to the effective handling of social, moral, and political conflict. In fact, it is the combination of perspective-taking and conflict that most studies point to as the moving forces in development." (Berman 1997, 98)

We can talk to students with respect, even when they have messed up, and redirect their behavior so they learn how to live within the rules, with consideration for themselves and others. The more they learn, the more we can loosen the reins, and the greater the sense of competence and autonomy our students will feel and exhibit in their journey toward self-management and academic success.

Fun

Adolescents love to play and laugh and move; their developing bodies crave the stimulation and excitement of good times. However, seeking fun, students might want to pass notes, engage in horseplay, chat, or tease. Although what students might do to amuse themselves can interfere with the learning process, their love of fun can also spark their learning, both social and academic.

Meeting the need

It is both our pleasure and our responsibility to make sure our students get their need for fun fulfilled constructively in academic and social contexts, or they will find pleasures that interfere with learning. For one thing, we have to let them move. Being confined to chairs and desks is challenging and could be physically painful. Let them move and play a bit—they live for light moments, and a school day of unmitigated seriousness is practically unbearable for them. And as an added bonus, mixing and matching teams in unlikely ways in the context of playful activities helps discourage exclusion and cliques.

In the area of physical development, young adolescents
- Need to release energy, often resulting in sudden, apparently meaningless outbursts of activity.
- Experience restlessness and fatigue due to hormonal changes. (NMSA 2003, 44)

Knowing their needs can help us diagnose student problems

Some problem behaviors adolescents exhibit at school can drive teachers right out of the profession. Underneath those behaviors, we can find mistaken attempts to satisfy the four needs we have noted. Identifying what a student is really seeking when he or she breaks the rules can be the beginning of solving the problem. See Appendix F for some examples.

An alternative approach [to creating responsible behavior] begins not with blame and control, but with asking why people are behaving irresponsibly in the first place.... This approach takes the individual's perspective, and focuses on the motivation underlying that behavior. It then addresses the factors that can lead people to behave more responsibly. (Deci 1995, 2)

In the first semester, I used the Take a Break room outside of my classroom 42 times. Asked to reflect on what need they were trying to fulfill when they disrupted the class, 23 students checked on their reflection forms "I wanted to have some fun." Almost as many just wanted to talk or relax. Simply put, fun and relating to others are very important to middle school students, and sometimes these needs can get in the way of learning. What I saw from my little study was that the more I intentionally built into my lessons opportunities for fun, social interaction, and learning in a relaxed environment, the better climate I'd have. It was clear to me that every period of my day—not just advisory/homeroom— needed to have a built-in opportunity for positive fun.

—7th and 8th grade teacher, Minneapolis MN

Scope of the Book

Meeting adolescent needs requires a variety of structures

It is one thing to talk about the importance of social-emotional learning and quite another to provide the means for achieving such growth. A variety of effective practical structures is necessary to help us through the complexities of building responsible, independent learners.

The structures described in this book are based on the *Developmental Designs* approach, integrating social and academic learning for adolescent students. They allow us to teach social skills, establish and uphold rules, and help students solve problems while we maintain good relationships with them. Each structure is shaped to address adolescent developmental needs, and all of the tactics and strategies have been classroom-tested, practiced by middle level educators in the United States and in Canada.

The tools we use to foster order and meaningful learning build social skills at the same time. They include structures for

- establishing relationship
- establishing purposes and goals for being in school
- establishing agreements about rules by which the community is made secure enough for all to achieve their goals
- living our agreements in our daily routines *model*
- engaging students in learning and away from misbehavior
- redirecting rule-breaking that damages the learning climate
- thinking reflectively about actions, social and academic, to maintain a course of constant growth
- problem-solving with chronic rule-breakers

Problem-solving structures address and help prevent chronic rule-breaking in the classroom, but these structures are useful and important for *all* students to guide them toward responsible independence. Throughout the book, we suggest teacher language that cultivates and preserves relationships while it supports the rules that bind the community, to ensure that the container is fit to carry the message we want to send: *I know you and believe in your capacity to grow, and I am committed to helping you correct yourself every time you break our agreements.*

Guidance with rigor and relationship

Our goal in this needs-based approach to behavior management is to use the most rigorous guidance possible with adolescent students while still providing the freedom to explore learning, and to nurture the relationships and fun that make that exploration safe and attractive. We use the components that work best as described in Robert Marzano's meta-analysis of research reports about classroom behavior management (note the percentage of decrease in rule-breaking that each produced):

1. An understanding that healthy relationships are crucial in all phases (28% decrease)

2. A set of clear rules and procedures that are carefully introduced with no assumptions that students already should or do know them (32% decrease)

3. Reinforcement of those guidelines and procedures and respectful interventions for all rule-breaking to preserve the integrity of the rules and the continuous progress of students in gaining social competency (31% decrease)

4. Cultivation of a teaching mindset—a stance relative to teacher "withitness" (see page 33) and emotional objectivity—that underlies and supports all interactions with students (40% decrease)

See Chapter 2 for a detailed description of the mindset and skills that educators need to draw upon to power them through the process of meeting students' needs and guiding them to responsible independence.

Classroom Discipline: Guiding Adolescents to Responsible Independence is designed as a practical guidebook for effectively preventing and handling misbehaviors in the classroom while building social competence and a strong connection with school. Rule-breaking that requires intervention beyond the classroom is discussed briefly in Appendix G, but the main emphasis here is on empowering the classroom teacher of adolescents to use behavior-management approaches that can launch our students into life with the power of independence and the strength and protection of responsibility.

Getting into Gear for Responsible Independence

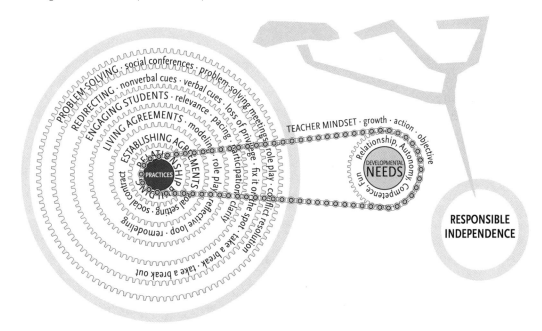

Teacher Mindset and Skills

I really do love these kids, and they sense that. I establish consistent routines. When I say something, that's the way it's going to be. I'm quiet about it, but I'm firm. Once we talk about the guidelines and they understand them, then every single time someone deviates, I have them Take a Break or another consequence we've talked about. This relies on my "noticing," because a lot of times I can correct a few papers and still notice everything. The kids know that, and it helps them feel safe; they know that I'm going to see them and they're going to have to sit out or do something to fix their mistakes. I think it relies on relationship, too, because they know I like them and have their best interests at heart. So they're willing to trust me. I think what works is that I take action every single time they step away from the rules. I'm never too tired or too distracted to do what I know I need to do.

—8th grade language arts teacher, Greenfield MA

What is at work when teachers remain steady and committed to a student's growth in the face of anger and rule-breaking? How does a teacher devise a consistent, dignified, effective response through the daily trials of a middle level classroom? There are no formulas, but we do know that successful educators call on inner strengths, moment by moment, in the classroom. We are interested in naming and exploring some of those strengths, because they are essential for meeting the needs of adolescents in an academic setting. We're going to begin with them, because the right disciplinary action taken without the right skills and the right mental/emotional package is not likely to succeed.

Facing the truth about what it takes to teach discipline effectively is dangerous—we risk scaring ourselves away from the task—but not seeing what is at work is even more dangerous. When discipline structures fail, what often happens is that we look at the action only, failing to examine the skills and mood with which we took the disciplinary action, and we say that the action didn't work, without understanding why. But it is the full picture of the steps we take, the skill with which we take them, and the attitude with which we flavor them that makes or breaks the corrective action.

Lest we give up on the structure and continue to struggle over discipline in partial darkness, in this chapter we will look at the frames of mind and skills necessary to succeed in behavior management, examine why they are important, and consider how they might be cultivated.

TEACHER MINDSET

What mental and emotional strengths does a teacher draw on to meet the considerable challenges of behavior management? Educational coaches and consultants working to support *Developmental Designs* implementation in classrooms across the U.S. have noted that successful teacher disciplinarians work from three fundamental frames of mind:

Growth mindset: The space of possibility that we hold for each student—our belief in their capacity for growth into responsible independence—as we guide them

Action Mindset: The active support of each student through good times and bad, which demands a commitment of heart and mind fueled by courage and a sense of urgency

Objective Mindset: The ability to interact with students without taking what they do and say personally

Teaching, like any truly human activity, emerges from one's inwardness, for better or for worse. (Palmer 1998, 2)

Growth Mindset

Everyone can grow. This simple but crucial idea builds power when applied to teaching:

- Every student has the capacity to grow and ultimately succeed
- Self-control and resilience are teachable and learnable (some students need more guidance than others)
- Given the plasticity of the brain, we can grow new and positive habits
- Effort, not talent, is the best path to mastery
- Teachers have the capacity to grow their skills so that all students' needs are addressed
- Challenges, setbacks, and criticism are welcome, because they provide a context for growth

Teaching in accordance with these understandings requires some conscious commitments: a declaration to keep on patiently trying in the face of pushback when solutions are not apparent, and a determination to build a pathway to success for even those students whose capacity is hard to see at times. The payoff is results in place of reasons why not.

Growth-minded students

Teaching is most successful when the teacher believes in the capacity of all people to grow, and when the teacher cultivates in the students a belief in their own growth. In other words, we must teach a growth mindset, model it as believers in our own growth, and "hold the space" for students who do not yet believe in themselves.

Consider the dangers of "fixed-mindset" thinking for adolescents: A physically awkward boy in his early teens had had several negative experiences on the playground;

he lacked stamina, had poor hand-eye coordination, and bumped into others. He decided he was a klutz (a fixed mindset), and did not embrace physical activity. The ungainly teen soon reached his full height and became more coordinated. He might have discovered a love of Ultimate Frisbee or soccer and gone on to spend several decades engaged in regular, healthy physical activity and the social satisfaction gained by being part of a team, had he kept a growth mindset, but because he had settled into a mindset that labeled his athletic skills deficient, he lost out.

Interestingly, the fixed mindset is just as dangerous when initially positive: An eighth grader did well in math and decided she was a "math whiz" (a fixed mindset) until she confronted algebra. Faced with a math struggle for the first time in her life, she quickly felt incompetent, and swung to a new summary judgment: math wasn't really for her after all. Chances are she simply wasn't developmentally ready to handle the abstract thinking required to integrate the algebraic mode, but by labeling herself first a "winner" then a "loser" in math, she closed the door on many career possibilities.

The impact of growth and fixed mindsets was the focus of a study of low-achieving seventh graders in New York City. All students in the study group began by attending sessions during which they learned study skills, how the brain works, and other achievement-related topics. The control group attended an informational session on memory (fixed-mindset ideas), while a second group learned that intelligence, like a muscle, grows stronger through exercise (growth-mindset ideas). The group that received the growth-mindset messages greatly improved in the areas of motivation and math grades; students in the control group showed no improvement despite the other interventions. (Blackwell, Trzesniewski, and Dweck 2007)

This research illustrates the importance of having conversations with all students about how intelligence grows—through exercise and effort. The pages that follow offer ways to talk with students about the importance of social skills and how they develop. The conversations take on life as social skills are taught and practiced. Mistakes are opportunities to fix things and try again. Through encouragement and reflection, students experience their own growth.

When students believe they can develop their intelligence, they focus on doing just that. Not worrying about how smart they will appear, they take on challenges and stick to them. (Dweck 2007, 35)

Numerous studies have found that students who adopt task-focused (mastery) goals are more likely to engage in deep cognitive processing, such as thinking about how newly learned material relates to previous knowledge and attempting to understand complex relationships. In contrast, students who adopt ability-focused (performance) goals tend to use surface-level strategies such as the rote memorization of facts and immediately asking the teacher for assistance when confronted with difficult academic tasks. (Anderman and Maehr 1994, 295)

Growth-minded teachers

I really disliked the raised hand as a signal for silence. The sight of a teacher with her hand raised, and all the students raising theirs in response, reminded me of a Nazi salute—rigid and slavish. And insisting that no one could speak while the one person was speaking, refusing to allow side conversations or just speaking out, seemed suppressive. I was proud that mine was an "open" classroom, and we had exciting conversations about things that really mattered to me and to the students. I was proud of that until a colleague asked me about the students who sat silently through most discussions. "Maybe," he said, "they feel that there's no room for them to squeeze into the conversation." I suddenly saw what he saw, and knew I had to change. I began using the signal and raised hands for permission to speak, and our conversations, although somewhat less dynamic and fast-moving, became thoughtful explorations, with all voices heard.

—Principal and former K-12 teacher, MN

Being growth-oriented in teaching means having the humility to acknowledge the gaps: *I don't know everything—there's still a lot for me to learn, and I can and will grow.* Such a stance keeps our minds open to learning from colleagues, workshops, books, and from students themselves: *I don't know everything, so I am willing to hone my teaching skills and learn from you and about you.* This open-minded receptivity infuses optimism into frustrating, potentially defeating moments: *I know this student can grow. What does he need from me to make this happen, and what do I need to learn about him?*

Knowing that we don't know everything gives tooth to strategic sharing of power with students. Reluctance to take chances gives way to growing awareness of what strengths are dawning in students that can be parlayed into independence and power, and what strengths are growing in ourselves to guide them there. It's like having a third eye—to see what isn't there yet in our students and in ourselves. An apt adjustment of the old adage would be: *I'll see it when I believe it.*

When we walk the subtle line between the authority we are obliged to exercise and the humility to remain open to learning from our students, we demonstrate great personal power. What a balancing act—taking charge while holding the thought that you don't know everything! Neither selfless nor powerless, this kind of humility is an act of strength and commitment in the service of our students.

Psychologist Carol Dweck responds to the question, how can growth-minded teachers consistently devote their energies and untold hours to even the most challenging students? "The answer is that they're not entirely selfless. They love to learn. And teaching is a wonderful way to learn. About people and how they tick. About what you teach. About yourself. And about life." (Dweck 2007, 201)

Teacher self-assessment

Admitting we don't know guides us to seek change in our teaching. It helps us identify our growing edges: *What works for most students doesn't work for this student. Is there something else I could try? Am I truly being consistent? Is there some important adjustment needed in my approach?*

When we recognize our capacity for growth and that our students and others contribute to our teaching, we look for ways to identify what and how we need to learn. One easy place to look is in the mirror. Periodically evaluating our teaching strengths leverages our professional growth, just as reflecting on the behavior of our students helps us help them. We can check ourselves against inventories that describe qualities such as:

I know how to teach content in ways that maximize student learning

I intervene when I see unacceptable behaviors

We can answer reflection questions in a journal, such as:

Did I increase student participation in fifth hour today?

Am I catching small misbehaviors before they escalate?

Or we can simply write in an unstructured way thoughts about what we did and how we did it during the day. Sticky notes stuck on a lesson plan or daily calendar can remind us to think about doing things differently next time. We can use a standard set of basic questions to review in our minds any lesson we've taught: *What did I teach? Now what? So what?* They help us think about how we did something, what would be a good follow-up to reinforce or extend the learning, and maybe most important, what was the purpose or meaning for my students in learning this knowledge or skill? The questions could be designed around behavior management or teacher language: *Which students were disciplined today? What follow-ups do I need to do? Did I avoid using sarcasm? Did I use open-ended questions to get students to think about their behavior?* For more on self-assessment through inventories and written reflection, see pages 232-239.

Colleagues can be another avenue for self-assessment and reflection. Even brief conversations, so long as they are specific and honest enough to be useful, can get us thinking harder or from a different angle. In some teaching cultures, observing and processing lessons together is built into the teaching day. Most American schools do not have that benefit, but we can find ways to process with each other, formally in staff meetings and staff development opportunities, and informally over coffee.

Action Mindset

Brittany was one of my students who spoke her mind, and usually as soon as the thought was born. Often her contributions were biting. In our first social conference she was polite until we had to identify what behavior in the Social Contract she was not living up to. She immediately went on the defensive and acted as if she were trapped in a corner. She admitted to disrespect, but the rest of the conversation was a struggle. She had several criticisms of others, including me. She was very bitter.

We agreed on a signal I would give her as an early warning when she was getting disrespect-ful in class, and we agreed to meet again in two weeks. The signal didn't really work because she was only slightly committed to changing. Next time we met, we changed the signal, but her disrespectful comments continued .

I stayed with my commitment to her growth. I did a little research, and learned that she slept on a couch at her grandma's house with her mom, grandma, and an aunt and uncle. As I grew to understand her, I could better see through her roughness. This helped me have the resiliency to keep coming back and checking with her.

I searched for her strengths, as she did her best to hide them, and I discovered what a talented writer she was. In one of our conferences when I shared this recognition with her, she acted as though no one had ever told her this before. My resolve thereafter was to find and draw out the talents and good in her. Our conversations never really became warm, but these recog-nitions seemed to help take some of the edge off. At one point Brittany was acknowledged by a fellow classmate for showing respect. She beamed a bit, and seemed to enjoy the moment.

—Middle level teacher, LaCrosse WI

Courage and commitment in teaching

Who's responsible for our students' education? They are. Their parents are. We are. The paradox is that all of us also have *all* of the responsibility. As teachers we have to consistently act on our responsibility to create openings for students to take responsibility for their part. In certain cases, this may not be easy. The data tell us that not all students succeed, but nevertheless, each year our active commitment to their growth will be a decisive factor in their lives. And it is not enough to merely *believe* that we are responsible. Commitment calls for us to *actively provide* the relationship and assistance needed for every student to move along his/her journey of growth, even if it means going outside our individual comfort zone. There are no throwaways, although some students may need a special environment that we cannot provide. Even so, it's our job to know what is needed, and to take action.

Acting on a commitment to teach each student effective *self*-discipline requires sufficient, steady strength and stamina. Moving students in the right direction is sometimes an act of will, requiring us to tap into our personal reservoir of courage. It takes courage:

- to hold the line for a classroom of adolescents, many of whom are sure to test your limits
- to be equitable
- to consistently intervene when students break the rules
- to maintain professionalism in the face of high emotions—theirs and yours
- to exude calm, thoughtful confidence
- to keep parents in the loop
- to maintain your belief in all students' ability to grow
- to try things you believe are good for students but are outside your comfort zone
- to work on your professional weak spots
- to admit mistakes, fix them, and move on
- to slow down and get things right rather than rush ahead and have to pick up the pieces later

It also takes great diligence to give attention to many details, and never just let things go. The switch is on from the moment you come into the building to the moment you leave.

For many teachers, the problem isn't that they lack courage *per se*, but that they have a specific fear that prevents them from trying something new, and the fear paralyzes them. For example, a teacher who considers himself a weak disciplinarian may fear conflict, and will resist using a redirect that requires a student to move. He doesn't know how the student will react, and if the student refuses, the teacher has a power struggle on his hands.

When we operate out of fearful reluctance, we are, in effect, trying to teach discipline with one arm tied behind our back, and we are stuck with what remains: repeated verbal reminders, pleading, cajoling, lecturing, using sarcasm, etc.—redirects that don't require the rule-breakers to do anything but listen (or at least be silent and act like they are listening) and are therefore responses to misbehavior that are too "soft" to make a difference. When our exasperation or anger takes over, we end up sending the student to the office, a strategy that might have been avoided had we used a stronger, more courageous intervention earlier.

How does one get over that type of fear that leads to paralysis? There is no formula, but when discussing the issue of courage as it relates to teaching discipline, Kristen Konop, middle level teacher at Crosswinds East Metro Arts and Science School in St. Paul MN, says, "Sometimes you just have to jump off a cliff. Nine times out of ten, you realize you always had it in you."

Each time I walk into a classroom, I can choose the place within myself from which my teaching will come, just as I can choose the place within my students toward which my teaching will be aimed. I need not teach from a fearful place: I can teach from curiosity or hope or empathy or honesty, places that are as real within me as are my fears. I can have fear, but I need not be fear— if I am willing to stand someplace else in my inner landscape. (Palmer 1998, 57)

Students who present the most challenging behaviors try my patience and wear me out. It sometimes takes all my energy and courage to keep coming back to check in, especially when they intentionally *choose* not to cooperate.

Forrest was an emotionally-challenged student who lost no opportunity to disrupt the class during the first week of school. When we put together a "gift puzzle" of what we each brought to the community/class, his gift was "hatred." He offered it in front of the whole class. He seemed so angry! I was a little afraid to take him on, but I did.

In a brief conference immediately following class, I asked him if he realized that his behavior was out of line. He admitted to being disrespectful. I asked him how he was going to improve. He stated that he was not going to improve. I asked him a second time, and again he said he was not going to improve. I took a deep breath, and said that if that indeed was his choice, then in effect he was surrendering his freedom to choose. I would be taking over control. I told him he was going to go back to his seat and compose an appropriate gift. He asked me, "When?" I said, "Right now." He replied, "Oh!" with a look of surprise. I said, "What will you do if you don't have a pencil?" He said he did not have one. I reminded him of our procedure for classroom pens and pencils. He responded, "Okay," and walked into the room, picked up a pencil, walked to his seat, and got to work. We had one more outburst a few days later, when he was having an especially bad day, and I reminded him about the Take a Break chair.

One of the reasons I believe the quick exchange with Forrest worked was that I set clear boundaries. He knew where they were, could more easily follow them, and knew that I would keep up with them. That gave him the sense of security and safety that allowed him to be a bit more relaxed and not so anxious, and he functioned more appropriately. I drew a line and let him know not to step over it, for his own good.

—Middle level teacher, LaCrosse WI

Urgency in teaching

Whether released or restrained by fear, feeling courageous or doubtful and tired, we must act decisively for the good of our students. Some call this quality of action "moral agency," the forwarding of others according to our highest moral commitments. One *Developmental Designs* practitioner describes this force within as "urgency": "I have no choice, really. I must do what I can, right now, to get this child straightened out and flying right."

A sense of urgency can lead to quick social conferences with students, well-timed conversations to convey the social-skill knowledge they need.

> Derek was my little comedian. He joked around all the time, not understanding when it was OK and when it was not. We had conversations about when humor gets in the way of instruction. I said, "You must channel that powerful skill appropriately. You must learn to manage it." After that, when he began to joke at inappropriate times, I would simply say, "Not now." He learned to stop, and the interruptions decreased. What could be seen as sabotage was better viewed as an enthusiastic young person with little self-control, and an itch for attention. By withholding negative judgment of Derek, I was able to teach him internalized self-control early on while maintaining, even reinforcing, our good relationship. I felt a great sense of urgency to act now, on his behalf, so I thought hard and worked with him to redirect his joking behavior. Derek needed me. I could help. The way I see it is that students are learning all the time, for better or worse, and my sense of how urgently important it is for them to grow pushes me to act to keep their learning positive and within my design.
>
> —5th grade teacher, St. Paul MN

A sense of urgency can call for both patience and impatience in teaching. Impatience is called for in the face of anything that stands between our students and their optimal learning—including student misbehavior, staff dysfunction, preconceived beliefs of others (or your own) about what individual students or groups of students are capable of, district policy blunders, physical plant issues, etc. The urgent stand is: We must put everything we've got into teaching our students, and we don't have time to waste.

Patience may seem an unlikely partner to urgency. Can someone be urgently patient? Yes, when we take time to teach, model, practice, set rules, create norms together, seek student endorsement through sharing personal experiences, ask open-ended questions, and work with students who need extra time to develop appropriate behavior. Change is hard—it can be slow, incremental, with false starts, peaks and valleys—and internalized social skills are usually hard-wrought. They are developed with patient, committed teaching and a willingness to share power for long-term payoffs.

Objective Mindset

Professional objectivity is part of the full complement of teacher equipment when we move from thinking of ourselves as mere disciplinarians to teachers of self-discipline. It's not about us holding the power to punish (although we do have this power); it is more about empowering our students to learn to discipline themselves. In fact, when things are working the way we really want them to, it's not about us at all.

Researcher Robert Marzano defines emotional objectivity as part of the necessary mindset of effective disciplinarians: "[A]n effective classroom manager implements and enforces rules and procedures, executes disciplinary actions, and cultivates effective relationships with students without interpreting violations of classroom rules and procedures, negative reactions to disciplinary actions, or lack of response to teacher's attempts to forge relationships as a personal attack." (Marzano 2003, 68)

Marzano tracked the impact of holding a professional distance in the heat of the moment in his meta-analysis and found that it added an additional 26% effectiveness in reducing behavior disruptions. He recognizes, "This is very difficult to do because the normal human reaction to student disobedience or lack of response is to feel hurt or even angry." (Marzano 2003, 67-69)

Student and teacher share a moment of connection with a playful greeting

On the other hand, Max van Manen in *The Tone of Teaching* reminds us that although we try to see students objectively, since neither they nor we are objects, in the name of objectivity we may default to summative labeling and automatic interventions, as if they were.

What happens then is that I forego the possibility of truly listening to and seeing the specific child. (van Manen 2003, 26)

When we lose sight of the individual child, our chances of making a difference in his life, especially when the child has many social deficits, are greatly reduced. It is by connecting to the individual that we can figure out what best to say and do, what best to have the student do, given his needs, his current skills, and his style of being. But it is by remaining enough apart that we can look clearly at the student without the fog of hurt or anger. It's definitely a balancing act, and the proportions of personal interest and objectivity that work for one may not work for another. Discipline is a process of careful decision-making and planning. We must:

- Offer clear choices when students cross the line, and communicate those choices firmly but without malice. "It's my way or the highway!" isn't a choice.

- Listen to students who are having difficulties, even if some of what they say may be directed at us. When students ask: "Why should I?" it takes humility to step away from the stock reply "because I said so," or to not run away, and to craft a thought-provoking answer that brings the students on board.

- Not take it personally—so easy to say! Only a clear mind and a powerful intention can help us pull it off.

"The teacher," says van Manen, "serves the child by observing from very close proximity while still maintaining distance." (van Manen 2003, 28)

A teacher colleague of mine had had a tough time with a student, and when she and I had to conference with him and his parent, she was afraid. The whole thing had become a personality battle. She had become too emotionally involved. The student was wrong in the first place, but it was the teacher's emotion that brought her down to his level in the matter. The student had had similar problems in 7th grade, and now in 9th those same behaviors were resurfacing. I showed him in the conference that there were times when he crossed the line and asked did he remember how to stop short of that the way he did in 7th grade. That helped him. The teacher got a chance to see where things tended to go wrong for her as a pattern when she interacted with students. She attributed too much meaning to everything, gave it a personal value, and then lost her own controls. When that happens, when you snap out with a student, he or she will run with it. You've got to keep from getting caught up, keep your power by keeping your cool.

—9th grade assistant principal, Harrisburg PA

TEACHER SKILLSET

The list of skills important to good discipline is sobering, because it is so long. Nobody ever perfects all of the skills; we all have partial skill sets. Like a good craftsperson, we shape and polish the skills we have and work to develop more along the way.

Knowing Your Students Developmentally

Honing and keeping our knowledge of adolescent developmental needs front and center influences the effectiveness of every move we make in behavior management. Developmental science tells us that adolescents are chemically prone to certain behaviors, almost promising struggles and strengths in predictable areas. Adolescent brains are especially active in the area of sensation and risk-seeking, and not as developed in the areas necessary for exercising judgment. Especially in early adolescence, there's a dangerous gap between the urge to take risks and the internal brakes that suggest the need to think first. Impetuosity and poor judgment are responsible for much of the rule-breaking in middle level schools.

[A] large and compelling body of scientific research on the neurological development of teens confirms a long-held, common sense view: teenagers are not the same as adults in a variety of key areas such as the ability to make sound judgments when confronted by complex situations, the capacity to control impulses, and the ability to plan effectively. Such limitations reflect, in part, the fact that key areas of the adolescent brain, especially the prefrontal cortex that controls many high order skills, are not fully mature until the third decade of life. (Weinberger et al. 2005, 3)

Acknowledging the force of developmental patterns and needs can defuse and depersonalize behavior confrontations and help us to view these potentially high-emotion exchanges as not about us, not unique to our relationship, and often, quite ordinary. The knowledge we have about the biology of young adolescents allows us to remain focused on our commitments and to maintain the objectivity required for effectively sharing power.

Once we focus on the four basic human needs identified by theorists —autonomy, relationship, competence, and fun—and understand that humans will do almost anything to get their needs met, we can simply *assume* the necessity of addressing them. The needs take on special force in adolescence, that threshold to adulthood, where autonomy seems just beyond our grasp, competence ever elusive, and relationships a matter of survival. Even the quest for fun presents a challenge, because it lures us to take big risks in our love affair with excitement and stimulation. So how do we use discipline to help our students meet their needs in a safe, productive way? The behavior management structures in this book incorporate knowledge of adolescent developmental needs, with indications for the reader of what forces are at work and how they are being responsibly satisfied. See pages 113-117 and Appendix A for more about adolescent development.

Dr. James P. Comer of the Yale Child Study Center Project proposes that "many practices in education that have been developed over the past two decades have been less successful than they might have been because they have focused primarily on curriculum, instruction, assessment, and modes of service delivery," neglecting the principles of child and adolescent development. (Comer 2005, 758)

Building Positive Relationships With and Among Students

Positive, inclusive, trusting relationships underlie successful behavior management. All relationships—between teachers and their students, among students, among adults, and our relationships with ourselves—color every move we make to discipline students. From the first moment you enter school each year through every moment of every class hour, tending to relationships is paramount. A huge help in this everlasting responsibility is using structures to shape life in school. This book offers ways to build community and get to know one another during advisory and class hours (pages 48-50) and careful consideration for building, maintaining, and strengthening teacher-student relationships with every rule-breaking redirection and intervention. The latter is done through structures that allow dignity and provide appropriate autonomy for the student, embodied in rigorous attention to respectful teacher language.

[In academic performance and in the area of health behaviors], young people who feel connected to school, that they belong, and that teachers are supportive and treat them fairly, do better. Some contend the business of school is teaching for knowledge acquisition and that attention to the non-academic aspects of school is a low priority. However, the health and education literature suggests these factors contribute significantly to school success. (Libbey 2004, 282)

In addition to ways that strong relationships between teachers and students allow for mentorship in social skills, positive peer-to-peer relationships also boost social and academic learning. Observing friends who know how to get along in school is the best way to learn and reinforce the skills necessary for smooth social interaction. Our students have their eyes and ears on us, but even more on each other. The community-building strategies described in this book are designed to provide the best environment possible for peer learning.

It is in peer relationships that [young people] broaden self-knowledge of their capabilities. Peers serve several important efficacy functions. Those who are most experienced and competent provide models of efficacious styles of thinking and behavior. A vast amount of social learning occurs among peers. (Bandura 1994, 78)

Using Encouraging and Respectful Teacher Language

One way we can create a friendly environment for learning together is to insert some fun or movement or personal interest into our teaching. But we also have a tool ready at every moment to make or break our relationships with students: our language. In every encounter, the tone of our voices, body language, and words can build connection or dismantle it, can help or hinder the process of students becoming responsibly independent. When responding to student mistakes, if our words are rooted in our belief that students want to and can do well in school, if we avoid rescuing them or debilitating them with praise, and invite them to solve problems and make choices, we can build social skills as we correct mistakes. Psychologist Lev Vygotsky, in his theory of language development, established an explicit connection between speech and cognitive development. The language we use with students shapes how they feel and think; it forms their behavior. (Vygotsky 1986/1934)

[L]anguage has "content," but it also bears information about the speaker and how he or she views the listener and their assumed relationship. (Johnston 2004, 6)

We need to maintain a tone of acceptance and encouragement that empowers young adolescents when we see positive actions *and* when we are correcting negative ones.

Armand, what do you need to get started? Alisha, the timer is on—where should you be?

Effective use of teacher language is like a steady infusion of caring support. It nudges students toward right action while maintaining a good relationship with them. It is most effective when we are specific, direct, and clear. Using language that invites reflection after rule-breaking maintains everyone's dignity, shows a relentless faith in each student's ability to learn, and is evidence of a shared-power relationship between a caring guide and a student moving gradually towards responsible independence. The subtext of every exchange is: *I am asking this student to think about what he just did so he can identify what he learned or needs to learn, and leverage the growth I know he is capable of.*

The teacher escorting students towards self-management avoids language that creates dependency through praise or punishment. We must avoid the temptation to give young adolescents broad strokes, when what they often need is specific information about what was effective in what they did, or help in perceiving their strengths on their own.

We must avoid purposely injecting pain into a correction in the mistaken belief that without it there will be no gain. To develop positive behaviors, students need guidance in the context of encouragement. We have to treat them well for them to behave well. What we're after, always, is to help students develop *internalized* good judgment through on-the-spot critical feedback that is firm, clear, and encouraging, all at the same time. Examples of encouraging and respectful teacher language are included in the discussion of every structure introduced in this book.

Students pick up where we are from our tone, our attitude. You don't have to praise them. The way I see it is there aren't "good" things and "bad" things that they do—there are just things. *We* put the value on it. I avoid putting value on student behavior. I think of the student and the role each needs to play. I acknowledge when they've got their role in action and when they haven't. I use no praise. I avoid value language across the board so no one sees me as playing favorites or being prejudiced against someone.

—Middle level teacher, Harrisburg PA

Cultivating Endorsement to Increase Student Motivation

There is wide agreement that self-motivated people have an advantage over those who need external motivators to get them to act. *Jazz Theory* author Mark Levine claims that music students need four things to become skillful practitioners of their craft: talent, good teachers, access to quality musical examples, and ambition. Of the four, he says ambition is by far the most important ingredient.

The million-dollar question for educators is: How does motivation work? In any class, some students will be self-motivated while others won't, so how can I motivate students to engage in the behaviors that support learning subject-area content and a healthy community: listening, putting forth effort, handing in work on time, participating actively, and following the rules?

Motivation has been studied for decades. According to psychologists Edward Deci and Richard Ryan, the best way to motivate someone else is to get him to *endorse* a rationale for engaging in the target behavior. When this occurs—and with plenty of practice over time—the desired behavior can become a part of who that person is. The result: the level of student motivation to engage in the target behavior becomes almost the same as it would be for something he was intrinsically motivated to do. (Ryan and Deci 2000) For more details on Ryan and Deci's self-determination theory, see pages 254-255.

Creating endorsement for behavior-management practices

Throughout the school year, the approach we present here creates endorsement for behavior-management practices both before and after rules are broken. If we can make the case that getting good at setting goals, creating rules, doing routines a certain way, and so on, are really useful to them, we stand a good chance of helping our students value social and academic competence enough to walk the road to success. In short, student endorsement permeates everything. Without it, they won't want to learn from us.

Whenever we teach a new behavior, we seek student endorsement. Then we continue to seek that endorsement when we tend to the behavior all year long. Every correction, every review of the procedure, carries with it an effort to keep our students with us, keep them allied in the understanding that this is important for our community and for them as individuals. Consider the following set of questions for creating endorsement when setting up group work routines. Each question invites students to look inward for reasons to endorse the behavioral goals.

Why are we here? What's the purpose of attending school? What are your personal goals?

Why is it important to listen to each other? What will be the payoffs?

What should group work time look, sound, and feel like if we're going to achieve those goals?

Now consider this set, which garners endorsement for maintaining this routine all year:

What should you be doing right now to be successful in this project?

Ask yourself whether your group worked together using the skills for success that we listed.

The research tells us that student achievement improves dramatically when we find usable, classroom-friendly techniques to increase student motivation. So we use language, relationship, shared goals, intentional structures, and incremental growth to steadily invite students to endorse the idea of building their academic and social skills.

Seeing Everything, and then Acting

"Withitness," as defined by educational researcher Jacob Kounin, is a teacher's communication through her *actions* that she knows what her students are doing moment by moment, all around the room. It's not enough to merely *say* to a class, "I know what's going on." The teacher must make her keen awareness of behavior apparent by what she does. (Kounin 1970) Teachers skilled in withitness see everything, and they take action—both to reinforce the positive and redirect the negative. Although this book focuses on discipline, this quality applies to all things academic as well. Teachers who possess the quality of withitness notice all students as they work, watching for those who are struggling, and offering ready assistance. When we quickly address academic needs, we also head off student frustrations that can manifest in negative behaviors. In such actions, we fulfill students' need for competence by diverting potential disruptions into recognition for growing academic skills. It's all connected.

Withitness begins with noticing. A teacher never has the luxury of focusing on one thing at a time. The radar is constantly scanning the room. Some moves and sounds are just the noise of productive work. Others are distractions which can escalate quickly into disruptions. The teacher makes hundreds of small corrective moves in response to the potentially disruptive items. *Carolyn, focus. Marshall, what's the first step your group needs to take? It sounds a little restless in here. Take a breath, settle yourself, and focus on your work. Raise your hand if you need my help.* She moves closer to one student, tells another to change places with a third.

To develop my withitness, I follow the wisdom of sweating the small stuff—I look after the little things. I am aware of how much I scan the room. Sometimes I think it is a curse to be so aware, to be acting on all I see. It is exhausting! But it is much more exhausting to not do so. Before I developed this skill, I was putting out bigger fires.

I do a number of things to support my withitness. I set up my room so I can see everybody all the time. When students are doing small-group work, I circulate throughout the room. I put reminders to myself in discreet places about things I need to do. I include prompts for teacher language, such as remembering to say "I notice…" when talking with students about their behavior. I remind myself to move slowly, use a calm voice, and consider proximity. I check in more with these reminders when I am feeling impatient.

When modeling expectations, I tell the students I will be noticing little things and correcting. Then they watch to see if I am doing what I said I would do. The payoff comes when our mutual vigilance shows that I mean what I say. I think the students feel like they are in an environment that is safe and respectful. They know I am going to do my best to not let things get out of hand. This can be especially important to bringing out some of the more introverted students.

I increase my vigilance in general when the students appear more active or unfocused, and during the typically more challenging times of the year—before break, near the end of the year, etc. In between these periods we have stretches where we are in the flow. The *students* are being withit! Essentially, when I use my withitness, I model what being on task, being effective in your job, looks like. Then they can mirror that.

—Middle level math teacher, Minneapolis MN

A defining characteristic of this kind of vigilance at its best is the nurturing element in it. The spirit of it is: *I watch for what might be going wrong because I want to help us keep things going right, and I know we can.* More like a herding dog than a wolf on the watch, there is no "pounce" in effective withitness, just a steady commitment to keep nudging things to where they need to be for excellence in learning.

It's a slow business, however, becoming highly aware and then able to act in many possible ways to avert, divert, and correct at the same time as I'm doing a demonstration or lecturing. It's definitely a rub-your-stomach-and-pat-your-head kind of existence—all day long! There is the quality of an alert animal to it—watching everywhere, scanning, making a quick move, then back to watching.

Structuring teaching for equitable participation supports positive learning behavior

Some ways to increase your capacity for withitness are:

- Arrange the room so you can see everything and everybody fairly easily

  - Consistently scan the room

    - Organize your lessons so you don't have to search for things while lecturing, demonstrating, or facilitating discussions

      - Separate students who trigger each other into rule-breaking so you avoid hot spots in the room that may distract you from other smaller infractions

        - Videotape your students while you are teaching, and watch for what you missed

        - Have a colleague observe you and tell you of *all* infractions that occurred while you were instructing, so you can learn about those you missed

It's definitely worth the effort. Researcher Marzano found in a meta-analysis of more than 100 reports on behavior management that "...the mental set necessary for effective classroom management requires teachers to cultivate a mindful stance relative to their 'withitness' [as defined by Kounin] and 'emotional objectivity.'" Of the different elements of classroom management Marzano noted, the use of withitness showed the greatest decrease in behavior disruptions—42%. (Marzano 2003, 66)

Engaging Instruction

When I was teaching, I never sent a student to the principal's office. I worked very hard to make all my lessons engaging. That was my main discipline method. Basically, it worked.

—Principal, grades 6-10 school, St. Paul MN

A behavior management strategy that is often not perceived as an element of good discipline is the way we dish up our lessons. One of the best ways to keep hallways clear, referrals to the office down, and everyone on the right academic track is to make learning engaging. And the most effective way to accomplish this is to make it active, interactive, relevant, choiceful, and fun. An engaging lesson is perhaps the best management tactic we have to avoid disruptions in the first place. We want our students to perceive our classroom as the place to be, so that missing it because of poor behavior is not attractive.

Student engagement is of primary importance to supporting positive behavior; this book devotes a chapter to it. See Chapter 6 for ways to structure lessons for a minimum of behavior disruptions and maximum participation through:

- good timing and flow
- variety
- differentiation
- personal connection to content
- content which is developmentally appropriate

When content is connected to the lives and concerns of students, they are much more likely to feel that we know and care about them. At every opportunity, we can ask the kind of open-ended questions that allow our students to make connections that engage them—connections to other experiences they have had, things they have studied, concerns in their personal lives. The more relevant the topics and the more we allow students to construct their own understanding of what we are presenting to them, the more they will trust us to guide them socially and academically.

Being Strategic, Not Formulaic

Developmental growth is gradual and irregular. We need to teach the skills necessary for social, emotional, physical, moral, and intellectual growth incrementally and systematically. We may begin each teaching year holding almost all the power, but slowly, methodically, and consciously, we can hand pieces of it over to our students. The approach we are after is a planned, organized introduction to students of all the routines and strategies they need to be successful in school. Chapters 4 and 5 describe those strategies in detail, including the order and manner in which to introduce them. The goal is to create a scaffold upon which students can climb, safely and steadily, to responsible independence.

When there are missteps in the journey, when students abuse privileges, break rules, defy our authoritative guidance, we can take back some or all of the power, and quickly act to get them back on the right path. We can use the structures described in this book to slowly build their competencies for handling things well themselves, one step at a time. See Chapters 7 and 8 about redirecting and problem-solving.

All of this takes planning, and a toolbox of strategies the teacher can use to build a scaffold to master each routine—logistical, social, and academic—of the school day.

The operating principle here is: *assume nothing and teach everything*. What to teach and when to teach it is guided by a carefully designed structure accompanied by, as always, encouraging and empowering language. In this manner, we can head off many behavior problems before they happen. We can even introduce structures to correct rule-breaking before rules are broken. But inevitably they will be broken, and then, after the consequences relevant to the misbehavior have been administered respectfully and realistically, we begin anew to build social capacity and nudge toward responsible independence.

Matching the support to the student

Here's where the strategic part comes in. The choice of *what* consequence—what reminder or redirection to use when, the decision about whether a conference is necessary and whether it's a quick exchange at the side of the room or a meeting with parents and perhaps other staff present—must be decided moment by moment, infraction by infraction, student by student. Although everyone benefits from the initial detailed introduction of a routine, the slow drip of friendly reminders, and occasional corrections, for some they are not enough. In other words, it is necessary for all, but not sufficient for some.

Some students need more frequent correction that goes beyond verbal and non-verbal reminders—perhaps temporary loss of privilege or quick problem-solving conferences, or perhaps they need to learn to repair the damage they do. And there are still other students for whom all of this is necessary but *still* not sufficient. For them, we have longer conferences, perhaps involving administration and/or family. We work out individual plans and strategize with colleagues about best approaches.

There are no formulas for action. There is no "step" plan, no pre-charted course when students require redirection or problem-solving. We don't count infractions and build a pyramid of punishments. Every day we begin fresh. Every misstep is corrected, and then we move on. Nothing is ignored. Every little bit of rule-breaking is addressed, but not with recrimination or the goal of inflicting suffering. Our eyes are on the prize: fixing what's broken so we can move on towards responsible independence for every student. Some may end the year remarkably able to self-manage; some may seem stuck. But we are in relationship with every student. All get caring treatment, but each response to misbehavior depends upon the circumstances peculiar to it.

This takes teachers who operate with their weight forward on their toes, ready to move in whichever direction their best judgment indicates. It takes good relationships with colleagues who help you figure things out, and it takes a commitment to reflection.

Collaborating with Colleagues: Being a team player

An element of our school day that requires the same commitment to good communication and support as working with students is the opportunity teachers have to help one another. When relationships among a staff are good, when teachers can go to each other for help and strategize together about how to best correct and guide an erring student, they are almost unbeatable. A healthy adult community within a school staff, with high levels of cooperation and trust, provides the kind of school climate young people need for success.

Anthony Bryk, among others, has found that successful schools are those where the adult community, including administrators, teachers, paraprofessionals, and parents, work together in positive, transparent, collegial ways. His study of effective schools within the Chicago Public Schools and in some inner-ring suburbs found that trust among adults and strong, positive administrative leadership were the two most important factors related to student achievement. (Bryk and Schneider 2002)

[R]elational trust supports a moral imperative to take on the difficult work of school improvement. Most teachers work hard at their teaching. When implementing "reform," they must assume risks, deal with organizational conflict, attempt new practices, and take on extra work.... Teachers quite reasonably ask, "Why should we do this?" A context characterized by high relational trust provides an answer: In the end, reform is the right thing to do. (Bryk and Schneider 2002, 43)

Appendix G touches upon the adult community in its discussion of school-wide discipline, but a complete exploration of this important subject is beyond the scope of this book.

The Habit of Reflection

Ideally, in life we would be granted a few minutes after each thing we did to take inventory of what worked and what didn't, and to plan adjustments for next time. This is the optimal learning cycle for excellence—for both teachers and students. In school, however, we have no luxury of time: our next group enters on the heels of the one leaving, and we make adjustments on the fly. The challenge is to make the best ones for the results we are seeking. For that we need to cultivate the skill of habitual reflection.

One group of researchers notes, "High levels of student learning require high levels of staff competence." They list a number of ways that reflection brings increased competence to teaching practice, including opportunities to continuously learn, avoid repeating aspects of your practice that aren't working, and generate a greater variety of perspectives when facing challenges. (York-Barr et al. 2001, 8)

A menu of standard reflection questions

Ideally, reflection occurs both individually and with colleagues. What help make it habitual are familiar structures that provide the containers for our thoughts. For example, a set of general reflection questions can guide us as we think about the progress we're making with students:

> How can I better meet my students' needs for autonomy, competence, relationship, and fun?
>
> What's working well? What's not?
>
> What should I change?
>
> What behavior routines and expectations do I need to revisit?

Where can I turn for help?

How specific and descriptive is my language when I reinforce my students?

What can I do to help a student who's having trouble?

How well do I share power in my classroom?

Am I remaining objective, even clinical, in the face of disruptions?

Imagine using the few minutes between classes, while you are gathering what you need to teach, to have a brief internal reflective dialogue with one of these questions (perhaps your "question for today") to help you better learn from your experience:

I had to redirect Stephen four times in class. He did finally get to work for the last 15 minutes of class. What was the last redirection that I used—the one that stuck? Oh, yes, I asked him to move away from the group and work on his own. Maybe his struggle is social. Write a note to myself to observe next time.

Reflection on the effectiveness of discipline practices practices are found throughout this book (for example, see reflection questions for the Social Contract on page 78, and about choosing the right redirection on page 183-86). We use the abbreviation *PWR* as shorthand for the cycle of:

P: Thinking about how best to do what you will do (plan)

W: Doing it (work)

R: Thinking about what you did so you can do better next time (review)

This is the cycle of learning that all successful people use. We call it the Reflective Loop. It gives us insight into who we are, how we are, and how we can better become the teachers we dream of being. Learn more about the Reflective Loop on page 101.

[K]nowing my students and my subject depends heavily on self-knowledge. When I do not know myself, I cannot know who my students are. I will see them through a glass darkly, in the shadows of my unexamined life—and when I cannot see them clearly, I cannot teach them well. (Palmer 1998, 2)

TEACHER REJUVENATION

Even just thinking about all the qualities it takes for optimal teaching can be tiring. In real school life, we know that our most rigorous growth-mindset and our most well-developed skills can falter if we don't take care to recharge our power-sharing batteries. What we know in our hearts is that tending to our own well-being, often the last thing on our minds in school, can leverage everything else we are doing and becoming.

As an aid to our task of tending ourselves, we offer here a few examples teachers have shared with us of ways they defuse and refocus in the face of difficulty or weariness. The suggestions fall into four realms: in class, during teaching time; in school, when students aren't present; with colleagues; and outside school. As this sample list suggests, avenues of rejuvenation are many, and each of us uses methods that suit us. Whatever it takes, we know we need to establish habits of living that nurture our teacher selves.

During class, I...

Sing a song; do a quick sketch

Use a mantra: whisper "Patience" to myself

Say "Stop" to the negative thinking

Say to myself, "If you're in a hole, stop digging!"

Play Mozart (or ____) during class

Smile or laugh with students—tell a joke or a funny story; read Shel Silverstein

Play a quick game or movement activity, perhaps student-led

Ask students to stand up and turn in a circle (turn the day around)

Do jumping jacks together

Sip something warm—coffee or tea

Take 5 while students quietly read

Soften voice

Take an impromptu class field trip within the school

Remember that students aren't out to get you

Mentally scan body & relax muscles

Count backwards silently

In school, when students aren't present, I...

Relax with a magazine article

Close eyes and repeat mantra "Relax"

Talk with colleagues who can lift my spirits

Organize or clean up something

Power nap

Eat an apple

Play games with students at recess

Call a friend or my partner to get moral support

Send an email to a friend

Cross things off my "To Do" list

Remember that students want to learn

Sit at the rowdy table during lunch

Write in journal

Visit the library or another quiet place

With colleagues, I...

Walk at lunch

"Primal scream"

Carpool and share positive reflections

Eat—healthy food, staff cookouts

Laugh

Say friendly hellos throughout the day

Have a staff wellness day with massages and bio rhythm readings

Share stories and get positive feedback from colleagues

Make wellness pacts (walking teams, weight-loss support)

Tell positive jokes

Use community-building structures for staff or team meetings

Outside of school, I try to remember what's not working and plan to fix it, and what *is* working, and celebrate it!

There's no question that maintaining a productive mindset and building a rich skillset are demanding challenges. Tending ourselves along the way becomes not merely a helpful thing to do, but a life-saver. It supports the whole. It is also helpful to realize that in interesting ways, the frames of mind necessary for successful teaching help support each other. Urgency feeds commitment. Commitment feeds objectivity and the courage to act. And a growth mindset helps us be patient and humble enough to seek solutions that work wherever we can find them. Getting in the flow of teaching through any one of these avenues can open the way to the others. So here we go, beginning where we are, and knowing well the prize we seek.

TEACHER MINDSET: Getting in Gear for Responsible Independence

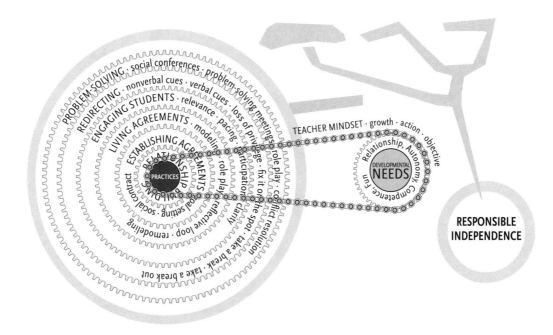

SECTION II

Establishing Relationship and Order

Relationship is the great elixir of behavior management. Throughout the ages, educators have made the impossible possible on the strength of relationship. Within the context of healthy relationship, everything we need to know can be learned.

The quality of teacher-student relationships is the keystone for all other aspects of classroom management. (Marzano et al. 1997)

In 1948 the great bebop jazz master Charlie Parker was introduced to a skinny, star-struck 14-year-old aspiring musician named Jackie McLean. Parker immediately recognized McLean's keen enthusiasm for jazz and invited him to carry his saxophone to gigs in and around New York City. The resulting master/disciple relationship lasted until Parker's death and included many sessions about how to play jazz, as well as informal discussions about how to comport oneself on the bandstand and in life.

Following Parker's untimely death, McLean devoted the rest of his life to continuing Parker's musical legacy, becoming one of the all-time great alto saxophone players in his own right and founding the Jackie McLean Institute of Jazz at the University of Hartford. He received an American Masters Jazz Fellowship from the National Endowment for the Arts in 2001. The disciple had become a master. Forty years after Parker passed away, McLean often remarked that he thought about Charlie Parker every day and was profoundly grateful for the time they'd spent together.

Jackie McLean was a quintessential adolescent when he met Charlie Parker: he longed for relationship and fun and hungered to become a competent, autonomous musician. His relationship with Parker became the means to fulfill McLean's other needs.

Every teacher, parent, aunt, older neighbor, grandpa, storekeeper, and anyone else who has contact with adolescents is a potential Charlie Parker! Adult mentors' impact on adolescents can be incredibly potent and affirming.

A girl named Tanya was known for being extremely aggressive, both to adults and kids. She had a hard time establishing relationships with other kids. She couldn't control herself, and in an instant she could snap.

I got her to come out for track team. We established a relationship there, and she learned to control her anger in track. Now she's in high school. She's still really strong in her ways, but not defiant, even when she's angry. It wasn't track *per se* that made the difference. It was the relationship we had. I encouraged her to go for success, and she had some. I taught her how to identify when she was going into crisis, so she could develop some control.

—Middle level teacher, Harrisburg PA

Teaching competence from a base of relationship

In the *Developmental Designs* approach to discipline described in this book, discipline includes that old idea that learners develop their skills in life in the context of their relationships with older, wiser, more accomplished "masters." What do adults who have decided to spend their lives mentoring youth know about getting along in life? A lot! We have well-developed social skills; we know how to work with others; we have cultivated the self-control we need to keep our attention focused on tasks at hand and avoid letting distractions derail us; we have principles and high values. Most of us became educators because we wanted to help young people succeed in the world. Our challenge is to figure out how to best accomplish that.

In the largest sense, how we help young people succeed is the topic of this book. An accumulating body of research about social-emotional learning tells us that social competency is fundamental to academic and work success.

Satisfying the social and emotional needs of students does more than prepare them to learn. It actually increases their capacity for learning. Social and emotional learning has been shown to increase mastery of subject material, motivation to learn, commitment to school, and time devoted to schoolwork. It also improves attendance, graduation rates, and prospects for constructive employment, while at the same time reducing suspensions, expulsions, and grade retention. (CASEL 2003, 7)

Our approach is to work on building that competency every day. Anchored in caring, friendly relationships, our task with students is to teach them how to help create and live within an orderly classroom by following rules and routines appropriately, getting good at relating to others and treating them well, and cleaning up their mistakes along the way. This takes a lot of demonstrations, repeated practicing, many conversations, and all the redirecting necessary when they go the wrong way.

The chapters in Section II are about establishing relationship and order in the classroom, and then maintaining them. It describes a method of teaching adolescents how to live an orderly existence in school. The skills they learn from us about handling themselves as they move through the day will help diminish the number of times they mess up. The social skills we discuss, model, and practice as often as necessary will keep most of them on the right path much of the time, and the corrective moves we make when we respond to student misbehaviors will be coupled with more discussions, more modeling, and more practicing.

We seek incremental growth in young people, who need us the way Jackie McLean needed Charlie Parker. One problem we have, however, is that unlike McLean, our students don't always welcome us as their mentors! Even so, we persist in nudging them onto the path to social success, and back onto it when they stray. And we'll do it in the context of a give-and-take relationship in which we share our adult powers with them bit by bit, until they can handle responsibly sharing power in the classroom.

Section II establishes the ground we will walk on all year. It sets forth our purposes for being together, learning how to relate well to one another, and practicing social skills so they become part of who we are, not something imposed upon us.

Students who internalize the values and skills of good relationships, courtesy, and self-control have a much greater investment in school and work success, and they find for themselves the moral compass that can guide them through a wholesome, productive life. For now, while they are in the classroom, those relationship and self-management skills will allow them to focus on their immediate task—learning.

This section also contains a chapter devoted to supporting order in the classroom through several basic, important, but often-forgotten ways to keep students engaged in their learning.

Purposes, agreements, routines, and instructional strategies that work set the table for a feast of successful teaching and learning.

Establishing Relationship

A food fight was about to begin in the cafeteria. A girl got mad at another girl and poured a glass of juice on her head. The girl who was doused grabbed a friend, they each grabbed some food, and they went after the one who poured the juice. She ran behind me for protection! I had to say something to stop the escalation, and fortunately I'd had a talk with the girl who'd been hit with the juice just the week before. We had chatted about her life, her family, and things she was interested in. I was trying to get acquainted with her. I think that's why she was able to let me talk her down at this moment. If I hadn't had that talk with her beforehand, I doubt that she would have listened to me at all. But we had some relationship, so she was open to me and I was able to help her to de-escalate.

—Middle level teacher, Harrisburg PA

The process of building adolescent social competence doesn't work well without the crucial ingredient of *relationship*. Every step of the process—setting goals, rule-making, establishing and maintaining routines, responding to rule-breaking—must be supported by positive relationships among the collaborators. For teachers, this means that from the first encounter on the first day with our advisory (or class hour), we make efforts to get to know our students, and to help them feel that they are getting to know us. In other words, we commit to building a climate of trust. Lacking trust, how likely are we to move our students toward success?

The causes of many classroom behaviors labeled and punished as rule infractions are, in fact, problems of students and teachers relating to each other interpersonally." (Sheets and Gay 1996, 86-87)

Researcher Robert Marzano looks at the impact of ways that teachers interact with students, and finds that when teachers use dominance, purposeful interactions that provide strong, unapologetic guidance (rather than submission to student misbehavior), and cooperation, concern for the needs and opinions of their students (rather than an attitude of opposition, me against you), they achieve the optimal teacher-student relationship for learning. (Marzano 2003, 42-43)

As you read this book, you will discover that everything is founded on relationships. So we will begin not with the discipline structures themselves, but with ways to create and maintain good relationships. The advisory period is a great place to start because it is focused on community-building, but relationships can be built all day long in content-area classes as well.

Building Relationship through Gatherings

Daily homeroom/advisory meetings

Daily community gatherings create space and time for relationship-building that can make a huge difference. Many secondary schools designate advisory time for purposefully launching students into each day, ready to learn both socially and academically. Without this time together, both students and teachers stand to lose a great deal. An effective advisory meeting structure gives everyone a chance to encounter and converse about behavior and the management structures we will be using. It allows us to increase student connection to school, practice and internalize social skills, and discuss problematic behaviors. It provides a home base, a place to get to know a group of classmates and a teacher, a place to feel connected.

Studies have shown that students who don't feel an attachment to school staff are likely to have poorer attendance and to drop out more than students who feel that they are part of a supportive school environment. In addition, healthy relationships between teachers and students appear to facilitate academic achievement. Successful advisories can contribute to this type of positive school climate. (Makkonen 2004, 11)

The *Developmental Designs* approach offers two basic structures to begin the day in advisory. Both build trusting, enjoyable relationships in school-appropriate ways. Without this consistent, daily, built-in structure, adolescents are likely to try to meet their need for relationship in exclusionary ways—cliques, gangs, etc.—which inhibit learning. The structures level the playing field among a panoply of personalities. One social skill we are trying to build in every student is assertion. A structured format tamps down a bit on extroverts (who may tend to otherwise dominate the proceedings) while asking for participation on the part of introverts (who may otherwise remain largely invisible to their peers).

The Circle of Power and Respect

A whole-group meeting format called the Circle of Power and Respect (CPR) is a circle meeting (15-25 minutes) ideally held first thing in the morning that lays the groundwork for a successful school day. In the circle everyone can see everyone else, the teacher can see everything, and all students are included. It is the perfect setting to model and practice healthy social interaction, and to respectfully intervene when behaviors slip.

CPR consists of four crucial parts, each of which fosters equity and trust: greeting, sharing, activity, and daily news. A daily greeting allows students to learn each other's names, practice courtesy, and welcome each other. After the greeting, all are more truly present to the school community. The second part, sharing stories about life in and out of school, allows students to get to know one another, practice the art of conversation, and make personal connections to learning. The third part, an activity, encourages students to have fun, engage, cooperate, be inclusive, participate, develop self-control, and learn skills that transfer to academics. Finally, the daily news—posted, written, or presented in letter format—greets, informs, and can be used to teach academic skills.

Activity Plus

Some days, advisory might begin with a quick greeting, and then most of the time may be spent on an activity (current events, homework partners, silent reading, a game in the gym with another advisory group, etc). A few minutes before the end of advisory, the group gathers again in the circle to reflect on what they have done during advisory—what they have learned, and the fun they have had. The important thing in advisory is that we are together, getting to know and enjoy each other, building our relationships into a climate that fosters learning. For abundant ideas on flexible, practical, effective advisories, see the Origins resource *The Advisory Book* (Crawford 2008).

You know the old saying, "Life is a box of chocolates"? Middle school can be like that. Kids come in a variety of shapes, sizes, colors, cultures, and tastes. A middle school can be filled with cliques and clans, but there is a time each day when we all melt together and form a united community. CPR is a time when friends and loners, students and teachers can all blend together and leave negative perspectives behind.

—Middle school advisory student, Hudson MA

Relationship-building all day long

Some schools do not have daily advisory times, or the time allotted is insufficient for relationship-building. Whether this time is available or not, teachers in middle schools and high schools can include quick community-building practices in all their classes. Regularly leading students in a quick greeting, or playing a team-building game on Mondays, or allowing students a few moments to share something about their lives outside school—and participating in these exchanges ourselves—fosters positive relationships.

A team of core subject-area teachers at Bemidji Middle School, in northern Minnesota, decided to integrate as many community-building ideas as possible into their content classes. Their school's schedule meant that they would never be able to run full community-building meetings, so they decided to insert a greeting during one class, a share in another, an activity into a third, an acknowledgment on Fridays—whatever they felt they could squeeze into the period without neglecting their content-driven obligations. They felt that the time they spent engaging students in these activities resulted in a stronger sense of unity throughout the school group, better peer relationships, and better group dynamics during independent work time.

We start out developing community by taking the first few minutes of every class (yes, every class of the day) to do a version of our morning meeting, the Circle of Power and Respect. Each teacher determines the degree to which he or she can fully do CPR daily, but there is always at least an abbreviated meeting to begin class. In this way, we have successfully built community. Students have let us know that they like the CPR routine. We will continue to fine-tune the balance between CPR and curriculum.

—Middle school 7th grade team, Bemidji MN

Class planning meetings

When we gather to plan an upcoming event and give students some input, we build relationship. Students quickly realize the culture in your classroom—and at their school

in general—is one in which voices are heard (and some decisions made) as a group. An extra benefit of planning meetings is that later, when a class problem-solving meeting is needed, students will have an established routine for meetings: a problem-solving meeting becomes just another way we all conduct business together.

Relationship-building outside the classroom

Every time students gather, there is an opportunity to create and reinforce trusting, inclusive connections. There are chunks of time during the day when students are not in class. These times—in the halls, at lunch, at assemblies or team gatherings, at special events—all offer additional opportunities to build relationships among the young people and between them and the adults in their lives. Although the focus of this book is on practices in the classroom, Appendix G provides some ideas for offering these opportunities. The better the relationships we build with our students, the more the rules will be owned and honored by them.

Students respectfully listen and contribute while interacting with the daily news message in their morning meeting

Building Relationship through Conversation

There is no better way to build positive relationships than practicing the art of conversation. Diplomats, business people, journalists, flight attendants, defense attorneys, barbers, police officers, politicians, and parents all know this. We teachers use our conversational skills to great effect, too. Having relationship-building conversations early and often, beginning even before rules are broken (which means you have to begin early!), provides a foundation for the learning that follows.

You get to know your kids so much better when you conference with them. You can be more effective in helping them to adjust and differentiate their learning. Sometimes creating a relationship, showing that you care, is all it takes for students to achieve what they're capable of. No matter what you say to the whole group, talking one-on-one to each student shows that you care in a unique and important way.

—Middle level teacher, LaCrosse WI

One- or two-minute chats

We all do this every day! You check in with as many students as possible during student work time, and you may chat briefly with students during advisory, in the hall or lunchroom, and as they enter or leave your classroom. These spontaneous conversations often do not refer to learning goals and objectives—there's no agenda. The result: positive relationships.

Leveling the conversational playing field

Sometimes our casual conversations with students —those we hold in the margins of the school day— happen with the same students, over and over. Whether we're aware of it or not, the extroverts, or those most comfortable with adults, or those most needy, or our favorites get much of our conversation time. Making an effort to chat casually with students with whom we might not otherwise talk may help level the "relationship playing field" for all students. The goal is to have a moment of relationship with all the students you teach during the course of a week or two. These moments transform teacher-to-whole-group relating to something more personal. *I know you see me because you spoke to me and me alone, in a friendly way.* That moment could make all the difference in a subsequent moment of correction.

You can monitor the degree to which you are spreading evenly your casual conversations within each of your classes. For example, at the end of the second or third week of each new term, you can look at your class rosters and place a check mark in a column for "Chatted with him/her." The following school days, you can take a minute here and there to have a friendly exchange with those whose names you didn't check.

Another way to reflect on student relationships is to scan each class and make a quick note of anyone for whom you can't recall much detail about his or her life, or with whom you haven't spoken for a while. Chances are those relationships could use a boost. Alternatively, you could use Donald Graves' exercise from *The Energy to Teach* (see page 234) to identify students you need to converse with in the near future.

Five-minute social conferences

In addition to quick talks with students, strengthening relationships by holding a more extended, planned conversation can have big payoffs. A five-minute relationship-building conference is an intentional conversation used to get to know students during a time when they are not "in trouble," i.e., when they are emotionally clear-headed.

At the secondary level, even the most gifted relationship-builders among us have few chances for extended one-to-one conversations with students during the school day. Who has the time?! Yet finding time to do so with those who need it most helps establish trusting, positive, teacher-student relationships.

Talking proactively with students who are potential behavioral challenges lays the groundwork for a successful problem-solving conference later, when we have to respond to those challenges (see problem-solving conferences on page 194). Taking time to talk to them up front helps us know how to build upon their strengths and interests, encourage them, and uncover potential obstacles to success before they manifest as rule-breaking. It enables the students to see that we have their best interests in mind— we really do care. They'll be more likely to accept our way of doing things if this caring attitude is expressed by us and received by them early in the school year.

Steps of a five-minute social conference

Becoming comfortable with a meeting structure you haven't used before takes time and practice. Until fluency is developed, following prescribed steps is helpful. For some, doing so will seem forced at first, but this awkwardness diminishes as familiarity increases and the structure itself becomes embedded in our repertoire of tools. Each step takes a minute or less. Don't make any speeches—just give a specific, descriptive acknowledgment of something the student is doing well.

1. Noticing strengths and naming their payoffs

Describe something positive you've noticed about this student. Be specific—don't give general strokes. Ask if the student has noticed this, too. If you find it difficult to come up with positives, comment on something the student appears to put lots of effort into.

Charlene, I've noticed that you've participated in class every day this week. Have you been aware of this, too?

I've also noticed you appear to have lots of friends here, that the other students like you. Do you see it that way?

Name the payoffs of the student's positive behavior. Describe how the behavior ultimately will get the student what she wants (supports her individual goals) and how it helps everyone else as well (supports Social Contract).

Your participation helps us live up to our rule: Do your best work.

Do you see how your consistent participation helps you meet your own goals and also preserves our rules?

Having friends should make you feel comfortable here, and maybe your good relationships will allow you to take on some leadership roles; others are more likely to accept being led by someone they like.

2. Understanding

Help the student uncover specifically what she is doing to make things work. Help her raise her consciousness about her behavior. Ask the student to think about the strengths she is using to behave positively.

Charlene, how are you keeping yourself aware and actively participating?

What strategies or strengths are you using?

How did you learn this strategy?

Devon, you have so many friends! In your opinion, what is it about you that others like? What do you do to get people on your side?

Help the student along if she has no ideas. If you get a shrug, a look of puzzlement, or an embarrassed, "I don't know!" from your student, prime the pump by offering a few possible explanations.

Could it be....

Is it that you....

Maybe it's because you....

But if it appears that she won't be able to come up with a reason for her success, say what you see and why you think it helps her make friends and/or succeed in academics.

3. Next steps

Help the student think about how he can use his strengths in other situations.

How can you use participation and making friends to help you in other situations in life?

Can I help you in any way?

4. Acknowledgment

Reinforce positive behavior.

Your high level of participation is paying off.

Your social skills are going to help us get a lot accomplished this year.

I have a lot of respect for anyone who works hard towards a goal.

By following our guidelines you're helping all of us. Thank you.

5. Check in

Suggest that the two of you talk again soon. Sometimes a check-in will simply give the student another moment of contact with a caring adult; it also begins to build a relationship within which she can be held accountable.

I'd like to help you keep a good thing going. Let's talk again soon.

Consider taking notes during (or after) the conference for future reference. If a problem-solving conference is needed later to redirect negative behavior, you can review the notes, using them to remind the student of his assets and his thoughts about them. If such a corrective conference is necessary, you will begin from a place of relationship, the only basis that works to help most struggling students.

Watch out for the pitfall

The language you use is one of the most important things to keep in mind during any social conference. There can be no veiled references to mistakes in the past, and no "buts" that move from acknowledging strengths to correcting weaknesses. We have to carefully avoid discussing a hidden agenda, even if we think it will help them change counter-productive behaviors into positive ones. Adolescents are always waiting for the other shoe to fall, for the "Now about getting assignments in on time..." endings to what start out as encouragement and acknowledgment. Instead, try to keep it to: *I see you. I see your strengths. I encourage you to keep building upon them.*

Pick a few students for five-minute social conferencing

At the beginning of each new term, target a few students who would benefit from five positive minutes with you. Student "types" with whom to consider conferencing:

Students who have been "red-flagged" by others

Take time to converse with a student whose negative reputation precedes him, i.e. a student who has been identified by others as a significant behavioral challenge. When a teacher warns you about a student he had last year: "Watch out for Billy! He's a piece of work," or when a parent pays you a visit prior to the school year to discuss her daughter's social problems last year, a positive social conference may be useful. It's best not to prejudge anyone based on others' perspectives, yet ignoring the warning may also be foolish. The proactive conference can help you head off rule-breaking before it happens—an approach that is a lot easier and more effective than correcting it afterward.

Struggling students who worry you

Confer with a student who appears troubled—lonely, angry, scared, or distracted, someone who appears to be living in her private, inner world. A short conversation with that student might be the beginning of a trusting relationship with an adult, something she'll need to make it to adulthood safely.

Students who show capacity for leadership

Consider conferencing to create a partnership. As we all know, students with the most social charisma sometimes lead their peers down antisocial paths. Forming a genuine relationship with a student who has influence with his peers can make things smoother for all.

Struggling students who have had some success

When a student who has struggled in a specific area (homework completion, tardiness, blurting, conflict with peers) finally succeeds, acknowledge it. Build on the success she's had by talking with her about it, and you may have the beginnings of a new leader, someone with the strength to conquer adversity.

Struggling students who need a fresh start

Facilitate a fresh start when the beginning of a new term or an extended break presents an opportunity for a struggling student to begin again and have a chance to shine.

Using conferences to build student leadership skills

Conferences are opportunities to help students learn important leadership skills. Talk about:

- Leading a CPR meeting or activity for the first time. Have the student check in with you to share his plan and make sure he's prepared. This is especially helpful to the shyer, more introverted student who may nonetheless be capable of leading others.

- Helping a struggling peer

- Welcoming or orienting a new student

- Orchestrating class acknowledgments
- Representing your advisory at an all-school meeting or student council

Opportunities abound! Your struggling students could end up doing wonderful things for the world, and school is a place to begin to develop their leadership skills—academic and social. Many struggling students are natural leaders who, left unguided, may lead others down the wrong path.

Building and Preserving Relationship Moment by Moment

Whenever teachers are with students—chatting briefly, in a structured conference, during instruction, or in other situations—they are in the process of creating relationship. Advisory meetings, class community-building, and conferences offer specific structures for building relationship, but every interaction can contribute to relationship.

Relationship emerges from our language and from our manner, how we are *being*—the climate we create for interactions. How can we choose tone, body language, and words moment by moment to support positive relationships with students? Most broadly, we maintain a positive, effective teacher mindset. The action, growth, and emotional objectivity mindsets outlined in Chapter 2 provide productive context for making the many decisions and adjustments that will support teacher-student relationship. The consistent subtext of all the messages, whatever the content, needs to be: *I accept you, I want to get to know you. I'm on your side.*

The message can be communicated in as many ways as there are teachers! There is not a formula for all, and although developing a vocabulary of effective, non-judgmental phrases helps, a belief in students' capacity to grow, and a commitment to their growth, no matter what flack we may get in response to our efforts, are frames of mind that can take many forms.

Two teachers from Minneapolis and St. Paul, Minnesota, are good examples of the wide range of expression possible. Marguerite talks straight and sometimes tough to her students:

OK. That's enough. You know where you're supposed to be and what you're supposed to be doing. Frances, remind us all.

Any opportunity to talk with a student is an opportunity to build relationship

Clara's language is straight, too, but warm, no matter what the message:

We didn't do very well at the start of class today. We must have had a lot on our minds, because some forgot to read the message and respond, and the noise level was way above the calm start we said we were aiming for. Tomorrow I'll put a reminder in the message, and who's willing to be at the door with me to remind everybody as they come in?

Both Marguerite and Clara make it clear that things must change. Both evidence a no-nonsense commitment to the belief that their students are capable of doing better, and neither one is taking things personally. But the vocabulary they use and the tone and expression are quite different, and that difference denotes the authenticity with which each teacher works. Other teachers may use a hybrid of these or other approaches, or vary their mode depending on the instance. Part of finding our ground as teachers is creating the authentic form that our expressions of understanding and determination will take.

Challenges of Building Relationship and Community

Q. *How much should I divulge about myself early in the school year? Should I keep my focus largely on academics to avoid having students think I am soft because I share about myself?*

Students can and do distinguish between a teacher who is soft because he is reluctant to enforce high standards, and a teacher who is soft as in friendly and approachable, but is very clear that rules will be followed or there will be consequences. The challenge is to show both sides of yourself. If you get even the slightest hint that students are beginning to take advantage of your friendliness, talk straight to the issue, and tell them to make no mistake about it.

I want to get to know you and I want you to get to know me. But at the same time, I am very clear that on my watch, no one will treat others in this room any way but respectfully.

Q. *How can I keep my students invested in our social skills development and community-building when other classes are not doing it, there are so many academic pressures, and even some of their families wonder why we're spending time this way?*

Familiarize yourself with the abundant research that supports social and emotional learning, and share this information with students and their parents. (The CASEL website, casel.org, is a good place to start.) You'll find plenty of data to support the idea that community-building and student attachment to both the people and the work of school greases the wheels of motivation and academic success. Investment in community-building is investment in academics.

Research clearly shows that in schools where SEL [social-emotional learning] is treated as a regular part of the curriculum rather than as something extraneous to it, students are better prepared to learn. Schools where SEL competencies are taught have been shown to foster student attachment to school and receptivity to learning, factors which are strongly linked to academic success. (CASEL 2003, 6)

A review of social and emotional learning programs involving 180 studies and more than 250,000 students indicated significant gains for students in the following areas:

- Increased social-emotional skills in test situations (e.g., self-control, decision-making, communication, and problem-solving skills);
- More positive attitudes toward self and others (e.g., self-concept, self-esteem, prosocial attitudes toward aggression, and liking and feeling connected to school);
- More positive social behaviors (e.g., daily behaviors related to getting along with and cooperating with others);
- Fewer conduct problems (e.g., aggression, disruptiveness);
- Lower levels of emotional distress (i.e., anxiety, depressive symptoms); and
- Significantly better academic performance (i.e., school grades and achievement test scores)

(Payton et al. 2008, 7)

I spend less time on behavior and I spend more time in discourse and discussion on class topics throughout the rest of the year because I sacrificed a little more time at the beginning of the year for social development. The work that I did in the beginning—developing the class contract, getting to know one another, teaching students what it looks like to listen to each other and respect each other during discussion or shares—these are things I don't have to spend as much time on throughout the year. There are fewer breakdowns and I don't have to stop the class to correct them. I can enjoy the students as individuals and get to know them better, instead of focusing on getting them to follow my orders. There's a real give and take in the class now because of the time I spent on the preliminary steps.

—High school teacher, Cambridge MA

Q. *I'm a teacher, not a camp counselor! Isn't my job is to instruct students in my subject area, not build friendly communities?*

Actually, your job includes both, if for no other reason than that you can't have one without the other. Time on task means time spent learning. You may be doing the things teachers do, but if students are scared, angry, or generally feeling vulnerable and unsafe in your room, they will not learn to their maximum from you. Spend some time building relationships so that you can create a vigorous learning climate within which you can teach and students can and will learn.

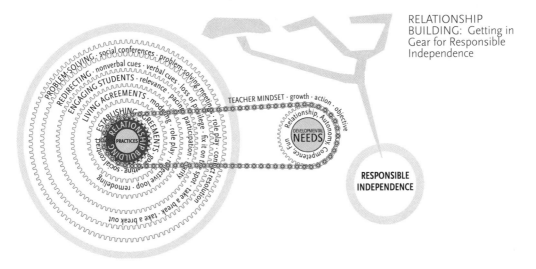

RELATIONSHIP BUILDING: Getting in Gear for Responsible Independence

Establishing Purposes and Agreements

—true for adults too! [handwritten note]

When a group of people set out to spend a significant amount of time together, they need clear understandings about how they will be as a group, what behavior is OK and what is not. In school, guidelines for the group can be set autocratically, by the adults alone, or by the adults and students together. Because we want to foster internalized social competence and responsibility and an authentic investment, rather than mere compliance, we share power with students and create rules collaboratively.

Democracy in the schools is a necessary bridge between the family and the outside society in providing experiences of democratic participation and community leading to the development of social responsibility. (Kohlberg 1985, 39)

How can we guide adolescents to invest themselves in a democratic rule-making process? How can they put enough at stake to be willing to control themselves and follow the rules? Goal-setting provides the motivation for them to do so.

Some students have never liked school very much, and may not see any connection between school and happiness in life. Developmentally, adolescents still lack what is called the "executive function," that part of the brain which guides decision-making and judgment, so planning ahead for growth in the future feels foreign to them. Even so, it is empowering for students to establish a purpose for their education, a goal, in the first few days of the academic year. If they can identify for themselves good reasons to put effort into school and find a positive direction for themselves, they'll be on their way toward linking school with happiness. We can help them do that.

Laying a path

This chapter begins to define *Developmental Designs* behavior management structures with the practices of

Assessing student strengths and areas of growth

Setting and reinforcing goals

Collaboratively creating and supporting rules

The process of identifying goals and then establishing rules to protect those goals offers behavior support to all students, no matter what capacities they already possess or need to develop. All students—those with excellent self-control and internal motivation and those who need assistance beyond the structures described in this chapter—benefit from a collaborative approach to establishing purposes and rules. For those who need additional support—especially those who generally lack social skills—the structures in this chapter are *necessary*, but not *sufficient*. Once you establish purposes and rules, you have a strong foundation upon which everyone can build social competence.

Steps along the path

Ideally, student reflections on what they have at stake in school occur in both advisory and class hours, in the form of goal-setting. With goals expressing student investments in having a good year, the rule-making process can begin. Coming to agreement about guidelines is most easily managed within the advisory period. Once each advisory group in the school agrees upon guidelines, representatives from each advisory can meet to combine their rules and establish team rules. A final step can be to create school rules by combining all the team rules. The school rules then are recognized by everyone, and provide uniform, agreed-upon parameters all day long and everywhere. All of these processes are described in detail in this chapter.

Individual goals and advisory rules

Advisory: First, students set for themselves broad social and/or academic goals for the year. Then students and teachers create rules for advisory to achieve their goals and guide behavior.

Class hours: Students can set specific, content-related goals for the semester or year in their subject-area classes. Those teachers can then report content-related goals back to advisory teachers.

Families: When families come to school early in the year for conferences, we have an opportunity to share with them what their children have declared as goals for the year, invite their comments and insights, and encourage them to support their achievement. If your school holds more extended individual goal-setting conferences early in the year, include families in the process and thereby create a partnership among student, teacher, and family around specific academic and social goals.

Extending the process to team and school rules

Teams: Representatives from each advisory meet to negotiate and agree upon rules for the whole team

School: Representatives from each team agree on school-wide rules. The school-wide rules then replace individual advisory rules.

Advisory: School rules are then signed and posted in each advisory. They guide behavior there and in class hours.

If a school doesn't have an advisory period, both academic and social goals can be constructed during a class hour and combined by sending a representative from each class to a team-wide or school-wide meeting. Even if you are the only teacher in your school who has decided to democratically establish rules with your students, you can do it—but it's more work. You need to go through the goal-setting and rule-making process for each one of your classes at the beginning of the semester to achieve the payoff of greater student investment in the guidelines.

GOAL SETTING

I wanted my 6th graders to help create a structure of support for their challenging first year in middle school. I decided to first engage them in an activity called Group Juggle to demonstrate the demands placed on middle school students. We began by tossing one ball around the circle in a pattern so that each student received and threw the ball once. As the ball was passed, students said the names of the students from whom they received the ball and to whom they tossed it. Once the pattern was established, I added more balls of different shapes and sizes until we were tossing several balls simultaneously. We stopped occasionally for discussion about how we could improve the game.

Afterwards, we discussed how this activity was like the dynamics of sixth grade. Students responded, "We have to work together to accomplish things;" "We have to focus on the task at hand;" "We have to be aware of what comes next;" and "We have to juggle our classes, homework, friends, and after-school activities all at the same time."

Next, students decorated one side of a 5" x 8" index card, including their names and symbols representing some of their interests and abilities. On the other side, they wrote two academic and two social goals for the term, goals that would help motivate them through the challenges of the year. Here are some of their goals: "I want to learn to be more organized." "I want to try hard to understand math more and pay closer attention in class." "I want to keep up my personal standard of good grades." "I hope to hand in all of my assignments on time and really be on top of my school work." "I want to improve my typing skills and learn how to touch type on the computer."

Our next step was to create rules together to guide us in fulfilling all our goals.

—6th grade teacher, Hanover NH

Why Set Goals

Goals fulfill adolescents' need for a sense of competence. It is difficult to experience yourself as growing in competence if you do not have a clear idea of where you are going, and a way of measuring whether you've made progress in getting there. All we have to motivate our students is what Mother Nature gave them—those powerful needs to experience themselves as competent, autonomous, and likable enough to have friends, all while they are having fun. Goal-setting feeds the first two very well, because it provides markers towards which students can move with strength and growing independence.

Goals provide a stake in the rules

Our aim is to involve students in creating for themselves authentic purposes for learning, and the guidelines (rules) within which learning will take place in our school. It is far more meaningful for students to follow the rules, and more meaningful for the teacher to require it, if they have an important stake in school. Goal-setting is a form of anteing up before the game. It says that we each have an investment in the way the year, the day, and each class period goes. It gives young adolescents a vision of the payoff for all the hard work it will take to manage themselves responsibly. They need to identify something that is important to them as a payoff for behaving the way a successful student behaves.

In his research on motivation psychologist Edward Deci identifies the qualities that make goals "autonomy supportive," that not only support focus on learning, but also appeal to the adolescent desire for autonomy. He writes: "To be most effective, goals need to be individualized—they need to be suited specifically to the person who will work toward them—and they need to represent an optimal challenge.... Goals that are autonomy-supportive are optimal goals to which people will commit because they themselves played an active role in formulating them." (Deci 1995, 152-153)

Preparing for Setting Goals

First, relationship

We always begin with human connection. Helping students think about their futures, their strengths, and their hopes happens in a climate of trust. Why would I tell you my hopes for my life if I don't know you and doubt that you know (or care about) me?! Hoping and dreaming out loud requires a certain amount of vulnerability, and probably will not happen until you and your students have begun to talk together, have some fun, and learn about each other.

There are lots of ways to spark students' thinking about what they want out of school and life (see below). In addition to these tools, when a teacher expresses friendly confidence that the student is capable of great things, great things usually begin to happen. People attest to this all the time:

It was my 8ᵗʰ grade language arts teacher who first read and responded to my writing with excitement. It had never occurred to me before that I could be a writer!

We can be the voice of the ambition that might not occur to them unless we say it. Our noticing their capabilities and possibilities occurs in the context of our relationship with them. The better the relationship with a student, the more we are likely to see his or her possibilities.

Teacher assessments and student self-assessments

School offers a fresh start every year. Teachers know that to take full advantage of it, they have to identify each student's starting place. How can you know where to go next unless you know where you are beginning? This involves more than simply reading student records from the previous year. In fact, many teachers avoid the pre-judgment that can come from looking back.

To assess where a student is beginning the year academically, teachers may select from several available inventories and baseline tests (written and oral); have students show the skills they have developed so far by writing, reading aloud, taking tests to indicate skills in spelling, computation, math and science vocabulary, and so on. Most schools build into the beginning of the year a period for school orientation; teachers can use some of the orientation time to assess each student's beginning point.

In addition to teacher assessment, we suggest having students look at themselves and take stock. A successful goal-setting process often begins with a good look at yourself—your interests, beliefs, values, talents, what motivates you, how you like to spend your time, what you don't like, what you don't do well, etc. We can help meet students' needs for competence and autonomy by inviting them to reflect before they set goals. They'll set better goals for themselves if we give them time at the beginning to explore who they are.

Developmentally, this is a great place to start with adolescents: your group may be extremely diverse academically, but everyone can succeed when it comes to identifying personal interests, motivations, hobbies, and favorites. In addition, sharing these self-explorations with classmates helps build relationships by providing low-risk opportunities to get to know each other, make connections, and thereby make school an emotionally safer place. And teachers gain insights about their students as they learn what students think about themselves.

We can go through this self-study process with them. We can offer appropriate information about ourselves, showing that we know good relationships are a two-way exchange, and we're willing participants. In this process, students begin to experience the importance of reflection and sharing personal information. They may take an initial risk in what feels like a safe place to do so, and the community begins to form.

There are many easy, enjoyable approaches to student reflection on their performance. Here is an example, and you'll find several others in Appendix B.

Bio poems for getting to know students' interests, families, and feelings

Use the categories to help students write biographical poems, or bio poems. When these personal poems are shared, the classroom community learns about facts, interests, and feelings of each of its members. Students begin to notice their common ground, a stimulus for peer connections.

Bio poem format

Line 1: Your first name

Line 2: Who is.... (words that describe you)

Line 3: Who is brother or sister of....

Line 4: Who loves.... (3 ideas, places, seasons, activities, pets, or people)

Line 5: Who feels.... (3 ideas)

Line 6: Who needs.... (3 ideas)

Line 7: Who gives.... (3 ideas)

Line 8: Who fears.... (3 ideas)

Line 9: Who would like to see.... (a place or event)

Line 10: Who wishes.... (1 idea)

Line 11: Who is.... (a quality or character trait)

Line 12: Who is a resident of....

Line 13: Your last name

Brainstorm a list of words with the class for any of the lines you think may be difficult. After the students write their bio poems, they can add illustrations or designs. They may share them aloud or post them on a "getting-to-know-us" display board. A guessing game may be played in which each poem is read aloud by someone other than the author and the audience is given three guesses to identify the author.

Bio poem example

Frankie

Who is energetic and intelligent

Who is the brother of Jacob and Rose

Who loves Ichiro Suzuki, James Brown, and good food

Who feels hyper, hopeful, and happy

Who needs food, freedom, and an allowance

Who gives friendship, time, and laughs

Who fears food poisoning, wild boars, and fear itself

Who would like to see all the Major League Baseball stadiums

Who wishes he could fly to all the Major League Baseball stadiums

Who is loyal

Who is a resident of Houston, Texas

McCreary

Guiding students to think about their behavior is a key to their social growth. And if they haven't thought about who they are first, reflection on their behavior (something I insist they do on an ongoing basis) is detached from their awareness of who they are.

—Middle level teacher, LaCrosse WI

Work from a growth mindset in the goal-setting process

Once we've thought about where we are, we begin to plan where we want to go. Teachers play a crucial role in motivating students to think deeply as they create their goals. Here, the teacher's *growth mindset* introduced in Chapter 2 is crucial (page 20). When we approach each student believing that he or she is capable of learning, we help establish a climate for growth. Our belief in the student's capacity for growth, reflected in our language and our way of being, is contagious. We are convinced that even students who feel the hopelessness of repeated failures can and will succeed this year in this class, and our commitment can shift them into possibility. How do we know? We don't, really—not the way you know the student's date of birth, for example. It lives as a conviction, a powerful intention: *under my watch, this student will succeed!*

Steps of Goal Setting

Teachers must carve out time to lead students through the goal-setting process. As soon as possible—the first week of school is ideal, right after the self-assessment exercises—invite students to think about why learning is important to them, and to declare their intentions, or goals, for the academic year. Goal-setting can occur in each class hour and in advisory time. Ideally, the process continues with goal-setting conferences with families, creating alliances around academic and social goals for the students.

i. Inspire students to value school enough to establish goals

Establishing the importance of school for fulfilling ourselves in life often requires inspiration. Many students have never seen the promise of their lives. Some come from generational poverty, and ambition is nowhere in their picture. Some lack a belief in their own capacity for growth. They may have a fixed idea of what they can accomplish and what they can't, and there may be no room in their picture for the possibility that they could become scientists or historians, musicians or politicians. Some live in the context of other people's fixed expectations of what they will do and how they will do it. If we can help our students see possibilities for their lives, they are likely to have the courage to declare hopes and dreams for themselves.

Build relationship

How do we inspire hope in the face of hopelessness or resignation? First, establish a personal connection. If a student can see that you care about him, he may begin to dream a little. In the course of a conversation in which you acknowledge a capacity you see in him, he may step out and declare a goal. You might tell your students a story about how important school has been in your own life, and how it helped you get what you want. You might tell about former students who took school seriously, and where they are now, or about a student who at first had a fixed mindset, how he or she transformed that into an attitude of possibility, and what doors opened for him or her.

Provide inspiration from others

Set the tone for positive, meaningful planning. Tell a personal story, read a narrative or poem, watch a film or film clip, display a work of art, or play a piece of music that inspires people to reach for a point beyond where they are at the moment. If you do this process with your subject-area students, tell them a story about something that touches you and why you chose to focus on this subject in your own education and life.

Often, we are up against the discouragement of prior poor performance and/or outcomes. Some students find it almost impossible to believe they can achieve a goal, big or small, in a particular subject or in school in general. Storytelling, poems, narratives, and other art forms bring warmth and build the community that may help the student open to his own possibility.

You might bring in a former student to talk about how taking school seriously has paid off for him, and now he's on his way to a high-school diploma. Perhaps an adult who has achieved in life against the odds could visit and share about the role school played in his success. You might find a film clip or a reading that inspires interest in achievement in school and life. A picture book such as *More Than Anything Else*, by Marie Bradley, the story of the education of Booker T. Washington, is worth the ten minutes it takes to read aloud to inspire the idea that what seems impossible is often achieved largely through the courage of committing to a plan.

See page 256, Stories and Conversations that Inspire Goal Setting, for ideas about books, films, exercises, and discussions to stimulate conversations about having the courage to invest hope and effort in your own future. Such conversations, combined

NT Community Connection

with our capacity as teachers to hold a hopeful space open for students until they can occupy it for themselves, can create new meaning for their school experience.

Extra support for some

You cannot simply turn goal-setting over to a deeply apathetic student. You'll have to manage the process enough to be sure he sets achievable goals, even if they seem very small. He may be able to move from success to success if you help him design goals limited enough for even a student who makes only half an effort to achieve. Step by step, you help him choose goals that could give him the experience, maybe for the first time in his life, of going from success to success.

Perhaps you need to find something larger than school learning, some other stake in life that the student has. Perhaps he wants to make a lot of money, or he might dream of becoming a professional athlete. In either case, success in school will enhance his chances, and you can help him make that connection. If you suspect that he has in mind working outside the law, helping him see the bleak possibilities for life after one has been convicted of a crime might expose the shortcomings of that plan. Perhaps you can get help from another teacher, another student, or his family. Building a personal relationship with him is a pathway to trust, and with trust comes the possibility of hope and a positive, meaningful goal.

2. Write goals

A student prepares to share her poem; setting goals connects students to learning

Have students consider this broad question: "What do you want to achieve in life? What would you like to contribute?" A young adolescent may rise to this with his own brand of idealism and her own sense of justice. Most have something they'd like to see happen in their lives. Connect this hope to school. "What do you need to achieve this year in school to move you closer to your life goals (or in this class)?" They may write their responses in journals, academic planners, or on loose-leaf paper. They can write one or more academic, social, study, leadership, and/or extracurricular goal(s).

Additional questions to guide goal-setting

What do you want most out of school this year?

What is your goal for reading and writing? Math?

What do you need to work on specifically to achieve those goals?

What is your goal for getting along with everyone?

What is one thing you can do to improve your relationships with other students?

What is your goal for living according to the rules?

What behavior might you do differently this year to help you stay within the rules? What is your goal for _____?

Your aim is for students to find and name a place to stand for investing in school and in the rules soon to be formulated. Almost any sincere goal can help provide that place. If a student's declared goal is to become a millionaire or a professional athlete, you can easily make the connection between those goals and the necessity for self-control. For purposes of creating a stake in the rules, it is necessary only to establish that effort and the habits of self-management will be needed to achieve the goal.

If you have the opportunity to develop student goals into specific goal plans for the purpose of assessing ongoing social and academic growth, students will have an extra advantage. See Appendix C for sample goal-setting forms, and for more information on expanding goals in conferences with families or in the classroom.

Public or private?

You may decide to keep goals private and confidential, at least for a while. They might be amended or changed in the future, and they may or may not be made public in the next step. This is one of those times when it pays to go slow to go fast. *It is always up to students whether to share their goals with people other than their parents and teachers.* In some groups, everybody shares easily. In others, perhaps where students have a history of low achievement, one way to encourage powerful goal-setting is to promise that all goals will be kept private.

3. Transform goals into declarations

Goals exist as mere wishes and hopes until students give them the muscle of *declarations*.

Consider the difference between "I want to improve my math skills" and "I *will* improve my math skills." In the declarations step, students identify themselves as *cause in the matter*. Each declaration begins, "I will...." Their goals become, in John Dewey's words, "an idea with a future," (1938) or, in popular parlance "ideas with legs." Declarations state what the student is committed to *doing*. Remind your students that the Declaration of Independence didn't merely state a desire of the colonists. It declared them change agents, shapers of the future. You might say:

One powerful thing we can do with the goals we just wrote is to turn them into declarations. By beginning each goal with "I will..." we declare to ourselves and the world what we're going to do to make sure our actions fulfill our purpose. A declaration is a call to action. You are stepping up and declaring, "This is what I will do!" Declarations tell people you should be taken seriously.

Imagining success

Learners can pause for a moment after having made a declaration of personal growth and visualize themselves in possession of the knowledge and skills they want. Their imagined consequences of success may be shared in pairs or with the whole group, or kept private.

If we're successful this year, what will the payoffs be for you? How will each of us be different? What impact will our new knowledge have on the world now and in the future?

Encourage students to set their own goals, share them with others, and talk about why they chose them. Ask students to put some stakes in the goals: "What will happen when you reach your goal, and what will you experience?" When students realize they may experience, for example, increased satisfaction, this discovery creates emotional hooks to the goals. (Jensen 2005, 37)

4. Teachers commit to goals

Students have expressed their commitment to their goals by making declarations. Now the teacher declares his or her commitment to all the students' declarations.

The declarations you've just written are important to me. I promise to do everything I can to make sure you all have every opportunity to achieve your goals.

Throughout the goal-setting process, the language used by teachers is paramount. How we talk to students, and whether what we say encourages reflection among them, can define the kind of relationship we have with each student. We need to be especially clear and forceful in our speaking when we express support for students' declared goals. Students need to understand intellectually and emotionally that the adults in their lives are committed to their success. If they *feel* it's true as they hear it said, the promise of our support will have more power.

Commit to our own teaching goals

We can strengthen the adult-adolescent connection by sharing our own authentic goals for the year. That declares our personal stake in how things go during the year, and solidifies our place in the community. It lets them know that goal-setting isn't babyish—it's for everyone—and we're all in this together.

Goals and declarations display

Reinforcing Goals and Declarations through Creative Display

Words are powerful. They can be calls to action. However, most of us have probably vowed to do something but not followed through. The fate of most New Year's resolutions is a good example of our often unrealized intention to keep promises at the forefront of our thoughts and actions over time. One way to help us remember to strive for our goals is to keep them visually present in our daily lives in the form of a declaration from each student as a reminder of his or her goals.

You can take this step either before or after initial goals have been expanded, but because this display is a symbolic device, it is best to record a single declaration as a reminder of each student's overall goals. Goal-setting forms will function as working documents for periodically assessing progress and making adjustments (see page 250).

Going public

To demonstrate commitment to their goals publicly (if you and they wish to go public), students can write one declaration (their favorite, or the most important one) on a sticky note, sign it, and place it on a group declarations chart. For a private approach, declarations can be written on pieces of paper which are then folded, sealed, and then perhaps arranged in a display. Or students can write letters to themselves that include their declarations, sign them, and seal them in envelopes to be opened when goals and declarations are revisited at mid-semester or mid-year, and at the end of the year. The letters allow for the possibility of going public later on.

Individual student declaration

Aesthetic appeal demonstrates importance

The visual vehicle for holding everyone's declarations needs to be attractive. You might decide to make your declarations display beautiful by using special paper, color, or calligraphy. You might use a beautiful container to honor the importance of the declarations. Some teams or schools pick a theme such as the nighttime sky, with each declaration written on a star signed or unsigned, as the student chooses. Other ideas for themes are parades, balloons, a garden, or a torch with the declarations as "sparks." Clusters of geometric shapes can be interesting, as can a display of goals folded into envelope shapes.

One team had students seal their written declarations in envelopes, which they then hung from the ceiling of the advisory room. They opened their envelopes on the first school day in January for reflection and revision as necessary, then hung them up again. Opening them again on the last day of school was part of their ritual goodbye to the year.

Students will come up with their own ideas for display, and art teachers may make exciting suggestions. When it's first completed, the display provides an opportunity for a formal dedication of the community to the hopes each person has for a successful school year, and thereafter it serves as a reminder that everyone in this community has a purpose for being here and is on a journey to success. Seeing our goals and declarations displayed on the wall or hanging from the ceiling helps everyone remember that we are all on our way to somewhere important.

When and where to create displays

In a school with advisory or teacher teams, each advisory teacher can create a display with one class of students. In the absence of advisory, the team can select a class hour during which everyone will set aside the subject-area curriculum and create a display of their declarations in the hallway. As the students move through the school, the visual reminder continues to evoke the vital context for their lives at school. For teachers who are working independently in this approach, consider creating small displays with each class to avoid overwhelming your space.

See pages 258-263 for more examples of creating declaration displays.

Reinforcing Goals and Declarations through Regular Reflection

Displays offer symbolic reminders of goals. But what makes declarations about the future truly powerful as a tool for remaining connected to school is the abiding presence of the goals in our lives over time. We can refer to students' goals for the year any time we are talking with them, either about their work or their behavior.

Salome, think about your math goal for this year as you work on these problems, and be sure to ask for help if you need it.

Shannon, your goal is to be more assertive this year. What are you doing to try to meet that goal during large-group discussion?

Damone, you want to be a rapper. That means you have to have some interesting things to say and a rhythm to your language. Let's look at this piece of writing for both.

Deirdre, you want to pass all your subjects this year. How are you doing so far? Are there any changes you need to make in your behavior in school so you get what you want?

Advisory students can also revisit their goals in a more focused way once or twice during the year to reflect on the progress they have made and to make adjustments in practice or in the goal itself, as necessary. Some advisory teachers allow time to write in journals about goals or for partner conversations, and then the whole group can gather to listen to revisions or reaffirmations of where each student is headed. These comments can be specific ("I've been reading more and I'm going to stick with this goal but set a target of reading five books in second semester.") or general ("I'm staying out of trouble for the rest of the year").

In schools where goal-setting involves each student in establishing academic goals for each class, the process of reflecting on goals can extend into a kind of individual learning plan for every student using goal-setting/tracking forms and conferences that may include families. See page 252 for more on academic as well as social goal-setting and monitoring processes.

Whether you extend the goal-setting process into academics or not, the thoughtful consideration of any objectives over time is very useful. The cycle is a simple one that successful people have always used: make a plan; act; reflect on the outcome and plan for next time. It's a continuous loop of reviewing each thing we do in order to improve it. Some describe the process as Plan/Do/Review; others call it Plan/Work/ Reflect; some refer to the cycle of growth, or the learning cycle. We call it the Reflective Loop (see page 101). The process is always the same, and the results are likely to be continuous improvement. The Reflective Loop is useful to just about everything we do in school or in life.

Challenges of Setting Goals

Q. *How can I help students who struggle to find meaningful goals?*

Settling on goals can be difficult for a variety of reasons. Common barriers include unwillingness to take a risk *(What am I supposed to say about myself? What's the point of some pie-in-the-sky goal?)*; a fixed mindset that leads to hopelessness *(I hate school. I never get good grades* or *I'm a jock—my goal is to make points in every game.)*; a budding academic narcissism *(I don't need goals. I always get A's anyway.)*; genuine inability to make a decision; student/teacher/parent disagreement about goals; and so on. Sending home a goal-setting form and asking students and their parents or guardians to write down ideas for goals can help. Develop a set of commonly used goals as a sample (see page 248). If your advisees need help setting goals for an academic area outside your expertise, you might consult with colleagues or discuss students at a team meeting, or refer a student who is having difficulty deciding on a goal in a specific content area to a teacher who is better able to guide him or her.

Students who are discouraged or confused and unable to set clear goals need a spark. Knowing the student well is a great advantage. Remind students of their interests-and-strength inventories. Tell about a challenging goal you've set for yourself, even though you doubt you will be able to reach it. Suggest what you believe would be a challenging but realizable goal for the student.

A language-arts teacher tells a student that his writing suggests that he might become a fine poet. A social-studies teacher suggests that a student is a tenacious arguer and might excel at debate or dramatizations of two sides of a social issue. What they are doing is holding the space of possibility open for the student until she has the courage to hold it for herself.

You have a strong, individual voice, Delores. Expressing it on paper would be a great goal for you for this year—and I would enjoy helping you.

Q. *I receive a lot of information about a student before he or she becomes part of my class. How can I integrate what I learn about a student's past into the goal-setting process?*

Teachers have struggled with this situation for years. Some choose not to look at student histories beforehand to guard against pre-judging. On the other hand, one might glean important insights from other teachers' observations. Remember that neither you nor last year's teachers know all that this student might be capable of. As discussed in Chapter 2, both the teacher and the student

I will sustain the energy and creativity to make the math light come on for every student.

Mr. George

Individual teacher declaration

benefit from a *growth mindset*, a belief in everyone's capacity to grow, no matter what their history. Whether or not you read records ahead of meeting students, be sure you do not close your mind. Use your first-hand understanding of your students to balance and color the perceptions of others.

Q. *After goals and declarations made in class and individual goal-setting conferences, some of my students seem to understand the purposes of education, but they don't appear to value it for themselves enough to strive toward goals. What can I do to lead them to value school for themselves?*

Some students just go through the motions of setting goals because they have to, but they don't believe the goals are important to them personally, or that they can lead them to success on their terms. For these skeptics, we need to connect school and its purposes with what they *do* value in life. Richard Frost, a teacher at Longfellow Middle School in LaCrosse WI, created a great way to do just that. He has students name what they would want to have in their "quality world," then devise a plan to achieve it. Such plans are very likely to include education. Identifying and expanding one's "quality world" is a concept developed by psychologist William Glasser. See page 253 to learn the whole story.

Adults, too!.

THE SOCIAL CONTRACT: ESTABLISHING THE RULES

Once initial goals have been stated and shared, we're ready for the next vital step: teachers work with students to create a Social Contract, a statement of guidelines by which the group agrees to keep relationships healthy and to achieve goals. Contracts can be created for each classroom independently or combined as part of a school-wide contract (see page 76). For all students to agree to the contract, all must have a voice in creating it. This is the power of democracy: a Social Contract created by and agreed to by everyone that will lead to an orderly classroom and an orderly school, free of threats, bribes, rewards, and punishments. The process of creating a Social Contract and living by it is a giant step toward responsible independence. It speaks directly to adolescents' need for autonomy and competence. *I want to take care of myself, and I want to do it well.* Making the rules is important to your students, and when they are included in the process in a meaningful way, they know they are seen as responsible: *I know you can do this well, and I expect it from you.*

The Social Contract process means that the foundation for authority in your room is the rules the community created, not you alone. Teacher-student conversations change from "I need you to..." or "It's my way or the highway," to "We agreed...." Far fewer power struggles occur, because in giving a correction, you direct students back to the rules they made for themselves. Students experience that they can handle the responsibility of both making the rules and abiding by them, with our assistance.

Children who attend a school in which they are asked to take responsibility for the... rules discover democracy; they also discover that in a democratic school, as in a democratic country, many problems have no clear-cut solution. Rather they learn that they have a responsibility for finding the best alternatives to a series of difficult problems, problems that they themselves help to pose. (Glasser 1969, 70)

The Social Contract in history

Individuals' pursuit of happiness must co-exist with the well-being of the community. For thousands of years, forms of social contracts have been used, seeking balance between the two interests. Socrates, Plato, Hobbes, Locke, Rousseau, and the founders of American democracy all wrestled with this important tension. In his 1762 treatise *The Social Contract*, Rousseau wrote that in a civil society, the good of the community is more important than an individual's desires if those desires are in conflict with the general good. He urged direct involvement by every member of society in the creation and maintenance of its social contract as essential to the contract's viability. Americans embrace these values in their Constitution.

Students in just communities learn that rules do not depend on the discretion of external authorities but are developed by mutual agreement and judged on the basis of their fairness to all involved. They learn about the processes that enable a group to come to agreement or consensus as well as the responsibility to preserve the right and protect the interests of the minority. In this way students learn about democratic values and basic political processes. (Berman 1997, 131)

Introducing the power of the Social Contract to students

Explain to students what a social contract is. Discuss the importance of the rule of law (the Social Contract) rather than autocratic decree and skills people need to get along well (compromise, communication, respect, etc.), so they can begin to internalize the value of a participatory, law-abiding society. Find a metaphor for the nature of the Social Contract: it grows from grass-roots; it operates from the bottom up, not from the top down. It's YouTube, not network television. It's of the people, by the people, and for the people.

You have an opportunity to share in the creation of one of the most important documents in our school, the Social Contract. Its purpose is to give us guidelines for learning as much as we can and getting along well. You have the power to help create the rules. With that power comes the responsibility to think seriously about what we really need, and to assert your own beliefs. Ask yourselves: What are the most important things for our class and our school? What rules will help us succeed as we work to fulfill our declarations?

Guidelines for rule-making

Characteristics of an effective Social Contract are:

- The contract is a description of ideal behaviors, not of forbidden ones
- Each rule is broad and general in its scope, therefore able to offer guidance in many social and academic situations
- Each rule is concise; just a few words should be enough for any rule, and brevity makes it easier to remember
- The contract itself is concise. Three rules are enough; five is the limit for people to remember
- The contract is an organic, dynamic document, agreed to by consensus, re-examined frequently in discussions about the extent to which the community is thriving.

The staff should decide whether you'll be creating contracts only in advisory or content-area classes, or will continue the process to create team or school-wide contracts. It is possible to have different rules in each class, but school-wide Social Contracts provide additional continuity, and they help build community by connecting all members of the community, students and adults.

Steps of Creating a Social Contract

Discuss with students how consensus works. Explain that consensus decision-making sometimes means that individuals have to give up something in order for the group to reach a decision that everyone is willing to live by.

Community requires compromise. At the end of this process, nobody will be able to look at our Social Contract and say, "These are exactly the rules I came up with in the beginning, so I got my way." Consensus requires that as individuals we submit, to a certain degree, to what's good for the group, perhaps giving up parts of our personal ideas about what would be ideal.

Our aim is to create a set of rules with which we all agree, so all of us can have a good school year and meet our goals. It's not about me or you, it's about us.

1. Brainstorm rule ideas

This is best done in four groups. Direct each group to create and agree upon a list of three brief, broad, positive rule possibilities. The groups consider: "What guidelines do we need to help us get along and learn as much as possible in school?" Each group should choose a student facilitator, whose job is to make sure all voices are heard, and a recorder. If a member of the group has such a problem with a rule that she is unwilling to endorse it, she must speak up, and the group must rework the rule until all agree that they can abide by it.

2. Merge the four groups into two

Pair up the groups so you now have two instead of four. In each new group the two reporters read the three rule suggestions their groups created in Step 1. Now each group has six rules to consider. Their job is to boil those six rules down to three new rules that express the meaning of all six. This is a serious responsibility in representative democracy: remember, every voice must be heard!

3. Whole class creates the final set of three to five rules

Each group writes their three rules so all can see, using large sentence strips, the blackboard or whiteboard, or on a piece of chart paper.

The six rules are examined and merged into a final set of three to five rules. Careful teacher facilitation is required throughout this step. Students generate several ways the six rules might be condensed into between three and five, without losing the meaning of any of the six. Everyone must listen carefully and assert himself or herself as needed: students should not be allowed to bully their ideas through, nor to passively accept ideas with which they do not really agree.

4. Ratify the rules

Someone reads aloud the remaining rule ideas. The teacher checks to make sure everyone understands each one. She then asks students to show their approval or disapproval using a system such as:

- Thumb up: *I like the rules and agree to abide by them*
- Thumb sideways: *There are parts of them I don't completely agree with, but I'm willing to abide by them*
- Thumb down: *I feel there is something seriously wrong with one or more of the rules, and I need to be heard now. I can't agree to abide by them until I have a chance to recommend a change.*

If all thumbs are either up or sideways, consensus has been reached, and the rules are ratified as the Social Contract for the group. If a student rejects the rules by voting thumb down, that student is asked to clarify for the rest of the group exactly what he or she objects to, and to recommend a change. The change(s) the student recommends must be considered by the rest of the class, then another vote is taken. This process continues until all are in agreement – that is, all thumbs are either up or sideways.

Note: To help make the rule-making process go smoothly, establish beforehand what makes for good small-group interaction (listen respectfully while each person speaks, invite everyone into the conversation so all voices are heard, sit in a circle facing inward, etc.) You can model appropriate group interaction, or at least have a short discussion about it (see Chapter 5 for more about modeling).

Who can describe for us what good group interaction looks like? sounds like? feels like?

5. Celebrate!

Completing the process of democratically creating a Social Contract is an important accomplishment. Everyone participated, and everyone will benefit from having clear rules for the class.

We did it! We worked hard to create a good Social Contract. Because we are here and now agreeing to live according to the rules in the Contract, it will help us get along and have a great year together. Let's celebrate with a cheer!

The teacher's role

The teacher facilitates the democratic process, contributes rule ideas, and may reject an inappropriate suggestion. Perhaps most important, the teacher will facilitate the enforcement of the rules throughout the year.

I am responsible for making certain that everyone abides by the rules. I am committed to helping each one of you reach your goals, and that's why I'm committed to maintaining the integrity of our agreement. I'll be watching carefully to make sure that each one of us abides by it. When anyone breaks our agreement, you can count on me to respond with a correction to restore it. Everyone makes mistakes, and we'll focus not on blaming the rule-breaker but on fixing the mistake. We made the rules together, and now we're working together to live by them.

Creating a Team- or School-wide Social Contract

Secondary schools may choose to take the rule-making process a step further by creating a set of agreements everyone can use. When an entire team or school comes together and agrees to one simple set of rules, feelings of trust, competence, autonomy, and interconnectedness prevail. Classroom representatives may bring the class rules to a larger forum—a team- or school-wide convention—where each contract is analyzed and synthesized into one set of three to five rules all can use, following the steps described above. Representatives can lobby for their classrooms' rules, understanding that consensus can't happen without compromise. Once the delegates reach consensus, they present the school-wide Social Contract at an all-school gathering. A copy of the contract is presented to each advisory and signed by each member of the school community. Here is one school's experience:

At the first meeting of our school's Continental Congress, students expanded our discussion about school-wide guidelines to include *why* certain guidelines are needed. The values-centered discussions about equity, control, independence, community, and management that followed enabled teachers and students to explore how and why communities establish guidelines.

During the Continental Congress, student representatives reported that students throughout the building were interested in examining how they interact. This process was a first step toward improving the social fabric of the school, and it led to many team-based discussions among students regarding social skills, respect, and individual responsibility. The Congress also stimulated many conversations among the adults.

As we moved through the year, there were many positive interactions with our agreement, and I see the effect it has had in the building:

- dismissal times are more orderly and peaceful;
- the cafeteria is cleaner because students clean up after themselves better and with less adult prompting;
- discipline referrals for common-area issues dropped dramatically (2 instead of 34 by the end of November!)
- vastly improved hallway behavior during passing times.

Because they were included in the rule-making process, students were willing to accept responsibility for their behavior. I was happy to find that throughout the year, students wanted a larger role in addressing school-wide issues. Also, having the Congress has changed the structure of our behavior management to more of a shared practice from what had always been a "top-down" administrative function.

—Middle school principal, Richmond VT

Students and teachers kindergarten through 8th grade gather for an all-school meeting

Supporting the Social Contract

Checking in and reflecting on the rules

Checking in with students about whether their behavior is in line with the Social Contract and about how well their teachers are working with them to enforce the Contract is a must. Check-ins can be done through meetings dedicated to the subject or by conducting quick rule reviews and reflections at the beginning or end of class periods, or both.

Just as beginning-of-the-year goals demand reflection or they wither away from neglect, the Social Contract requires frequent review, lest it be forgotten.

Abiding by our rules maintains the order that we need to achieve our goals. How well did we follow our Social Contract during small-group time? Was everyone treated respectfully? Did everyone participate? Rate your group on your exit card, and I'll collect the cards as you leave.

Goals and rules are living things or they are nothing. Once we commit to them, we must keep them alive through reflection. We plan our social climate, we live our lives, and we think about how well our living matches our plan. The loop of reflection never ends. See page 101 for a description of the process of reflection throughout the school day.

In our school we develop a class contract early in the year. The students develop five rules for the classroom. They work together to find out what the five rules are that they want the class to hold to. It's one of our first community activities—how we want our community to run. It takes a couple of days to put together a solid Social Contract. They all sign it when the rules are completed, to say they're going to adhere to them. Then it's my job to ensure that everyone in the classroom, including myself, keeps to that.

I refer to the Contract at least three times a week during the last part of class. I ask, "What did we do well today in relation to the Social Contract?"

It's important to take plenty of time in the beginning of the year to set the rules, since they need to stick with us for the whole year. The rules need to be broad enough to follow while allowing us to be ourselves. Last year we revisited the Contract halfway through the year, and everyone was confident that they were the rules they wanted to keep.

—High school teacher, Cambridge MA

Teacher reflection on the effectiveness of the Social Contract

Here are some questions we can ask ourselves periodically during the year to make certain we are doing our part to uphold the Contract and preserve the community order:

- Which rules are being followed by students? What's my evidence? What can I do to reinforce this?

- Which rules are not being followed? What's the evidence? What do I need to do to better guide them?

- Which students might need additional guidance? What are some ways I might help them become more content community members?

Responding to rule violations

The Social Contract is the basis for order in the school. Misbehavior is an infringement of the Contract and needs to be framed as such in our response to it. The voices of authority to uphold the rules in the school are the administration, the teachers, and the student body itself (in addition to parents and the legal system). Because we all made the rules together, *every* violation of them must be addressed; the quality of our shared school life depends on it. Others, including adults, can help rule-breakers repair the damage from their misbehavior. Everyone has a big stake in the repair, because it mends the fabric of the community.

See pages 267-269 about keeping the rules alive and Chapters 7 and 8, which focus on responding to rule-breaking.

Display of Social Contracts

Social Contracts should be written large and displayed in clear view for easy referral. School-wide Social Contracts should be posted in hallways, building entrances and exits, the cafeteria, the gym, media centers, and other common areas.

Sample Social Contracts — Points of Pride

Sparta Meadowview Middle School, Sparta WI

Be respectful to one another and property.

Be responsible for actions, privileges, and homework.

Be honest, be trustworthy, and have fun.

Jack London Middle School, Wheeling IL

Respect each other, everyone's ideas, and property.

Have an open mind and a positive attitude.

Take responsibility for our own learning.

Crosswinds Constitution 2008-2009
- Follow CARES
- Show Respect Mentally, Socially, and Physically
- Be Responsible
- Do Your Best
- Challenge Yourself

W. Harry Davis School, Minneapolis MN

We will come to school with a positive attitude and be friendly to others!

We will respect ourselves, others, and property.

We will work to the best of our ability, stay on task, and ask for help when needed, while having fun.

We will wear school uniforms while at school.

Example: Connecting goals and declarations to the Social Contract

One middle grades teacher started the process by asking her students to think big and share their future career aspirations and long-term hopes and dreams. Starting with the largest view, the students were able to connect their goals and behavior in school to possibilities for the future.

Connecting to larger aspirations when making our goals for the school year allowed students to understand the cause-and-effect relationship that our behavior has with the long-term goals we set. Students shared aspirations such as becoming politicians, fire fighters, interior designers, solar technology scientists, architects, and teachers, having families, becoming rich and helping the poor, running marathons, and learning Mandarin Chinese.

These long-term visions were then translated into here-and-now specific goals for the school year, including aims to work steadily (not procrastinate), make new friends, help fellow students, do our best work on all homework, get more fluent in Spanish, learn and practice better note-taking and better essay writing, and improve our athletic and artistic abilities by practicing more, among other things.

Finally, after forming a Social Contract to support our school-year goals, the students identified and declared their commitment to the behaviors that would uphold the Social Contract we made.

We, the students of Room 6, agree to:

Be respectful: We *will* cooperate, listen to others, respect our own ability to learn, take care of materials, and clean up together

Follow the Golden Rule: We *will* treat others the way we want to be treated, include and treat everybody as a good friend, help and encourage others, be a good role model, help others learn, pay attention, and be kind

Do work: We *will* contribute with a positive attitude, complete assignments on time, stay focused

Have fun: We *will* watch to see that everyone participates, and finds the joy in work

The process allowed me to say, "We want to be brain surgeons, computer programmers, chefs, agents, and more. We want to make enough money to help poor countries, travel the world, enjoy our jobs, do everything we were ever told was too dangerous, and more. Now we have said the actions we could take every day, in our classroom and in school, to help us achieve these things. In other words, we made a commitment today to the behavior that would help us get the results we want in the future."

—Middle level teacher, Minneapolis MN

Challenges of the Social Contract

Q. *What if students show no interest in helping to create rules? What if they say it's a stupid idea, and don't really believe that it means anything in real life?*

If students have had no experience with shared power, if they've never had a say in how things will go in school, they may be skeptical. Urge them to participate:

This is an opportunity for you to have a say about our school. Take a chance – you have nothing to lose but the time we spend doing this, and I believe you'll gain a lot.

Q. *What if a student refuses to agree to the rules everyone else has consented to?*

One of two reasons likely lie behind this refusal. Either the student doesn't understand the consensus model you are using (including the notion that everyone has *to give* something *to receive* the benefits of being united) or is looking for attention and/or power in the wrong place.

In either case, temporarily suspend the rule-making process and move to something else. Later, meet with the holdout. Ask him to describe the consensus model, including the part about having to be flexible. If you can see that he doesn't understand, clarify it for him.

If he understands the process but refuses to agree, ask him what reasonable rules adjustment he needs in order to consent. His participation is vital; tell him so. Review the goals he has set for himself for the semester or year. He needs to understand the connection between what he wants and how the Social Contract will help make it possible. If he lacks meaningful goals, review page 66 for more about creating goals with students who need support holding a hopeful vision for themselves.

Think about the rules we have so far: What do you need to add or subtract in order to agree to them? We cannot reach consensus without you.

His right as a member of the community is to propose adding or subtracting one *reasonable* thing. For example, it would not be reasonable to insist on wording that already has been rejected by the others, or to rewrite an entire rule. Help him formulate the change he wants to ask for.

Reconvene the meeting. Have the holdout propose the change he wants, and submit it to the consensus process. It may or may not pass, but at least you've brought the naysayer back into the process. Keep at the process until all agree.

You may want to have a conversation with the person who seemed to obstruct about appropriate channels for getting his needs for power and/or attention met, so he can learn to be a constructive participant, rather than an obstructionist or an outsider.

Q. *How can I help students quickly consolidate the rules from many to between 3 and 5?*

Ask someone to write each rule suggestion on a separate piece paper. Place them in everyone's view, and have students group them according to common themes, such as respect or open-mindedness.

Discuss each proposed move before moving a piece of paper, to be sure everyone understands and agrees with the move. These discussions are valuable, because they can deepen students' understanding of behavior, and they require higher-order thinking.

Q. *When attempting to create a team- or school-wide Social Contract, what if my classroom's student representative doesn't really have the approval of the rest of the class? Won't some students balk when told that whatever is agreed upon at the convention will be the final word, with no further opportunity to ratify?*

The teacher should select the class representative carefully, since the student who attends the convention must be able to both negotiate in best faith for *his* classroom's rules and compromise for the good of the others. Also, the selected student should be in good relationship with his classmates; a positive, well-thought-of leader is a natural choice. Before sending the representative to the convention, be sure to inform the entire class about the representative's role:

We expect our representative to do his best to make sure our group's ideas are reflected in the final document. He will have to compromise, just as each person in our class did when we made our rules together. Under no circumstances will groaning, complaining, or refusing to abide by the final school-wide (or team-wide) contract be tolerated. We trust the representative to do his best, and agree to abide by the will of the larger community.

Our experience has been that students are almost always satisfied with the final document; disappointment is rarely expressed. Some part or parts of each room's rules are sure to be evident in the final document, which helps everyone have confidence in the process.

Q. *In a K-8 school where students have been making rules every year, how can I keep the process fresh each fall?*

Middle grades students attending K-8 schools at which rules are constructed anew each fall may feel tired of the process. One possibility is to do the process every other year instead of annually. An alternative is to begin the rules-making process by examining last year's Social Contract first, and work from there to ratify new rules.

Starting with last year's rules

After declarations are complete, write last year's rules on a chart or board. Ask students to read their declarations to themselves and think about whether last year's rules would help them:

- to reach this year's goals
- to get to know each other
- to get along
- to learn as much as possible
- to have fun
- to make school and the world a better place

Would last year's rules work for us this year? Which ones might be just right? Which ones might not be? What rules might need to be added to help us achieve our goals? Which ones might need to be reworked, and how?

After students write answers independently, they form four groups. A facilitator and a recorder are assigned in each group. The recorder copies down last year's rules. Group members then share what they wrote independently as the recorder adds new rule possibilities to the list or modifies last year's rules. All members have a chance to share or add ideas, and everyone should participate. Each group emerges with three to five rules that may or may not reflect changes from last year's rules.

Now return to the rule-making consensus process, Step 2, outlined above: the facilitator in each group reads the updated list and helps consolidate the rules following the consensus process, and so on.

Building consensus from last year's rules calls for the same rigor as does starting from scratch. All must be heard, their suggestions noted, and their ideas voted on, and consensus must be reached. New students will be encountering the process for the first time; an explicit process with an opportunity to weigh in on the rules is critical for them.

Quality Ed   *Miracle Question*

ESTABLISHING AGREEMENTS: Getting in Gear for Responsible Independence

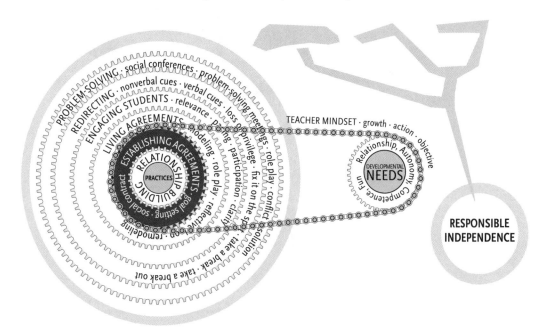

Living Our Agreements in Daily Routines

The agreements in a Social Contract are broad, general, and abstract. Each one is broad enough to apply to many situations. To make clear to students what to do on a practical, daily basis in order to fulfill their commitment to the contract and meet their goals, we need to create routines and expectations. To accomplish this, we recommend using the following structures:

Modeling

Recording norms with

lists of steps to follow

lists of must-do's and may-do's

Look-sound-feel charts

Role play

Reflective Loop

Reinforcing

Reminding

Remodeling

Setting expectations is worth the work

Take the time to teach students how to behave and how to perform routines that will fulfill the contract and allow everyone in the room to learn more, learn better, and get along. This investment helps launch students toward the independence that they want and need with the level of responsible self-management that we want them to have. If you take the time to model and practice many of your daily routines early in the year, and keep the routine fresh with review, you'll actually save time by having fewer mess-ups down the road. The *Developmental Designs* slogans for the practice of taking time to teach behavior expectations are: *Go slow to go fast* and *Assume nothing, teach everything.*

As you read through the structures below, you may question the need for so much attention to establishing standards for the routines of school life. You may think that the students should already know how to enter the room, listen, line up, raise their hands to speak, get quiet, participate in meaningful discussions, move classroom furniture, use school materials respectfully, hand in their work, etc. But unless we help them by establishing clear expectations, many of them won't rise to the occasion. If we teach the little steps, provide the incremental learning needed to shift toward productive learning habits, we'll have a much greater likelihood of our students doing what has been declared as right for the community.

Making the rules clear and concrete

In most cases, our practices teach behavior expectations through direct experience, *doing* the routine the way it should be done. Most people are visual and/or kinesthetic learners, and verbal or written instructions are not enough. Many need opportunities to practice the task under the watchful eye of a mentor who can set them straight when they miss the standard. Experience is the best teacher. Few, if any, athletes, writers, craftspeople, etc. can claim to have become proficient without lots of practice. Practicing the correct way of doing something allows it to get into our muscles and bones, helping us to remember.

Concrete experience is one of the best ways to make strong, long-lasting neural connections. These experiences engage more of the senses and use multiple pathways to store—and therefore more ways to recall—information. We remember what we have experienced much better than what we have heard or read. True, it is not possible for students to experience everything we want them to learn, but we probably miss many opportunities to engage students in more authentic learning. (Wolfe 2001, 188)

Practice helps create memory and new habits, which empower students to succeed in the classroom and in life without constant adult supervision.

Autonomy support... means actively encouraging self-initiation, experimentation, and responsibility, and it may very well require setting limits. But autonomy support functions through encouragement, not pressure. Providing that encouragement without slipping over into control would seem to be possible, but by no means easy. We already knew that being autonomy supportive can be more difficult—requiring more effort and more skill—than being coercive. (Deci 1995, 42)

When to establish behavior expectations

Behavior expectations need to be established, practiced, and revisited from time to time throughout the year, especially at the beginning of the school year, the start of each new term, and the return to school after a vacation.

Set the behavioral expectation for a routine immediately prior to using it for the first time. For example, teach procedures for walking in the hallway just before the first time students move from one class to another.

Teachers in schools that divide students into teams or houses often begin the year orienting students to daily student life and building relationship-based team communities. They delay the start of academic classes for a day or two in order to work together to set expectations for several important routines during this time. *(Go slow to go fast!)* Teachers who work collaboratively on a team, sharing a larger group of students, might gather two or more classes together for the process of setting expectations, or the entire team may do so, if space is available for the large group. There are several benefits in doing things this way:

- All the teachers deliver the same message, and every student receives the same message

- Students are less likely to have to go through the same expectation-setting exercise multiple times

- A sense of communal expectation and support can be established in the large gathering

- Games, songs, or other fun, community-building activities can be included at the gatherings to ease the work at hand and to strengthen the community.

All students learn and practice the routines. By the time regular classes begin, students are primed for a successful year.

Working independently

If you plan to implement this approach at first without the support of colleagues, you'll need to set standards for procedures in your classroom, with each of your classes. Try practicing one or two basic routines that will be used frequently in your class each day for the first few weeks.

Clear expectations support all students

Whatever an individual's capacity may be for self-control and internal motivation, all students need clarity about what is expected of them. For many, establishing expectations will be sufficient to keep them on the right road most of the time. For some, additional work and monitoring of social skills with adult mentors will be necessary. And for all, when they miss the mark, the expectations must be reasserted.

MODELING ONE ROUTINE AT A TIME

I assume nothing. I assume they come in not knowing how to move around the room, move desks, or even sharpen pencils. I model everything starting on the first day of school, from behavior expectations like listening to announcements, hallway and library procedures, how to use the laptop, and how to use our desk tops, to academic ones, like using our literature strategies in our writing units. I've learned when to go slow and when to go fast. If you model everything at the beginning and the students know the expectations, it saves time in the long run. They know what's expected of them, and they feel they have ownership and a say in everything we do. They participate in everything. I've relinquished some of the control and become the facilitator, which is an amazing feeling!

—8th grade English teacher, Tabernacle NJ

Modeling creates accountability

When we show our students exactly how we expect something to be done, we create the basis for accountability: we know that everyone has seen it, has participated in a discussion about what they saw, and has practiced the right way. Assumptions are replaced with expectations, and then we can hold students accountable. After discussing and practicing to make the expectations clear, we can redirect with confidence when students make mistakes. Modeling is part of teaching the skills necessary for autonomy and competence, and it facilitates holding students accountable for knowing and doing the right thing.

Example: Modeling listening expectations

It is likely that some students in a class already know how to listen, and use good listening skills regularly, but it is equally likely that some do not know the skills, or from time to time choose not to employ them. Slouching, ignoring, interrupting, texting, daydreaming, sleeping, and a host of other behaviors, left unchecked, can quickly become habitual, and taking a moment to model good listening is a great way to help students get back on track. It's like planting a flag that says, "In this classroom, this is the process that is acceptable." It is also likely that some students have never been taught how to listen well, and would benefit greatly from a tutorial. Take time on Day One to model with everyone your expectations for listening. Afterwards, you can hold everyone accountable.

What to model

Model any routine or behavior for which you have clear expectations. No matter how simple or basic it is, don't assume students know how to do it correctly. See Appendix E for examples of modeling the signal for silence and safe tagging during a game.

Common modeling routines (see a complete list in Appendix E)

Responding to the signal for quiet

Entering the classroom

Listening

Raising a hand and waiting to be called upon to speak

Greeting a classmate

Moving chairs, desks, or tables

Getting ready to learn

Sharpening pencils

Moving around the room during activities

Using materials and tools (compass, textbook, etc.) safely and respectfully

Sharing your work results with a partner

Simple vs. complex routines: two formats

When the routine you want to model is simple, and when there is just one way you want something done, use the Simple Procedures modeling steps below. When the routine is more complicated, takes longer to demonstrate, and/or involves the active participation of many people at the same time, use the "Fishbowl" modeling approach that follows.

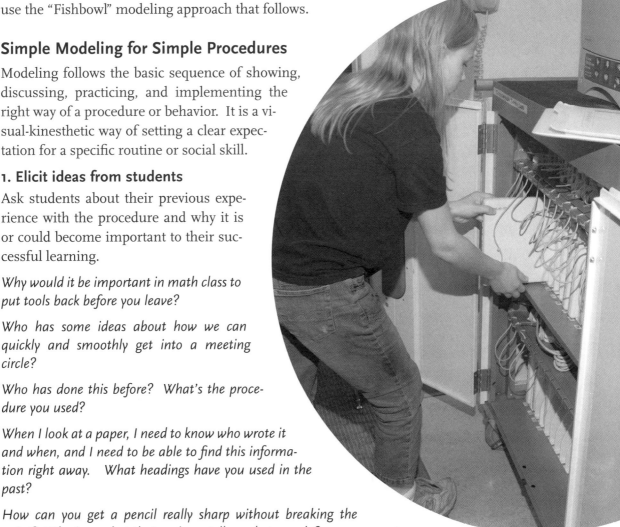

6th grade student follows the routine for returning computers

Simple Modeling for Simple Procedures

Modeling follows the basic sequence of showing, discussing, practicing, and implementing the right way of a procedure or behavior. It is a visual-kinesthetic way of setting a clear expectation for a specific routine or social skill.

1. Elicit ideas from students

Ask students about their previous experience with the procedure and why it is or could become important to their successful learning.

Why would it be important in math class to put tools back before you leave?

Who has some ideas about how we can quickly and smoothly get into a meeting circle?

Who has done this before? What's the procedure you used?

When I look at a paper, I need to know who wrote it and when, and I need to be able to find this information right away. What headings have you used in the past?

How can you get a pencil really sharp without breaking the point? Who is good at that and can tell us what you do?

2. Demonstrate the right way

Model the routine *exactly* the way you want it done. Never model a wrong way! Although modeling the wrong way may seem to clarify the difference between proper and improper behavior and may bring some humor to a serious process, students can easily forget the right way and remember the wrong way when both are demonstrated —perhaps partly because the humorous part sticks in their minds.

Watch carefully as I model this for you. In a moment, I'll ask you what you noticed.

Either teacher or student may model

The demonstration portion of modeling may be done by a student or the teacher. Modeling by a peer is more interesting for students, but there may be some routines which present too much social risk for an adolescent to demonstrate. If necessary, lead him or her through the demonstration step by step.

Notice what Damon is doing as he enters the room and gets started, and then we'll discuss it.

Celine, show us your quick, no-break way to get a good point on a pencil. Everyone watch carefully.

3. Notice the details

Ask students about what happened during the demonstration. Ask specific questions about what you want to be sure they understand, including how doing the routine well is consistent with the rules.

What did you notice? What did I do first?

What else did you notice?

Who saw something we've not mentioned yet?

What was the key thing Celine did after she turned the handle a couple of times?

Look at our Social Contract. Where does the routine we just modeled fit into our agreements? For example, how are we being respectful to others by following this routine?

Clear chair-return protocols facilitate fast and orderly transitions from working in circle to desks

If a written record of the group's ideas would be useful, make a list and post it for future reference. An alternative approach is to make a chart that lists "must-do's" (and "may-do's" if there are extra options—a T-chart works well). You can also use a Y-chart showing how the routine looks, sounds, and feels, done correctly. These will become the expectations for the group, so filter out any student comments that don't support the way you want it done. See page 96 for more about recording ideas. For many of the basic, simple routines, a written record may not be necessary.

4. Practice

After you model, have students practice the procedure before you hold them accountable. As they practice, watch the group carefully. They may need correction, or you may need to clarify something. Have several students—or everyone—practice the procedure.

Who else would like to try?

Let's all try now.

How did we do?

What can we change for next time?

Tell students that what you've just practiced is now a behavior expectation. Refer to the list made earlier if you decided one would be helpful. Add anything that you feel is valuable, especially anything that came up while practicing.

From now on, I'll expect you to _____ the way we just practiced.

5. What-if's

Now you're ready to think about things that might go wrong and plan for what you will do. Look ahead and ask students about problems that might occur.

What if there's no empty chair for you in the circle?

What if you come to class without a pen or pencil?

What if you're not sure what the date is?

What if your friend is three tables away from you and you want to talk to him?

Have students role-play some of these situations. This makes a much stronger impression on students than simply being told, so it could save time in the future. See page 99 for a description of a quick role-play structure.

Simple routines can be made more interesting by inserting a challenge. For example, mentioning some ways sharpening a pencil can go wrong (too short, broken tip, not sharp enough, pencil gets eaten up entirely, etc.) can transform a mundane task into something worth students' careful attention. Be sure you've modeled the routine first before you discuss potential problems.

"Fishbowl" Modeling for Complex Procedures

Protocols for complex routines that involve several people are effectively taught using a sequence and "fishbowl" modeling. More complex routines that benefit from this introduction include:

- working in pairs
- book groups
- small-group lab work
- small-group homework reviews
- peer assessment of completed work
- interactive learning structures (e.g., partner sharing, Carousel)

Use fishbowl rather than simple modeling whenever a procedure includes options or a number of steps. In the fishbowl protocol, as in simple modeling, all students see a procedure done correctly, and there is time for discussion.

1. Select and prepare students for the demonstration

Select one or several student(s) to demonstrate the procedure or activity. Teach them how to do it, and make sure they understand the specific expectations you want to get across. Create a chart listing the steps of the procedure. Post the chart so all can learn from it.

2. Prepare the fishbowl space and student expectations

The students who will demonstrate stand or sit in the center of the class circle. They are now in the "fishbowl." Set a clear expectation that observers do not participate in the modeling in any way except as careful, quiet, respectful observers.

3. Elicit ideas from students (same as simple modeling)

Ask students about their previous experience with the routine and why it is or could become important to their learning.

4. Demonstrate the right way (same as simple modeling)

The student demonstrators model for the audience how the procedure should be done. They don't offer explanations, running commentary, or helpful tips; they just model the procedure while the others watch carefully and use the written steps to keep track of what's happening.

5. Notice the details (same as simple modeling)

Ask specific questions about what you want to be sure they understand, including how doing the routine well is consistent with the rules.

6. Practice (same as simple modeling)

After the discussion, all students practice the procedure, with the newly crafted set of expectations as a guide. Tell students that what you've just practiced is now a behavior expectation.

From now on, I'll expect you to _____ the way we just practiced

7. What-if's (same as simple modeling)

Discuss with student potential problems with the procedure.

Follow Up to Reinforce or Redirect after Modeling

Doing something once is rarely enough. Young adolescents naturally push boundaries, and you are there to uphold the integrity of the rules—the rules that they helped create and that help them fulfill their goals. If several students are failing to follow the expectation, you can re-model it. Teacher language is a powerful tool, too. Follow up all modeling by using reminding language before putting a routine into action:

Who can remember how we agreed to safely carry chairs?

Correct deviations from the modeled norm as they happen, or re-do the procedure.

We didn't follow expectations in coming to circle that time. What do we need to change?

Marguerite, that isn't the way we practiced coming into the room and getting to work. Go back out and try it again.

The written and posted record of the steps or must-do's or a chart of how the routine should look, sound, and feel can be useful when a reminder or re-do is called for.

Phil and Maury, what does the Y-chart say about how partner work should sound?

When students' behavior begins to deviate from what you worked hard to model, you may be tempted to think that the modeling protocol doesn't work. But it is human nature—especially adolescents'—to stray from, forget, and/or test the rules and their enforcer. The fact remains that observing and practicing the right ways of doing things is more memorable that simply listening to or reading the rules. When students stray from the protocol as we have described it, they need more guidance from adults. For detailed follow-up strategies, see the Reflective Loop, page 101, Reinforcing, Reminding, and Remodeling, page 106, and Chapters 7 and 8 about responding to rule-breaking.

Challenges of Modeling

Q. *How can I address those students who resist modeling, saying it's unnecessary or childish?*

For most, the short time it takes to model a routine or procedure is at least mildly interesting. A few will dislike the level of detail involved (perhaps because this preempts claiming later that they didn't know the expectation), or feel the time spent reviewing something "obvious" is a waste of their time, or resist the protocol in other ways. You can avoid some of these objections by keeping things moving along. Except for unusually complex procedures, the entire process should take only 3 to 5 minutes (recording ideas to a chart will take longer) once you and the students are good at it. Remember that the simpler routines can be demonstrated by the teacher quickly, especially if students would likely feel embarrassed to demonstrate a simple procedure in front of their peers.

Taking time to show you how I want you to listen to each other might seem unnecessary, but we just brainstormed several reasons why listening to each other will be important to our success. I want everyone to succeed, and I know each of you can do it. I also know that real listening—paying careful attention and noticing the details—is a skill, and it takes practice. Watch carefully, and notice the details, as I show you how I want you to listen in our class.

Sometimes a student who complains is challenging you because she wants power in the class. Find opportunities for her to lead. For instance, she may find modeling more palatable if she's given a chance to be the person doing the modeling. But if a student is simply in the habit of resisting, tap into your commitment to the student's growth and the Social Contract. Stand your ground using your redirecting tools; see Chapter 7.

Q. *What if a student—or several students—don't do the routine the way I modeled it?*

If a student was at the modeling session and you're sure he understood what you modeled, redirect him. See Chapter 7 about redirecting students. He may have forgotten, or he may be testing your diligence. On the other hand, someone who fails to follow the model may need to see the routine done correctly again, and may need more practice. Use your discretion; remodeling for that one student or for everyone may be in order. If you did not create a written chart of expectations for the procedure at the time it was modeled, do so now. (See page 96 for a full discussion of recording charts and page 106 for reminding and remodeling.)

Q. *Can we afford to use precious class time to model behaviors?*

It is essential to lay the structural and social foundations for academic rigor and success. Adolescents need structures and routines to succeed in academics, and it does take time to develop, practice, and enforce them. Truly, go slow to go fast. Students will slip from time to time, and this calls for your diligent maintenance. When you model it, mean it, and be prepared to enforce the behavioral expectation. If you are the only person in your school working with this approach, plan modeling time in each class in the first week of school. If your entire team is implementing this visual/kinesthetic approach, use advisory time or share the task of modeling across the team during class hours.

In the absence of advisory, we (all the teachers of our 100-student pod) agreed to use class time at the beginning of the year to establish routines for the year. It was important enough to forgo teaching curriculum for the first week or so. Each teacher took his or her share of routines, developed them with their first-hour class, and communicated the routines to the other teachers. That way each routine became pod-wide.

Once school started, fourteen routines like entering class and working in groups were developed with student input, and put into effect. We used Y-charts to develop these, and we practiced the routines so that everyone knew them.

—Middle school 7ᵗʰ grade team, Bemidji MN

Q. *In the first few days of the year, before I have rules to build on, how can I use modeling to create order in my classroom?*

At the start of the year, you will not have a Social Contract in place, yet you'll be modeling things from Day One, so connecting modeling to the rules during those first days presents a challenge. Until you have a ratified Social Contract, you may choose to temporarily

- model without reference to a set of rules—*This is how we will do it until we establish our own rules*
- use last year's Social Contract
- create and use teacher rules for the time being (how about the Golden Rule?)
- use a dictated set of behavior ideals, for example from a character-education curriculum

One payoff for using temporary rules the first few days is that you'll be able to get students in the good habit of reflecting on their behavior as it relates to general guidelines. Whatever course of action you choose before the Social Contract is created, be sure to enforce the rules once you have them in place.

Q. *Do we need to model for students how to use the equipment and materials in the classroom? They often mess up when using them.*

Modeling will save time and aggravation by reducing mistakes. Some materials and tools have more than one possible application; build time into the modeling process for students to explore possibilities with the materials or equipment.

RECORD IDEAS TO SUPPORT EXPECTATIONS

A handy reference to reinforce students' understanding of how to behave positively during any procedure is a written record of what you modeled (this is useful for brainstorming sessions, too).   A chart may not be necessary for a simple procedure, but if the procedure is complex, or if students are not generally adhering to the rules, then a written chart is useful. There are several kinds of charts for this purpose. In all of them, because the ideas come from the students, they *own* the expectation and are more likely to observe it.

Record the Steps of a Procedure

The teacher or a student can make a written record of the steps of any routine. For example, students can name the expectations for the start of class and then put them in order.

Entering the classroom (Chart example)

Walk in calmly and quietly.

Read the chart or board for instructions of what to do first, "Do-now's"

Take your seat and complete the Do-now's.

Take out your homework, ready to check it.

After you have completed your work, chat quietly if you wish, in a low voice.

A posted chart of steps is a reminder of the protocol, and can be used whenever a student strays from the steps it lists.

Devonne, what's your job after you have read the instructions? Check the procedure chart.

Chart of "Must-do's" and "May-do's"

You can make a T-chart for required and optional actions. On one side are listed all of the required behaviors of the routine (the must-do's), and on the other side, some options (the may-do's). Students then have a written record of what they are responsible for and what they can add if they wish.

Hallway Passing Time (T-chart example)

Must-do's	May-do's
Keep hands to selves	Use restroom
Keep voices low	Chat quietly with friends
Walk	Greet someone you don't know well
At locker: drop off materials from last class, pick up materials for next class	Maintain physical appearance: comb hair, etc.
Be on time for next class	

Look-sound-feel Y-chart

Use a Y-chart graphic organizer to record in its three areas what a routine looks like, sounds like, and feels like (you could add a quick sketch of an eye, an ear, and a heart). The teacher or student leader leads a discussion about how a specific behavior should look, sound, and feel. Students and the leader contribute ideas. The leader or a recorder writes the ideas in the appropriate space in the chart, which becomes a collectively generated document that specifically describes the look, sound, and feel of the procedure when it's done well.

Example: Small-group discussion

Use the fishbowl modeling format for a complex routine like small-group discussion. As students discuss what makes small-group work effective, and after they see the protocol for small-group work during the fishbowl demonstration, they can create a chart about how the room will look, sound, and feel using the protocols.

We'll have discussions in small groups often this year. We want everyone to participate, and we want everyone to be heard. How shall we create the right balance so that everyone participates but we don't have noisy, chaotic, unfair discussions? What will quality small-group time look like, sound like, and feel like?

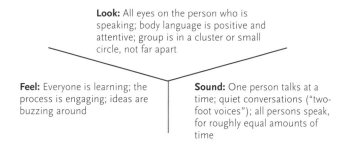

Example: Transitioning from circle to desks

A simple modeling would work better than a fishbowl for this process. As you collect ideas from students and after it has been modeled, transfer their suggestions to a Y-chart.

We need to move to our desks after each advisory meeting. What will the transition look, sound, and feel like so we stay true to our Social Contract?

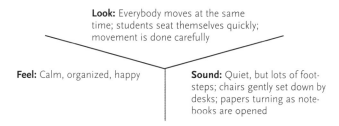

Because students participate in creating the chart, everyone owns the expectations. Students' need for autonomy and competence is respected and partially fulfilled. We have shown respect by sharing (but not abdicating) power, which strengthens our relationship with students. Later, if the routine is not going well, we can refer students to their own expectations.

Martin, check the Y-chart on transitioning to desks after circle meeting. Teresa, look at the chart and remind us how our group work should sound.

Use the Charts!

Avoid the mistake of taking the first step of establishing expectations, posting them, and then letting them fade away like wallpaper. Refer to them. Ask students to read them aloud. Use them during reflection at the class period's end. They should be used, or they're not worth the wall space.

When you find that you do not need to refer students to a particular chart anymore, you might want to take it down. If behaviors deteriorate later, you can repost it to remind students of their standards for behavior. You can also make a *Routines and Procedures* class book: students copy into a notebook for future reference Y-charts, Must-do's and May-do's, and steps to procedures.

I keep a small copy of my classes' "Hallway Use" chart near the door. Whenever students' hallway behaviors start to slip, I pull out the copy of the chart and silently show it to them as they exit class. I point at it, clear my throat a few times, or attract their attention to it in other quiet ways. Even if they don't read every word, they recall the main idea: Let's keep things calm and orderly in the hallway. They respond very well to the chart. I think they appreciate the fact that it spares them a lecture -- and, after all, the chart is full of their ideas, and one of them actually wrote it.

—Middle level teacher, Minneapolis MN

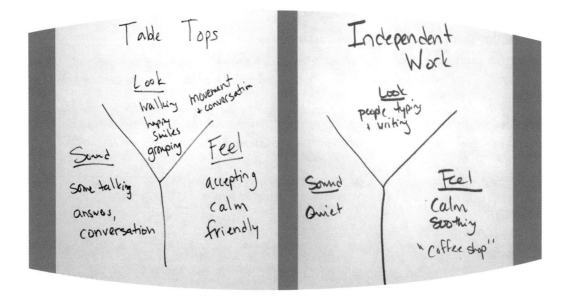

ROLE PLAY TO SOLVE DILEMMAS

To create a very clear memory for students of how to deal with moments when a rule seems hard to follow, turn the what-if step of modeling into a mini-dramatization, or role play. If students struggle or resist using the routines and procedures for which you have created clear expectations, it may be because situations arise that present dilemmas for them. For example, you have carefully practiced how to circle up for whole-group time. Two students want to sit next to each other because they are going to teach an activity to the class, but there are not two adjacent empty chairs. What should they do? Try acting it out.

Steps of Role Play (Example: dilemma presented by circling up)

While modeling a routine (in this case, circling up), insert these role-play steps to address what-if's.

Setting

Everyone is sitting in the circle. There are two empty chairs, but they are not together.

Action

Two students, one played by the teacher, are talking about the game they will teach the group. They approach the circle and see that there aren't two chairs together, and express mild exasperation through facial expression or body language.

The first few times role play is used, the teacher should be one of the actors. In scenarios where one of the actors must face the dilemma more directly than the other(s), the teacher should take this role. After role play becomes an established part of the culture of the classroom, students may be able to take on all of the acting roles, and the teacher can move to the role of director.

Cut

It is always the teacher who decides when to cut the action. Discuss with the whole class:

What's happening? What's the dilemma?

What are the characters feeling?

What can each one do to get at least some of what they want and follow our rules at the same time?

Action

"Rewind" the scene and play it again, this time trying one of the suggested solutions. Afterward, discuss how well the solution worked. If time allows, role play another possible solution, and discuss it. Now we have a concrete, visual/kinesthetic experience of following the circle-up guidelines, even when it's hard.

As the group gains skill in acting out role plays, use them to deepen and clarify any what-if's that arise during modeling.

Understanding Adolescent Dilemmas

When students are tempted to disregard a rule, their need for relationship, autonomy, competence, or fun may underlie this urge. At those moments of dilemma, they need to choose to follow the rule and feel good about it—to think and feel at the same time, then make a good choice for action. That isn't easy, and they need to practice, to see and feel what it's like to do that. Role play gives them a preview of maturity. It allows them to experience how responsible, ethical behavior looks, sounds, and feels.

Example dilemmas

If students are slow to respond to the signal for quiet, the dilemma may be that they want to keep talking to a friend or working on something they are engaged in, but you are requiring that they stop and pay attention to you. If students are gossiping, the dilemma might be that it appears that gossip is necessary to be accepted in a particular social group.

Acknowledge the Dilemma to Students

Acknowledge the humanness of the dilemma the role play will address. As you describe the scenario, show compassion for the students by siding with them about how difficult it is to deal with feeling pulled in two directions. For example, if you decide to do a role play about the powerful pressure peers can put on each other to not tell on a classmate when they know she did something wrong or dangerous, start by telling students that you understand how difficult such predicaments are. After all, adults deal with similar challenges—you might briefly share a time when peers pressured you to keep something secret, or an example from current public events.

With your understanding established, refer to the Social Contract, and point out that we have to follow the rules, even when it means risking the disapproval of friends. Ask: *Why is it important for us to help each other be successful in school? Why stand up for our agreements?*

By acknowledging the difficulty of dealing with a dilemma directly, we increase our credibility, empathy, and relationship with students and nudge them toward endorsing our main objective: to teach them to do the right thing, even if it means facing fears and going against what appears to be socially acceptable.

REFLECTIVE LOOP, A HABIT OF THOUGHTFUL PEOPLE

Much of the work of guiding students towards responsible independence centers on teaching kids to think, both before and after they do something.

—Middle level principal, St. Paul MN

The Social Contract and goals for the year are powerful only if they are kept in mind and used as resources for assessment through check-ins and reflection all year long. And modeling the daily routines of school to set clear expectations is effective only if it is supported by daily reinforcement, especially through reminding and reinforcing language and regular reflection.

The *Developmental Designs* structure for reflection is the Reflective Loop, a cycle of planning, working, and reflecting. It helps adolescents develop the competence and independence they need for success in life. When we use the Loop in school, we teach students to stop and think about their academic and social actions before and after they act. Include the cycle of plan/work/reflect to help students construct understanding of their activity: together, we figure out what's to be done; together, we do it; together, we think about how well we did. Then we begin another trip around the Loop by thinking about ways we can do better the next time. The Loop is a powerful assistant for students' social and academic growth.

Constructivists Marlow and Page state that if one of the goals of having students build knowledge and meaning through experience is independence, then having students create and reflect on their assessments will serve this goal. Teachers need to spend less time acting as judges of correct answers and more time helping students become better self-assessors of their own work. (Marlow and Page 1998, 61, 99-100)

Brain researcher Eric Jensen describes the process of making learning meaningful: either you can have your learners' attention or they can be making meaning, but never both at the same time. Meaning is generated internally, and it takes time. External input (more content) conflicts with the processing of prior content and thoughtful reflection. Students rarely get training in how to be calm, thoughtful, or reflective, and they are given little time to practice these skills in class. (Jensen 2005, 36-37)

Using a cycle of planning, work, and reflection is essential to establishing a non-coercive classroom. Without planning, results are random. Without reflection, there is no self-realization, little development of self-control, and a lost opportunity for moral development. It is up to teachers to help students think about what happened when things go wrong and when things go right.

When to use the Reflective Loop

There are few classroom activities that are not improved by thoughtful planning beforehand and reflection afterwards. Every time students play a game or observe a demonstration or participate in a role play or work at their desks or lab stations, careful planning about how things will go (including guidance from the teacher as necessary) and reflection together afterwards help them prepare and do better next time. This is how habits are formed, and reflective living is a habit with life-long payoffs.

The Reflective Loop also supports an already-established expectation. Once a routine has been modeled and practiced, the Loop can be used as often as necessary to keep the expectation fresh for all students.

Steps of the Reflective Loop

The three steps of the Loop are simple and easy to remember, but much of the Loop's power will be lost on students if we simply tell them about it and then tell them how they did in its execution. To let them discover the Loop and construct a sense of its value, ask them questions that encourage thinking, and invite them to share their thoughts with the group.

1. Plan

Ask students open-ended questions that engage them in a brief discussion about ways to do an activity successfully, in accordance with the Social Contract. Students may respond to the questions by writing their answers, by pairing up and discussing, or in a whole-group discussion.

Example: Preparing for small-group work

What do we need to do to make this work?

What might you do to go above and beyond the usual?

Who can make a connection between this activity and our Social Contract?

If we're successful in this activity, what will the payoffs be?

What voice level will be appropriate during this activity?

What might get in the way of success? How will we overcome these obstacles?

When is this due?

Who will summarize for us: What's our job today?

2. Work

Students do what was planned. Teacher facilitates learning and watches for behaviors that meet the criteria set by students during the planning time, and for behaviors that fail to do so. Make work-related specific comments to individuals or groups, reinforcing behaviors that foster student growth and redirecting behaviors that don't.

Example: During small-group work

That was a really quick response to the signal!

Your group looks focused and on task.

Your voice levels are right where we agreed they should be.

It's getting too loud: Who can remind us what it should sound like at this time?

I notice everyone is following our "Group Work" Y-Chart. Look around if you want to see productive work going on!

(Privately) *Tim, you're not adhering to our agreements. Go take a look at the Y-chart, then come back and get going again.*

(Privately) *Jane, you sometimes struggle to participate in group discussions, but today you jumped right in! What's different about today?*

3. Review

Ask students questions that engage them in a discussion about how they did—what worked and what didn't, how well they followed the rules, and what changes, if any, might make the process more successful next time. (A written record of this discussion may be valuable, such as a look-sound-feel chart, page 97.)

Example: Following small-group work

What went well?

What worked?

What didn't?

Did this move you closer to achieving your goals?

Did you put in as much effort as you thought you'd need to? Explain.

What obstacles did you encounter, and how did you overcome them?

How well did we adhere to the rules we agreed to before we began?

How well did you and your partner work together?

How did our Social Contract help?

In what way(s), if any, did we not live up to the Social Contract?

Example: Planning for next small-group work time

We'll be doing this regularly; how can we make it better next time?

Will you need to put in more effort next time? Why?

How can we follow the Social Contract better next time?

If you could highlight one thing you could improve next time, what would it be?

The next time they do that routine or activity, they begin the Reflective Loop again, this time planning with the benefit of whatever insights emerged in their reflection.

Example: Recalling reflections on small-group work

Last time, what did we say we needed to work on?

Who can remind us what Charlie said would be a good way to clean up our supplies after work?

Our group-work time has been getting better, but there's always room for improvement. Who remembers something we said we'd like to improve after our last group-work session?

Let's check our notes from last lab period to see what we need to concentrate on today.

After a few weeks of using the Reflective Loop, I saw it paying off. Students were more than willing to take the extra minute it took to collectively set the rules of engagement for an activity before we got started, or to plan things like effective small-group work, or whole-group discussions. It didn't come naturally to me the first two or three times I tried it -- I'd always wanted to "get on with it," and often skipped setting expectations or just told them what I wanted. But I got used to it, and it started to feel natural. Now I don't have to think or refer to a chart. I just slow down and say, "Before we start, who can tell us what we should keep in mind in order to be successful?" Students raise their hands, ready to share their ideas. They're setting their own expectations.

—Middle level teacher, Minneapolis MN

Student-led Reflective Loop

Once the Loop becomes integrated into your teaching practice, try handing over the questioning job to a student leader. This provides another opportunity for lively teaching practice and gradual, responsible assuming of power, satisfying the adolescent appetite for autonomy and competence. It's also leadership training for students, and is a great way to keep some of your best-behaved students actively engaged in the life of the community.

Students can record reflection suggestions for next time, remind you when it's time to reflect before the class hour is over, and ask reflection questions that you give them or from a general list. Eventually, some will begin posing their own reflection questions. This is especially likely to happen after students teach a game to the class. They can think of appropriate questions such as:

- Was the game fun?
- On a scale of 1-5, how would you rate it?
- Were the instructions clear?
- Do you have any suggestions for improvement?

Interest and participation increase when students themselves lead.

This year, I've added the Reflective Loop to my teaching habits. After my lesson, and just before we hit the lab, I ask a student to remind us of our safety rules, or how we're going to proceed in the lab. When we conclude an experiment, instead of just checking to make sure they have their homework assignment written in their planners, I have them circle up, and we review what we learned. I ask, "What did we learn today?" "What's important about what we learned?" "Who remembers what we're going to do tomorrow?" We close lab time by looking ahead, planning for next time.

—High school teacher, Red Lake MN

Challenges of the Reflective Loop

Q. *How can I rationalize the time it will take to add the Reflective Loop to my subject area lessons?*

It may feel awkward the first time you ask, "What do we need to keep in mind to be successful at this?" You may feel pressure to move directly into the work time. It may be difficult to get into the habit of reserving a few minutes after work time to reflect on learning. But as you see student behavior improving because of the consistent, quick, competence-enhancing planning and reflection sessions, you'll agree that it's a little time well spent.

I review the Social Contract at least three times a week during the last part of my class. I ask, "What did we do well today in relation to the Social Contract?" Students might say that one of our rules is to have fun, and we had fun today. Another rule is to respect yourself and others, and someone might comment that we did so by respecting each other when we did a particular activity. Reflecting on a regular basis allows the Social Contract to become more than a paper on a wall, but rather a constant reference point. —High school teacher, Cambridge MA

Q. *In the flow of my busy class hours, how can I keep track of what was learned the day before?*

Remembering the learning from last time at the start of next time is often the most difficult part. Because what's constructed at each step of the Loop is usually done only verbally, it's challenging to remember on Wednesday what we agreed on Monday to try to improve!

Of course, you could write it down. A sticky note written on Monday tacked to your Wednesday lesson plan would solve the remembering problem. Better yet, turn to your students for help. Ask: "Who remembers what we said we'd work on to improve the next time we _____?" Or appoint someone to be the recorder of ideas for improvement, and have him or her keep the list of ideas handy. A well-organized eighth grader can handle this job, and might appreciate the chance to lead.

Q. *Does writing down the plan help?*

Often the planning portion of the Reflective Loop is done verbally and quickly, but there are benefits of writing down the plan, either as a list of steps or as a Y-chart that describes how the action or routine should look, sound, and feel (see page 96). You can post a written version, and refer to it the next time you do the routine, or whenever a review might improve performance. Written versions of the plan are especially helpful for activities and routines that have several steps.

REINFORCING, REMINDING, AND REMODELING

Modeling, practicing, and connecting behavior to the Social Contract all guide students to think before they act and to behave so learning is maximized. To support this new learning, notice and acknowledge behavior that helps the class community live by the Social Contract. Proactively remind students of an expectation. Remodel especially after vacations or even weekends, if you have reason to think students might have lost rigor during the break.

From time to time we all need to review how something is supposed to be done. Chefs review their recipes; coaches go over game plans with their teams in the midst of games; managers send memos to workers to remind them of deadlines and encourage them to achieve goals.

When students do not live up to the expectations that have been set and made clear for all, reminding and remodeling are again useful tools. Adolescents are at a volatile time in life, learning daily about judgment and discretion. Consistent support from caring adults is crucial for them. Their tendency to obsess on their social concerns, their search for identity, their lack of sustained confidence, and their urge to push boundaries can cause them to lose focus. We can help by reminding and remodeling when they stray from behavior agreements. By paying attention to the details of students' behavior, we show them we care about their success and believe in their ability to do things right. Just as is the case with practice, reviewing norms builds student understanding and mastery.

Chapter 7 goes into detail about redirecting students when rules are broken; here, we will show how to use reinforcing, reminding, remodeling, and other strategies to build positive behavioral habits over time.

Education researcher Robert Marzano's meta-analysis of over 100 reports on behavior-management approaches showed that using reinforcement as a discipline technique created a 31% decrease in disruptions. (Marzano 2003, 29)

Reinforcing Positive Behavior

When you've modeled a behavior and it's working well, *say something!* Occasional verbal acknowledgments of little successes encourage students and make it more likely that they will continue along the same right path.

I noticed that everyone came in quietly today and got to work on the assignment.

We haven't had anyone arrive late to class all week!

Our work flow is moving right along. At the end of this period, we'll celebrate with a few minutes of social time.

Amanda, I see that the supply shelf looks orderly after your group used all those materials for your project.

Your work is in on time, and you put it exactly where it belongs. Thanks, Avery.

Reminding

When you notice that a behavior you've modeled is starting to slip, don't just let it go! Merely hoping behaviors will change for the better never works.

Example: Reminding students about good listening behavior

Students' listening habits are slipping, and a little whispering and squirming have crept in to circle conversations or sharing times.

Interrupt by using the signal for quiet. With clear language that fosters reflection about the proper way to execute the behavior, ask open-ended questions:

Who can remind us why it's important to listen carefully during sharing?

What connection can you make to listening and our Social Contract?

We modeled and practiced how to listen on the first day of school, and our listening habits have been excellent during sharing until today, but we're slipping a bit this morning. Who can remind us of what good listening looks and sounds like? Raise your hand and I'll call on you.

Have students describe good listening. Then say: *We need to get back to listening in the way you've just described. Listen carefully between now and the end of today's CPR meeting. After the meeting, we'll check in again and reflect on how we did.*

By asking questions, we give students a chance to remind themselves about the agreements they have made, and how they said they would carry out those agreements in specific routines. We avoid getting trapped in the role of the only rule-minder: we established the routines together, and we'll keep ourselves on track together.

Once something is modeled, revisited occasionally, and students know expectations, you don't have to constantly take the time out from class. Sometime the students do it for you. They'll say "Hey, we agreed on this. We all agreed we'd take on this expectation and follow it." They will remind each other, for example, that no one else should be speaking when someone is sharing in the literature circle. When we meet in the morning, they'll say, "We're not supposed to move the furniture like this."

—8th grade English teacher, Tabernacle NJ

Remodeling

Another way to restore the integrity of a behavioral norm is to remodel the proper way of doing it. We can reinforce their "physical memory" by modeling and perhaps practicing it again.

Example: Remodeling transitioning from whole-group to small-group activities

1. Elicit ideas from students

Who remembers why it's important to quickly and quietly transition from our large-group seating arrangement to our small groups?

2. Demonstrate the right way

It's time for a reminder. I'll show you again how I expect you to do this. Afterward, I'll ask you what you noticed.

3. Notice how behavior follows the rules

What did you notice?

Which rules in the Social Contract connect to what I modeled?

4. Practice and implement again

Let's try it again. As soon as we've completed the transition we'll talk about how we did. Now that we've gone over it again, I'm sure we'll be able to get our transitions back to where they need to be.

Follow up to reinforce remodeling

Check in with students after the remodeling to measure success.

How did we do?

If a student gives a nonspecific answer, like, "OK," require more specific information.

What's your evidence?

Asking for evidence in this non-academic discussion teaches the importance of verification of facts in content areas.

Once I practice the routines with them, I consistently ask them to tell me how the routine should go. After we do it, I ask them to reflect on what we did: what did and didn't work. I find that through practicing and noticing each thing that we do, we've needed to do very little remodeling. Last year we did a lot. The students have carried that learning over and it's become part of who they are. It makes sense to them innately. They know what's expected. It's structured, consistent, and fun. So they do it extremely well.

—8th grade language arts teacher, Greenfield MA

Don't remodel too much

Think about whether remodeling a particular procedure is likely to help. In some cases, you know they know what it looks and feels like, but they (or at least some of them) are still not doing it right.

If students continue to deviate from the modeled expectation and you know that everyone knows how to do it properly, don't remodel it more than once. Use another strategy instead, such as reminding language beforehand, reinforcing language to acknowledge times when things go well, and/or role play if the routine seems to present a dilemma. You may want to bring out the Y-chart and have students remind themselves of the protocol.

Remodeling repeatedly is not a good solution when individuals who fail to follow the model need to be redirected. Failure to enforce appropriately will damage your relationships with the students. They'll tire of incessant remodeling, and will begin to resent your not addressing directly the students who are messing up. See Chapters 7 and 8 for more about redirecting and problem-solving.

Student-led review

Eventually, some students may lead the review of routines. Watching a peer will likely bring renewed interest. You can invite a student to direct the class through the routine (using reminding language and a visual chart if one was created). Students can also lead a reflection on how the group did with a routine.

Elaine stepped to the front of the 6th grade advisory classroom and said, "Please stand for the transition to circle." Everyone stood. Elaine had a stop watch and said, "Ready...go!" Students began moving all the desks to one side of the room, even setting one on top of another, making very little noise. In short order, one side of the room was empty of furniture and students stood in a circle. "That was 64 seconds—not a record, but close to the record of 59 seconds." She recorded the time in a book, and said to the group, "Please sit down. Would someone comment on whether we were quiet and careful enough this time?"

—6th grade teacher, Portland OR

Other Strategies for Supporting Behavior Expectations

Tell a story about working to change your own behavior. Or, if execution of a routine seems to be generally deteriorating, it may be time for a problem-solving meeting where the whole class discusses how to make things better (see page 205). Pausing for a little fun can reduce tension and raise spirits: see if taking five minutes to enjoy a game or to chat together helps. And reflect on your language: are you keeping a balance between positive feedback and redirection? Think about the general tone of the room, and how you can lighten it up, if that's what it seems to need.

Watching and analyzing behavior

Another way to revisit expectations is to watch carefully how things are going, diagnose groups or individuals with problem behaviors, and suggest remedies. The problem may stem mostly from one or two rule-breakers who are setting the tone. If a student is having difficulty following an expectation, a quick remedying session with him or her might help.

Start by observing the learner in action. Watch for both strengths and weaknesses. When you notice something, approach the student and comment. Students thrive on nonjudgmental, non-evaluative feedback. Your relationships will flourish if you get into the habit of moving around the room, watching and offering comments. To be noticed by your teacher is to feel known by her. You can interrupt the student right when he's erring, and remind, redirect, or give *specific* verbal and/or nonverbal advice. The steps are:

1. Observe carefully
2. Diagnose the problem
3. Suggest specific way(s) to change the behavior
4. Allow those who need it to practice using your suggestion(s) as you observe

Simply being carefully watched may cause some students to remedy their misbehavior without further interaction between teacher and student. Teachers can also use these times to reinforce positive behavior:

You got it right this time. I knew you could do it! Get yourself back on track and do it this way from now on, whether I happen to be watching or not.

When entering my advisory class at the beginning of the day, students were in the habit of reading a daily question on my daily news and announcements chart and using a marker to write brief answers in a space provided—usually the bottom third of the page. In November, one student—someone who usually arrived at the last minute—had started writing her responses very large: she was using too much space, and sometimes she wrote over others' responses.

I met her as she entered one day, and while others chatted and finished eating their breakfasts I told her I wanted to watch her add her contribution to the chart. She read the chart, grabbed her marker, and was about to write her response. I stopped her and reminded her to write neatly (she was good at this) and to make her letters approximately the same size as everyone else's. "Like this," I said, and wrote my response, so she saw it modeled properly again. Then I handed the marker to her, and she wrote perfectly. After that, she kept the size of her responses acceptable.

—Middle level teacher, Minneapolis MN

Challenges of Reinforcing, Remodeling, and Reminding

Q. *How can I maintain my commitment to what could be the tedious, frustrating work of remodeling and reminding?*

Remember that adolescents need us to intervene when things start to slip (much more on this is in Chapters 7 and 8). They want to be positive members of the group, but they disappoint themselves and those around them frequently with their impulsive behavior, and sometimes they just forget. Wanting to do what's right is one thing; succeeding at it is another. Behaving appropriately with consistency takes a lot of self-control. When we intervene, some students may resist. If two or more students are allowed to slip at the same time, resistance tends to be more intense. Having the diligence to intervene early and often is critical in maintaining an orderly classroom. What saves those moments from becoming battles is our commitment to remain objective but caring, straight-talking but not shaming. Our language is crucial. Respectful, empowering teacher language is discussed in Chapters 7 and 8 as part of redirecting and problem-solving with rule-breakers.

Q. *What if reminding and remodeling don't work?*

There are many reasons why that might happen; a common one is late timing. Proactive and prompt intervention can prevent slips, and can right them quickly while students still have enough self-control to rein themselves in. Once an adolescent escalates the behavior, however, it becomes far more difficult to reverse. See page 140 for more on the need to respond to smaller infractions.

There are many strategies we can use when a few words or a look are not enough to redirect behavior. Some focus on righting wrongs and repairing damages; others involve consequences like temporary loss of privilege or time to cool off and try again. For some students and situations, the best recourse is problem-solving, either one-on-one or with a whole class. It isn't that reinforcing, reminding, and remodeling aren't effective strategies—they are!—but sometimes situations require further action. See Chapters 7 and 8 for a thorough discussion of these strategies.

Keep it varied and lively

Variety in your responses keeps the demanding work of learning self-management fresher and more attractive to young people. Watch your language to make sure that it doesn't start to sound formulaic. Like a good baseball pitcher, we need to vary our pitches—some remodeling, some redirecting, some referring to recorded reminder charts to revisit how we agreed to handle a procedure. Think about what is really going on and why: perhaps a role play will help for a social situation that seems to be giving several students trouble, or a private conversation with one student to build relationship while we redirect behavior.

Marcel, I know you love to have fun, but we've got to focus on learning these map-making skills right now. Can you do it, or you need some help from me?

Don't forget the power of play! One of the best ways to keep management from getting stale is to add fun. Sometimes you can turn around a potential slide into class disorder by providing the stimulation and fun of a game, or making a game of a routine by using a timer to make a transition quickly (while preserving the rules).

You want to make sure you're upholding the classroom contract for the students. It's about watching your language with the students as well as watching their language, making sure that you're keeping to what you promised them. The minute you break that contract with them, you're really breaking down the community. Your role as a teacher is to hold on to that trust. Consistency is key.

—High school teacher, Cambridge MA

LIVING AGREEMENTS: Getting in Gear for Responsible Independence

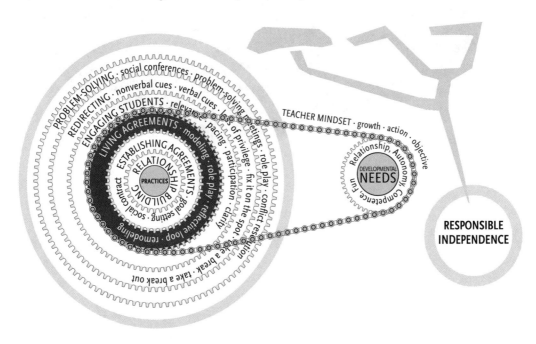

Engaging Students

One of the best ways to reduce behavior that impedes learning is to engage students in lessons that address their needs for autonomy, competence, relationship, and fun. When students are engaged in learning, their prodigious energy supports their work. We know how important content is: what students learn is at the heart of any school. Yet *how we deliver* that content is equally important. This chapter presents in detail teaching approaches that encourage successful learning and its ally, positive behavior.

For optimal student performance, we make learning engaging. Best practices include planning lessons that will be personally relevant for students and matching lessons to their cognitive maturity. We present content in a variety of ways, allow for students to make choices, and include opportunities for them to plan, work actively, figure things out, and reflect—all with a lot of variety and interaction with peers. We manage time to promote focused attention and absorption. We maximize active learning and minimize passive learning.

Various methods have been developed for facilitating student motivation. The ones that are most effective are learner-oriented. They include providing as much choice as possible; allowing students to work together on projects; calibrating the material to the interests of the students; being sure that the material represents optimal challenge for all students; and allowing students to be active in their learning rather than just sitting and listening. (Deci, from 2006 interview with Kevin Bushweller)

MEET STUDENTS WHERE THEY ARE DEVELOPMENTALLY

Intellectual Development

To make learning relevant, we need to match what we want students to learn to their cognitive development. Young adolescents are rapidly increasing their cognitive capacities, especially their ability to think abstractly. Year by year, concepts like justice and point of view, and interest in academic skills like making successful arguments, are of greater interest. Understanding child and adolescent development empowers teachers to design lessons that keep students focused. For a comprehensive look at cognitive development as well as other aspects of adolescent development, see *Yardsticks: Children in the Classroom Ages 4-14* by Chip Wood (2007). See Appendix A for more about adolescent development.

Create lessons that are challenging but not insurmountable

Young adolescents need to be challenged by difficult work, but not defeated by it. Their desire for competence and autonomy impels them to take risks, and this can lead to rapid academic growth when teachers keep the gap between what they already know and what they are to learn next (what Vygotsky calls the "zone of proximal development;" 1978) small enough for them to successfully make the leap. Good piano teachers make sure that each new piece builds on what the student has learned recently, and is slightly more difficult, but not overwhelming. Similarly, when we design lessons to match what students are able to do at their stage of cognitive development and then ratchet things up bit by bit, we help them build one success atop another.

Ultimately, students' legitimate successes—whatever they may be—are the most valuable components of any curriculum at this [middle] level. Youngsters' belief in themselves as capable learners must be our most venerated goal. (Stevenson 2002, 181)

Physical Development

Adolescents learn best in situations where they have things to make, materials and peers to work with, interesting problems to tackle, and frequent opportunities to move.

Experiential learning

Activity can make the difference between staying focused and straying. When students engage with materials as they investigate a topic, they maintain their interest. They need to discover and experiment with ideas and information, not simply ingest them. In math, this may mean that they create math-based art, play math-based games, do simulations such run mock businesses or invest in the stock market, use manipulatives, or deal with real-life number problems. In reading, they might use graphic organizers, or hunt through literature with Post-its or highlighters to find evidence, or re-enact scenes or represent characters visually or through imaginary interviews. In history, they can use primary source materials, re-enact events in simulations, or create timelines. And science labs are intrinsically engaging.

Whatever the subject, when they experience it they are in it, not merely hearing or reading *about* it. The process of using the materials or engaging in action casts learning into memory. It also provides a certain amount of movement and manipulation, which is always welcome.

Movement breaks

Adolescent students need lots of movement and plenty of food. This is no secret to middle and high school teachers or parents of teenagers. A teacher in Minneapolis has a simple but apt mantra: "Feed 'em and move 'em." She makes sure her students get up and move at least twice during every period, and serves a snack if students haven't eaten for over two hours. Building movement into lessons pays off in focus time gained, not lost.

In his book *Teaching with the Brain in Mind*, Eric Jensen provides evidence of mind-body links that "demonstrate that movement can be an effective cognitive strategy to 1) strengthen learning 2) improve memory and retrieval, and 3) enhance learner motivation and morale. For example, he describes research that "traced a pathway from the cerebellum [the brain's center for motor control] back to parts of the brain involved in memory, attention, and spatial perception. Amazingly, the part of the brain that processes movement is the same part of the brain that processes learning." He recommends that educators include role play, energizers, quick games, cross-lateral activities, and stretching during class to access the boost that movement brings to learning. (Jensen 2005, 60-61)

Using engaged learning activities or games that require movement gets students moving (and a little excited) while they learn. Team-building and trust-building activities also get them up and moving, and have indirect academic payoffs. (See www.originsonline.org for activities appropriate for class hours at the middle level.) Simply giving students a minute to stand, stretch, or do a quick exercise can be very helpful, as students need frequent breaks to function at their best.

Students' need for movement and quick breaks makes transitions (from whole-group to small-group desk configurations, from classrooms to common spaces, passing between periods) part of best practices. Done properly—we model and practice first, then enforce expectations—transitions give students another chance to stretch, move, and chat.

Social Development

Adolescents need to interact with each other. Some are preoccupied with peer relating, and most have a strong desire for it, but all young people need to learn how to do it well. They need to learn how to collaborate with others as they work, for example, as well as when they play. Psychologists Piaget, Vygotsky, and Rogoff have all shown that cognitive development occurs best within a mutual apprenticeship. Social interaction leads to dialogue, and dialogue leads to higher mental function. Build into your lessons time to meet the need for interaction with peers in structured, appropriate ways.

Communication and shared problem-solving bridge the gap between old and new knowledge and between the differing understandings of partners (whether their understanding is at the same or at different levels), as individuals attempt to resolve contradictions or search for the common ground of shared understanding.... The participants gain in understanding and may have difficulty determining "whose" idea an insight was; many claim an insight as their own and cannot trace it to the group discussion. Indeed, it was theirs, but not theirs alone. (Rogoff 1990, 196)

Limit teacher-directed time

Ten or 15 minutes of teacher-directed ("sage on the stage") time is about all most students can handle; after that, their attention wanes. In the course of presenting information or demonstrating skills, provide a minute or two of partner sharing to reflect or to share a personal connection. The energy level of the room goes up, and attention is refreshed for the rest of the lecture or instructions. Learn more about switching learning modalities below, page 124.

Incorporate partner and small-group work

Increase learning and address adolescents' need for social exchange at the same time by structuring opportunities for students to work together. Set up students for success by modeling, practicing, and reviewing as necessary how appropriate social interaction looks, sounds, and feels. Consider making with students a visual reminder, such as a Y-chart, for the routine, or a list of steps, or a Must-do/May-do T-chart (see Recording Ideas, pages 96-98, for examples).

Skillful discussion with peers boosts engagement and learning

Excellent engaged-learning strategies that teach content through small-group interaction are available online. Before setting students to the task of a small-group discussion, define the format. For example, use a round-robin cycle in which the first person reads the book selection, the second person paraphrases, the third person interprets, and the fourth gives an example from personal experience. Putting such a format into a fishbowl modeling first is a great way to maximize the potential of small-group work. See fishbowl modeling, page 91.

Example engaged learning strategy: Think, Ink, Pair, Share

Use engaged learning strategies, like *Think, Ink, Pair, Share* described below, to teach content through small-group interaction. Many other strategies are available online, such as *Say Something* and *Missing Piece*, at www.originsonline.org.

1. Students think about a question or topic for 1-2 minutes

2. Students write down their thoughts

3. Students share with one or two partners about a given topic for a given amount of time (assign one partner to be first; be strict about time so each one gets an equal amount of sharing time)

4. One student shares the small-group comments with the entire group

Take 1 minute to think about and write down two ideas you have to improve writing in our school. After this, each partner will have 2-3 minutes to share ideas and answer questions from his or her partner.

Provide a peer audience

Another powerful way to utilize adolescents' absorption with each other is to provide a peer audience for student work whenever possible. Young, often insecure adolescents look around all the time: *Who's listening? Who's looking to see what I've done?* The best answer is "We all are!" Students whose work is assessed continuously, not just by their teachers but by peers, other adults, and themselves have a heightened awareness of doing good work and achieving a goal. Peer audience response to a display, a partner share, or a presentation of small-group work is the most readily available way for students to see that the quality of what they do matters to more than just the teacher.

Develop social skills in multiple ways

Assisting students in building the relationships they crave pays off in fewer disruptions. Spending time each day during a homeroom/advisory period teaching them how to greet, share, play, and celebrate together, and creating a sense of connection and community in class hours, help build individual social competency and the safe, friendly school climate in which learning best occurs. (For more on advisory structures teaching social skills, see page 48, and *The Advisory Book*.)

Students pay attention to content only when it is safe to do so. Many do not feel safe enough to ignore teasing from classmates and bullies. To student brains, that outside influence is a potential predator, like a saber-tooth tiger. Some teachers call on an unprepared learner just to embarrass the student. In this risky environment, some learners cannot focus on content processing. Many schools ignore student safety issues, yet act surprised that students can't seem to focus in class. (Jensen 2005, 36)

Keep behavior expectations present

When you limit your whole-group, teacher-directed time and give students opportunities for interactive work, remain vigilant about enforcing your listening and participation expectations.

During (independent or group) work time, make sure you hold yourselves accountable to all our behavior expectations governing work time. When I ask for your attention, I expect it to happen right away.

Follow through by redirecting those who fail to meet your expectations. (See Chapter 7 about redirection).

ENGAGE STUDENTS THROUGH RELEVANCE

When students see a lesson's relevance to their own lives, they are much more likely to take interest in it and much less likely to push back, disrupt, or sink into boredom. When a lesson seems to have nothing to do with them, they lose interest fast. They may resent what they see as an attempt to force them to do something uninteresting, and push back: "This is stupid!" "Why do we have to do this?"

Creating and presenting relevant lessons helps build solid relationships with students. It shows that we know them and respect their interests, that we care enough about them to connect their lives to their learning, to attend to their hunger for autonomy and competence. When students are invested in their lessons, their behavior improves.

Help students connect what they are learning to their own lives and experiences. This is the "prior knowledge" link, made more dynamic by our willingness for "knowledge" to include students' personal life experiences and interests. The more they make connections to what they already know about life, and the more they see links to things they already care about, then the more open they will be to the lesson, and the more likely they will be to internalize and remember it.

In her book *Brain Matters*, science writer Patricia Wolfe says, "The more fully we process information over time, the more connections we make, the more consolidation takes place, and the better the memory will be." (2001, 128) She writes about a kind of learning called elaborative rehearsal: learning strategies that require students to reflect on the information being taught, relate it to something they already know, and form meaningful mental associations.

Connect through student interests

You can help keep students engaged by having them study what the age group in general tends to find interesting: sixth graders are often interested in history, biography, the human body, science fiction, and non-fiction; by eighth grade, there is often greater interest in investigating social issues, historical conflicts, and world problems. One topic of endless interest to all of them is identity, since adolescence is the prime time for figuring out who we are and what we will become. Learning organized around points of view such as what scientists do or the lives of children in the westward movement grabs onto that interest in identity. Inserting biographical information about particular scientists in their youth or how young people struggled sparks attention and provides a personal connection.

Connect through surveys and choice

The best sources of information for targeting curriculum to interests are the students themselves. Interest surveys can reveal specific topics that have appeal. Exploratory studies of a variety of topics from which students get to choose provide further information. Making choices—charting their own course, exercising their own ideas about how to do things—is an efficient way to differentiate according to interest, and it also is an effective avenue to differentiation according to skill and knowledge level. Students readily embrace the opportunity to select a path of learning on which they can most likely succeed. Choices feed their desires for competence and autonomy and make their academic pursuit personal.

Having a say in what they learned was important to these students. They reported that having choices made learning both relevant and fun.... Self-direction created feelings of empowerment for students as they became leaders in their own learning. They fulfilled their need for responsibility and meaningful work, as they gained leadership qualities. (Boyer and Bishop 2004, 1)

Connect through your enthusiasm

Students watch us carefully. They quickly pick up on our moods, our habits, our preferences, and our mannerisms. A teacher who is passionate about her subject matter and about learning sparks student interest. We all remember teachers who shared with us their good energy. They enthusiastically invited us into their academic worlds, and we eagerly—or at least willingly—accepted.

Connect through thought-provoking questions

Other personal connections can be stimulated by open-ended questions that invite students to think about how they might use certain information, or how they have experienced what is being discussed in their own lives. If you hook them, if you bring in a relevant, personal connection or a connection to something they know well ("Charles, how does the principle of an inclined plane relate to cross-country skiing?" "Maylene, what do bicycles teach us about weight distribution?") you will reduce mental and physical wandering.

The openness of the question helps immensely. In place of short-answer, fill-in-the-blank queries that call for mere recitation and one and only one right answer, draw students in with open-ended questions whose answers might include examples from their own lives, or their own point of view or opinion.

Examples of open-ended questions

- Process questions: *How does this work? What should be the order of events?*
- Ethical questions: *Should we...?*
- Questions that require a decision: *What would be the most beneficial to all? What would be the best route to travel? What criteria would you use to decide who participates?*
- Questions about your own survival: *How can you best...?*
- Questions that invite lots of answers (e.g. brainstorming, listing possibilities): *What ways could you solve this problem? What are all the things we could do?*
- Personal experience questions: *How would you/did you...? What experience have you had with this? What have you read about this?*
- Hypothetical questions: *What if...? Supposing that...?*
- Noticing questions: *What do you observe? (see, hear, smell, etc.)*
- Causation questions: *How did this happen? Why did s/he decide...?*

What makes it do this?

- Contraries: *On the other hand, what about...? Now switch to the other side: what do you think...?*

- Point-of-view questions: *How did or might the main character experience this?*

- Beginner's mind: *Pretend you are completely new to this issue. What do you notice? What do you think? Pretend you have no opinion about this, and speak about pros and cons of the issue.*

- Emotional, empathetic questions: *How do you think s/he felt? How would you feel if...?*

- Drawing conclusions: *What does this show us about this character?*

- Practical applications: *If you were starting a business, how could you use this information? If you were lost, how could you use a compass?*

- Connections to the real world: *How does this relate to current events?*

- Opinions on controversial issues: *What do you think about this issue? Whom do you hold responsible?*

We seek a balance between externally-defined curriculum requirements and personal interests—the students' and our own. In *Teaching Ten to Fourteen Year Olds,* Chris Stevenson quotes 13-year-old Caitlin: "The problem with this school is that they want you to know all of this stuff except that I'm never going to use it. It's a big waste if I'm never going to use it." (Stevenson 2002, 174) Preserving this balance will both help adolescents advance academically and intellectually and present lessons that Caitlin and her cohort are likely to perceive as useful.

Our middle school built its entire curriculum around three questions, one for each grade, and then spent the year exploring those questions. Grade 6 explored "Who am I?"; Grade 7 explored "What are my relationships to others, to government, and to the world?"; and Grade 8 explored "What is the meaning of life?" We addressed just about every state standard in all of the curriculum areas beginning with these questions.

—Middle school teacher, LaCrosse WI

ENGAGE STUDENTS THROUGH PACING

Many behavior problems originate with students' restlessness. They want action, interaction, play, movement, and variety, and when we ignore these needs disruption is likely. Instead, use their restlessness to support learning and build social skills.

Adolescents pursue fun in both childlike and newer adult ways. Through this pursuit, the teenager learns about more complex relationships.... Having fun in relationships creates intimacy and forges a "pleasure bond" between people that helps maintain the relationship. (Fall, Holden, and Marquis 2004, 252)

There are many ways to keep things lively. All of the strategies described here can energize the classroom and engage student participation.

Strategic Timing

Make the most of prime learning time

Primacy-recency theory suggests that learning is most likely to occur at the very beginning of a new time frame, when student attention is greatest. But teachers often use this best learning time to handle administrative details with students, intending simply to get them over with. Although that may seem efficient, there is a sizable cost to spending the beginning of a class period this way.

New information or a new skill should be taught first, during primetime-1 [the beginning of the class period], because it is most likely to be remembered. Keep in mind that students will remember almost any information presented at this time, so it is important that only correct information be presented. This is not the time to be searching for what students may already know about something. I remember watching a teacher of English start a class with, "Today, we are going to learn about a new literary form called onomatopoeia. Does anyone have any idea what that is?" After several wrong guesses, the teacher finally defined it. Regrettably, those same wrong guesses appeared in the follow-up test. And why not? They were mentioned during the most powerful retention position, prime-time-1. (Sousa 2001, 38-39)

Exploit the power of primacy-recency! Get students engaged in learning the minute class begins. Don't attend to administrative details first—and don't start with a lecture. Students' first question, spoken or unspoken, is "what are we doing today?" "First, you get to listen to me talk for 25 minutes" is bad news—not an invitation to engagement!

Many teachers who understand the importance of getting students going right away use a programmed approach to their content, like daily oral language, math fact drills, word of the day, or five-minute freewrite. This tactic meets the need for getting started right away, but it falls short if the learning during these first few minutes is not connected to what follows.

Create lessons in which for the first few minutes they write, discuss, problem-solve, read, reflect—right away, while they're primed for learning. Follow that lively beginning with the lecture or demonstration or instructions connected to their initial exploration—the information they need to learn from the expert. Two or three straight weeks of starting this way should establish the habit. Do things like taking attendance while students are working independently.

Ways to get started

Use one of these structures, or one you devise, to make the most of those potent first few minutes of class:

- Review last night's homework in small groups

- Access prior knowledge by journaling in response to a question you'll use as a springboard to the day's lesson

- Write a prediction about how much effort they'll put into their work time that day

- Prepare a brief statement about what was covered yesterday, then share the written statement in a small group

- Read a paragraph or page, or participate in an activity that will spark interest in the day's learning topic

- Respond to a planning question, such as: *Who can make a suggestion about how we can be successful today?* or *How much effort do you think you'll need to put into our work time today to finish on time?* or *What do you need to keep in mind today to abide by our Social Contract?* Responses could be given aloud to partners or the whole group, or they could be written and kept private.

Some days, you might want to launch right into an active, teacher-led discussion that makes use of a participation technique such as those outlined on page 129.

Getting started after lunch

Right after lunch can be an especially difficult time to get students to focus at the beginning of class. Try creating a "soft landing" for students by using quiet time or hot topics upon their return to class. Quiet time requires a conscious shift from free social time to classroom self-discipline; the hot-topics approach harnesses the natural social energy of lunch time and infuses energy into the after-lunch doldrums. Both are meant to be brief—five to ten minutes—and both lead students' minds away from the events and distractions of lunch, readying them for an afternoon of learning.

Quiet time

Establish with students a routine of entering your classroom after lunch and engaging in a brief (5 to 10 minutes), silent learning period. This period should be active (drawing, writing, reading, solving for Y) but should focus on learning in an inward rather than social way. The silence may help students center themselves for the rest of the class.

Hot topics

If you feel that students need interactive time, have them form small groups and discuss a hot topic for about ten minutes. The topic should be either academic or social in nature, and the discussion should be structured (page 116) to ensure full, fair participation.

Academic example: In groups of five or six, students discuss yesterday's reading.

The teacher appoints a facilitator in each group. The facilitator asks each person to look at his notes from yesterday and share one point in the reading that stood out to him. The facilitator is also responsible for making verbal transitions from one group member to the next, like "Thank you, Antonio. You're next, Stephanie; what do you have to say about yesterday's reading?"

Social example: In pairs, students discuss the use of cell phones. Topics for discussion may include what students' rights and responsibilities are with regard to cell phone use in school, and the cell phone etiquette in general.

Addressing after-lunch problems includes mitigating them by creating lunchroom and recess environments that reduce opportunities for conflict and support harmonious social time. Appendix G touches on creating school-wide routines for common areas but a full address of this topic extends beyond this book.

Reflect at the end of each class period

The scenes are familiar; are they from movies about schools or horror films? A bell rings to signal the end of a period. The teacher raises his voice uselessly as the students tear out of the room: "Uh, we'll finish up tomorrow... dismissed...." No completion of the lesson, no closure of the class period, no order, and very little hope for an orderly start for the next class. The last few minutes of each period are second only to the first few in primacy-recency learning.

Closure should take place during prime-time-2 [the last few minutes of the class], since this is the second most powerful learning position and an important opportunity for the learner to determine sense and meaning. (Sousa 2001, 39)

To take full advantage of the power of the last few minutes, conclude your lessons with:

Student participates in reflection at the end of the day

- Learning reviews (*What did we learn today?* or *Here's what we covered today...*or *On your exit card, write two things you still need to do to meet the requirements.*)

- Reflections about the learning process (*How did we do? How much effort was necessary to complete the task? How well did you focus? How well did your group interactions go?*)

- Acknowledgments (give students an opportunity to thank others for something that contributed to their time together)

Move administrative duties to times when students are working independently, and use stretching, snacks, breaks, or games in the middle of the period, when they may need to reenergize.

Variety

Change learning modalities frequently

To increase focus and decrease disruptive behavior, design lessons that demand listening, writing, talking, reading, thinking, making, and viewing in segments of twenty minutes or less. In a 55- or 60-minute period, plan for learning in at least three different modalities, and perhaps as many as five or six. Middle level students need variety, movement, fun, and interaction. Their adolescent brains thrive on variety.

55-minute lesson example

Mode 1: (5 min.) Write complete-sentence answers to a five-question about the day's topic

Mode 2: (5 min.) Discuss answers with partner and/or in large group

Mode 3: (2 min.) Orally reflect on learning (what's been learned, effort, obstacles, next steps, etc.)

Mode 4: (15 min.) Teacher leads mini-lesson on the topic

Mode 5: (20 min.) Read, create, problem-solve, etc. to apply and enrich teacher's mini-lesson. (During this segment, students may pause and play a quick game)

Mode 6: (5 min.) Review and plan for next time

By switching among learning modalities, you align your lessons to adolescents' natural capacities for paying attention, and you help them stay on task throughout the class period. See *Lively Learning* by Linda Crawford (2004) for ways to use the arts to add variety and increase engagement.

Expertise in the form of modeling, demonstrations, mini-lessons, text, or short lectures is a necessary ingredient of good teaching—they mediate the learning experience. But don't expect students to focus on you and on teacher-directed activities for more than twenty minutes at a time. Opinions vary about how long an adolescent should be expected to pay attention—defining "attention" is one of the problems in determining this—but they benefit from changes in learning modalities, with brief breaks in between. In *Teaching With the Brain In Mind*, Erik Jensen writes: "Remember that the human brain is poor at nonstop attention. It needs time for processing and rest after learning." He specifies that middle level students (grades 6-8) should receive no more than 12 to 15 minutes of teacher-guided learning at a time. This time frame can be increased somewhat if teachers use best practices (asking interesting questions, allowing students to briefly discuss their answers in pairs or small groups before returning their attention to the teacher, making the content relevant, etc.), because the variety of interaction enhances attention. (Jensen 2005, 37)

Over time, you may be able to increase the amount of time you spend in one modality, but watch carefully. Neural development can be erratic during adolescence, and expecting students to steadily increase their ability to sustain attention doing one kind of activity could backfire. Keeping them engaged by using a variety of modalities is more dependable.

Build in differentiation by giving assignment extensions

Students can do extensions on assignments through use of "must-do's" and "may-do's." Separate assignment components into the categories of 1) requirements and 2) options. Expectations for rigor, such as rubrics and checklists, are included in the must-do's. Extension possibilities—deeper study, adding aesthetic value, making more connections, etc.—are listed in the may-do category. Students who finish early then have specific additional options they may choose to explore, and they don't have to think up what to do, although such initiative is always welcome. You may require that in addition to the must-do's, students choose a may-do. As long as they have a choice, and the may-do's are carefully selected so as to be interesting ideas, students are likely to engage.

Example of must-do's/may-do's: Molecular structure of elements

Must-do's	May-do's
1. Choose ten elements	1. Write about the discovery of each element
2. Make an accurate atomic model for each	2. Describe the elements' uses for humans
3. Label each model accurately, including	3. Explain benefits and/or dangers to live organisms
Atomic symbol Atomic number Atomic weight	

Include a standard independent lesson extension

In addition to the specific may-do choices, there can also be a standard extension for students who finish before the end of a period. Some students complete assignments well and more quickly than others. For them, "down time" near the end of the period should be redirected to learning extensions:

- In language arts, students could always have at hand an independent reading or extended writing project to work on
- Language students may access a software program that engages them in multiple learning modes
- Math students might engage in an on-going financial game
- Science students may plot daily weather patterns for a city or a region
- In social studies, students may monitor and chart or report on current events

Select extensions that are relevant and enjoyable, offer choices, and model and practice how to do each one before offering them. Create a system to record the extra work done by each student. After these preliminary steps, students can quickly confirm with you that they have completed the assignment, and begin the extension.

Use a learning cycle for routine with variety

Some teachers like to establish a routine for their lessons, a sequence that is repeated daily with a range of topics and has variety built in. These "learning cycles" can help us be sure that more than one learning modality is used. Many learning cycles have been developed, and you can create your own. Remember to provide variety, and include reflection and social interaction. Here are a couple of examples.

Reflective Loop learning cycle

The Reflective Loop emphasizes planning, working, and reviewing what was done. This process is used to ensure quality work and steady improvement. The format has just three steps (see page 101 for a detailed description):

Plan: Prepare for the learning; decide what you are going to do and how you will do it.

Work: Do the work.

Reflect: Think about what you did and plan improvements for next time.

The Loop can be used for almost anything you do in the classroom. In the context of a game, for example, begin with brief instructions (expert input from teacher and/or students); plan how you will do it. Play the game, then take a couple of minutes to reflect together on how it went. The payoffs of using this format are that it supports readiness for the task and closure at the end, which increases understanding and builds competence and feelings of autonomy. The work period generally includes some social interaction and relationship-building, always a plus. The time it takes to complete a Loop can vary greatly, from just a few minutes for an activity to as long as several days for extended assignments.

Loop example: Introducing students to the physical features of the African continent

Plan: Students are paired. Every pair selects an aspect of the physical environment of Africa to study briefly (define time). They prepare to teach others about what they have learned, and they plan a visual addition to the map the class is creating to accompany their lesson.

Work: Partners select from a list of physical features such as rivers, lakes, mountains, deserts, swamps, forests, etc. and read about it in resource materials. Then partners teach the class about their physical feature, adding to the class map a visual representation of it on the continent of Africa

Reflection: Students write an affirming comment about each presentation and pass them to the presenting partners, and/or partners self-assess their content, map, and presentation. A quick alternative would be for everyone to respond to a reflection question, e.g., What is a one-sentence answer you would make if someone asked you to describe the physical features of Africa?

Loop example: Reviewing homework

Plan: *Muriel will lead the homework review. Get out your books and your work, and a pencil to make corrections. When she calls on you, speak in complete sentences. Are you ready, Muriel? Everyone else?*

Work: Students review homework under student direction.

Reflect: Students consider one or more of the following questions:

Are there any questions remaining for anyone?

If you were going to pursue this topic, what would your next question be?

What is one thing you learned from this assignment? Turn to your neighbor and share.

What is one way we can make this work better tomorrow?

Plan for next time: Teacher fields student responses and may take one or more of the students' ideas and try it out next time.

ReSET learning cycle

The four-step ReSET learning cycle has reflection at both the beginning and the end.

Reflect: Students think alone, perhaps organizing their thoughts by writing, editing, listing, creating a table or other graphic organizer

Share: Students share their thoughts with each other

Expert/teacher input: The expert/teacher builds academic content into students' reflections and shares

Test the ideas: The learning from the first three phases is experienced in an active way, for example by applying it to a project or a piece of writing. Students should reflect on what they learned.

Engagement increases as we meet students' needs for autonomy, competence, and relationship using ReSET. Students get into the habit of being responsible for completing a brief, often open-ended initial task, which builds competence. They interact when they share so they practice their social skills. During expert input their academic competence increases, and they experience autonomy when they actively try out their new knowledge in the last step.

In the ReSET learning cycle, the teacher, while she may need to offer quick directions in step one or two, is often a "guide on the side." Even the expert-input step may be led by a student, or a guest presenter, or be provided by a text, film, or other experience. Expert input may also consist of the teacher leading a discussion with students about their learning, in which case the "expert" role is shared by many.

Examples of ReSET beginnings

Consider several ways to structure reflection in of the ReSET cycle. In each example below, note that the reflection forecasts the sharing structure. Whenever you plan to have students share information with others, tell them ahead of time.

Ponder a new topic: *Today we're going to begin to study local water quality. For the next two minutes, write down some reasons why this is worth exploring. You'll share what you've written with a partner afterward, so be ready for that.*

Access prior knowledge: *Take out your rough drafts: they're due today. Begin class by reading them aloud, in a one-foot voice, and correct any mistakes you discover as you go: misspelled words, punctuation or capitalization problems, faulty sentence structure, and so on. Afterwards, you'll share your corrections with a partner, so look carefully! Let's each try to find and fix at least three errors.*

Make a personal connection: *Think about the poets we've studied so far this year. Select the one who speaks most directly to you, and write as many reasons and examples as you can. Don't worry about making your writing perfect—just let it flow. We'll share these in a minute. Ready, begin.*

Spark interest in what will come later in the lesson: *Write about a time you slipped on an icy sidewalk or a wet floor or some other slippery surface. Describe the feeling as you noticed you were out of control.*

Example of ReSET: Poetry lesson

Goal: Students will understand what constitutes an elegy poem and will be able to write one.

Reflection: Students brainstorm everything they know about Abraham Lincoln

Share: Students partner up and share everything they know about Abe Lincoln

Expert Input: Class reads Walt Whitman's "Oh Captain, My Captain!"

Teacher defines "elegy" and presents its characteristics; students then return to "Oh Captain, My Captain!" and analyze the poem, comparing it to definition and characteristics of elegy.

Test the idea: Students use the information learned as a guide to writing their own 24-line elegy poems, which could be in honor of someone they knew or a famous historical figure.

The reflection and sharing portions are 1-4 minutes each. Keep expert input to 15 minutes, not allowing it to run over twenty minutes if at all possible. That allows students 20 or 25 minutes to work, and 2-5 minutes to reflect on what's been learned and what the next steps are.

ENGAGE THROUGH PARTICIPATION

Full, fair participation by all students in whole-group academic and social activities is crucial to overall engagement. A community works best when all are involved. When even one person drifts off on his own, the community is weakened. To encourage engagement and participation of everyone in a class discussion, use a variety of ways to invite students to answer questions and share their thoughts. Several are described below. Always be clear about which format you want them to use at any particular time: set the expectation, and stick with it.

Formats for participation

Sometimes you want to conduct discussions that feel safe for everyone; at other times, it encourages growth to introduce a little risk. Start the year using safer, low-risk techniques, building a trusting environment before moving to formats that pull students out of their comfort zones. Build success on success, one discussion at a time. The following techniques are listed in order, starting with the safer techniques and ending with the more risky.

Visual surveys of the class: Each student can answer a question silently, using fingers indicating degree of agreement on a scale of one to five, or thumbs (thumb up = "I agree," thumb sideways = "I'm on the fence," thumb down = "I disagree").

Rate the degree to which the author's argument persuades you. Flash a "fist of five" to indicate your opinion, five being 'extremely persuasive,' one being 'not persuasive at all.'

Sticky-note response: Students write an answer to your question on a sticky note and display it.

Write your answer on a sticky note. We'll analyze them together in 2 minutes.

Partner share: Ask partners to briefly share their ideas about a topic.

What do you think? Share your thoughts with your partner; you'll each have 30 seconds.

Call and response: Students say an answer in unison. This works best for reviewing factual material students already know. At the point where an answer is required, the teacher pauses, creating space for the students to say the answer. The pause may be accompanied by a gesture to invite response.

Teacher: *How did we come up with this answer? Let's go through it step by step. Thirteen goes into 130 how many times_____?*

All: *Ten*

Teacher: *Right. 15 times 3 is _____?*

All: *45*

Kitchen Table Talk: Students act as members of a big family, contributing to the discussion at random and without raising hands, but without raising voices.

Let's brainstorm a list of the causes of the fall of the Ottoman Empire. No need to raise your hand to respond; just say an answer. Give me time after each response to jot it down.

Raising hands (volunteering): Students raise their hands to signal that they would like to give an answer. They remain silent, hands raised, until called upon.

For the next ten minutes, we're going to review problems 1-6. Raise your hand and wait for me to call on you before answering.

Volunteering plus: After hands go up, push a little: say how many additional hands you need to see before you will call on anybody.

I see 3 hands; I need 2 more. Who's willing?

Partner share followed by random calling: Partners share their ideas; when the partner share is complete, randomly call on individuals. You could call for volunteers to share out, rather than calling on individuals, to lower the risk.

Round-robin input: Each student gets a chance to respond to a question. You may allow students to pass temporarily, but return to them for a response.

Peer-to-peer calling: Students call on each other. After the leader calls on the first student to get her input, that student calls on the next student, and so on.

Variation: Students may pass a symbolic object—a decorated "talking stick" is one possibility—from one speaker to the next. The only student allowed to speak is the one holding the symbol.

Random calling: Leader calls on students by randomly pointing to names on a class list, pulling papers or sticks with student names on them out of a container, or some other randomization method.

As we look at this projection of the night sky together, I'll be calling on you at random to ask you what you notice. Pay attention and have a response ready—you won't know who I'm going to call next.

As a variation, each time a student is called, offer him the choice to:

- Answer the question: participant gives an answer
- Ask a friend (if s/he isn't sure of the answer): the student gives what s/he knows, and then asks a friend to help out with the rest of the answer
- Pass (if s/he does not know and doesn't want to guess)

ENGAGE THROUGH CLARITY AND ORDER

Set the ground rules, steps of the process, or method for participation every time. To build competence, students need to be clear about specific expectations before a lesson begins. Then we can hold them accountable, because we know they have the information they need to be successful.

Participation

Model and practice how to use each method for participation before using it for the first time, and before subsequent use, if a review is necessary. (See Modeling, page 88)

I'll call on you at random; no need to raise your hand. Listen carefully and quietly to the discussion until I call on you.

In the example above, the teacher framed the discussion and let students know how she would call on them and how they needed to behave. It's simple, but when we forget to make these norms clear, the results can be blurting and interrupting.

Use both written and verbal instructions

Reduce confusion and disorder by posting written instructions to reinforce oral directions whenever there are more than a couple of steps involved. During work time, students with questions can refer to the written instructions, rather than asking the teacher to repeat: this is a step towards responsible independence. All we have to do if some students ask anyway (which we know they will!) is point to the chart.

Check for understanding

If students are asked to work independently or in small groups without a clear understanding of the instructions, they are likely to waste time or disrupt the class. How can we check to see whether students understand what they're supposed to do next? It doesn't do to ask: "Are there any questions?" or "Are we clear on this?" Many students aren't willing or able to admit they aren't clear, and some mistakenly believe they understand the instructions. Instead, ask for student participation:

Who can restate the assignment?

I'm looking for someone to repeat the assignment aloud; who's ready?

We need to hear from someone new; what's our task?

Have more than one student restate the instructions. If someone volunteers, the teacher listens to make sure he or she gets it right. If no one volunteers, call on someone. If two students attempt to restate the assignment and neither is able to do so accurately, reteach it (or the parts that were unclear). Once everyone is comfortable with this technique, you can check for understanding by calling on students at random: "Pete, tell us what our job is going to be for the next twenty minutes."

Explicitly checking that students are clear about their assignment may seem awkward at first, but the process assures students and you that they understand what is expected. Then they experience competence, and you can hold them accountable.

SUMMARY

Meeting student needs in our teaching maximizes focused learning. The more clarity we provide in lessons, the more our students can manage themselves and solve their own problems. The better pacing and greater variety in the ways that we teach, the less we have to push and prod to get and keep attention. The more we teach with content and methods that connect to adolescents developmentally and speak to them personally, the less we face the upsets that come with boredom and disconnection. The more we structure lessons to satisfy adolescent needs for relationship, fun, autonomy, and competence, the less students will resort to disruptive entertainments.

Seldom ... do engaged students walk in the door; creating the climate and conditions for genuine engagement is our work. (VanDeWeghe 2006, 91)

ENGAGING STUDENTS: Getting in Gear for Responsible Independence

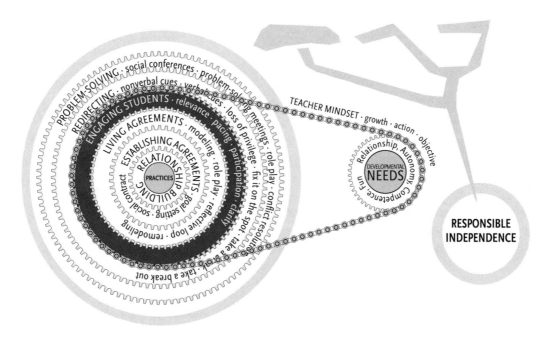

SECTION III

Responding to Rule-breaking

No matter how diligently we work with students to establish goals and commit to agreements about how we need to behave to support those goals; no matter how carefully we set up routines and model and practice them, no semester will pass without rule-breaking. It's part of the business of all children to test limits, but adolescents, especially, are figuring out how power works, and to what extent they can operate independent of the adults who have so much of it. It's part of healthy growth toward adulthood to try things out on their own, and it's part of the job of educators to guide that process so students are safe and respectful to others while they learn to be responsibly independent.

Guidance includes helping students grow socially and morally even when—perhaps *especially* when—they step over the line and break the rules. We can use rule-breaking as another opportunity to build resilience and teach responsibility and the skills of self-control by responding to it carefully. As we hold a student responsible to clean up a mess or take a few moments to pull herself together, our underlying objective is to build social skills so that next time the student will make better choices.

We teach young adolescents how to shift their behavior one small interaction at a time. When we are scrupulously honest with ourselves and willing to take risks, we can choose to give students chances to share power in such a way that they become larger, not smaller, from a correction of misbehavior. What we do and why we do it must not seem arbitrary to our students, or we will get pushback. By making sure our reasoning is transparent, and by involving adolescents in decision-making and problem-solving in both the rule-making and rule-enforcing processes, we encourage students to make good choices. Then they grow in character as well as in social competency.

Sometimes this process takes unexpected turns. There are no formulas, as the following story from a middle level teacher from Woodbury, Minnesota, shows. She describes a moment of choice for her as a teacher.

Vic was a charismatic seventh grader with a contagious smile and a fun-loving manner. He loved to play, until he perceived something as unfair. Then all bets were off; he would quickly escalate into all-out temper tantrums. He blew up, kicked and threw things, yelled, swore, or a combination of all of these.

One day Vic was on edge when he came to my class. I asked him if he wanted to put himself in Take a Break, so he could get focused and be ready to learn. He refused, insisting that he was fine. I gave the signal and class began. Things were smooth until I noticed Vic with a handful of rubber bands entangled on his fingers, shooting them off like a machine gun. I walked over to him and said, "You need to put those in my hand. You are not holding up our agreement to keep each other safe." His response was, "No, they're mine, and I am not giving them to you."

Sending him to my partnering teacher's room for a break would have been appropriate at this point, but instead I made a huge mistake. I grabbed for the rubber bands and got my fingers tangled in the elastic strands. Vic looked like a spider that had just captured its prey. Before I knew it, *snap*! Vic let go of his end of the entangled rubber bands, slapping them against my hand. He said, "There you go, Ms. K." As the red marks grew brighter on my hand, several students said, "Oooooo, now you're in trouble." The entire class was now involved in this power struggle.

I wanted to get even with this kid: *He needs to pay for this!* But the reality was that I needed to calm down, and I reviewed my options. I decided less was more, and I said, "Go to the teacher office." I sent another student to alert the staff in the teacher office, and Vic left.

Now I needed to repair what I had helped break. I sat in our classroom Take a Break chair and repeated to myself: *All children want to be good. If I want their behavior to change, then my behavior needs to change.* After a minute in the chair I went back to teach the class. I had a plan. I needed to have a discussion with Vic.

I instructed the class to read and reflect individually on some math word problems and then share their reflections with their assigned partners. As they started this process, I stepped in the doorway of my room and signaled to Mr. R in the teacher office that I was ready to talk to Vic. He signaled that Vic was ready, too. Mr. R went into my room with the class, and I stood right outside the door so Vic and I could discuss and repair the situation.

As Vic approached, he looked as if he expected a verbal lashing or a lecture about what poor choices he had made. But I decided to stand on my belief that he wanted to grow, and the best way to get his behavior to change was to adjust mine. I said, "I am sorry." Vic looked at me with surprise. I continued, "I shouldn't have tried to take the rubber bands out of your hand. I didn't respect your space." He looked away and then back again, gave me sort of a half grin, and said, "Ya know, Ms. K, I'm sorry too. I shouldn't of done it. It wasn't safe. Sorry if I hurt you."

I almost passed out from surprise, but I didn't let on! I said, "How are we going to make this right so our class feels safe again?" Vic thought a moment and said, "Why don't we apologize to the class? We need to let them know we're okay." I added, "We need to let them know what we are going to change for next time, so this doesn't happen again. Let's think about what we could do differently." Vic and I discussed this for the next few minutes, and then we walked to the front of the class together.

—Middle level teacher, Woodbury MN

When we model and guide students towards self-management even in the midst of rule-breaking, we communicate to them that we believe that although we all mess up from time to time, we can learn. When we watch closely and work to catch minor infractions, small successes begin to accumulate. Students experience incremental steps forward and begin to believe in their own capacity for steady growth. They need to see that by developing an *internal* locus of control that forwards their success in life, they gain real power.

We cannot expect children to accept ready-made values and truths all the way through school, and then suddenly make choices in adulthood. Likewise, we cannot expect [students] to be manipulated with reward and punishment in school, and then to have the courage of a Martin Luther King in adulthood. (Kamii 1991, 387)

The Developmental Designs Approach to Rule-breaking

We need a dynamic, flexible, empowering, non-coercive way of responding to mistakes in which we work with students to increase their self-control. The *Developmental Designs* approach provides an array of strategies that include dominating students *only to the degree necessary* to right a wrong or get them back to learning—not to cause pain. The strategies are meant to be used in as understated a way as possible to get the job done. Most are brief and low-key enough to barely interrupt the flow of lessons.

The purpose underlying every practice in this approach is growth, not mere compliance. We know from research and experience that corrections must preserve the dignity of the mistake-maker in order for him to grow from them. Therefore, the practices, although implemented in a clear and firm manner, avoid having teachers hold all the power, make all the decisions, or solve all the problems. Judicious sharing of power is a means to the end of launching our students into successful self-management.

Content of Section III

Chapter 7: Redirecting

The structures outlined in Chapter 7—nonverbal and verbal cues, Loss of Privilege, Fix It on the Spot, and Take a Break (in and out of the room)—all provide ways for students to 1) receive a cue from their teacher whenever they break a rule and 2) respond with a rehearsed, student-controlled process for getting back in the groove. The objective is for students to calm themselves, consider how to alter their behavior, and resume class participation in a discrete, quiet manner that doesn't get in the way of others' learning. As with goal-setting, rule-making, and modeling and practicing, all students go through this correction process multiple times during the year, some more often than others. For many, it is sufficient to keep them on track. For others, problem-solving with adult help is necessary.

Chapter 8: Problem-solving

Sometimes redirection that calls for students to self-correct is not enough structure to set them right, and they need adult help to regain self-control. Chapter 8 describes structures for private teacher-to-student resolution (social conferences), whole-class resolution (problem-solving meetings and role play), student-to-student resolution (conflict resolution and act of apology). These are used when students are unwilling or unable to quickly fix their mistakes on their own. The chapter offers quick formats for these problem-solving structures that many times can take place on the margins of a lesson. All are designed to provide behavior management within the classroom.

Appendix G: Problem-solving interventions beyond the classroom

Interventions that require the support of adults other than the content-area teacher, or significant time outside of class, are identified in Appendix G, Behavior Management beyond the Classroom.

Chapters 7 and 8 include suggestions about language to use as you employ behavior-management tools. Language is the vehicle of the message, and communicates how we feel about the student we're addressing and how we rate his prospects for growth. In a way, our language itself *is* the message. Our tone, choice of words, volume and speed of delivery, and all the nonverbal communication that surrounds the content, express to the student the feelings and thoughts we have about him. Because our language, spoken through words or the body, can sometimes make or break the effectiveness of any correction, you'll find many examples throughout this section to give you the tone as well as the content of effective responses to misbehavior.

Sustained, internalized growth frames the approach

What responses to rule-breaking *don't* support responsible independence

It can be helpful to identify what the *Developmental Designs* approach to discipline is not. It's not a prescribed, inflexible, arbitrary approach. It's not a system in which, for example, upon the third tardy, students automatically receive a detention, to be served after school on Wednesday. It's not a system in which a series of threats is given before disciplinary action is taken—we don't write a student's name on the board to let him and everyone else know he's breaking a rule, adding a mark next to his name each time he breaks the rule again, with the understanding that if he gets to four or five marks, he'll be in trouble. Likewise, we do not display visual assessments of students' behavior.

We also don't call attention to a student who is following the rules. There are no rewards, verbal or tangible, for doing what we all agreed to do. We don't praise students who do the right thing—we simply give them more opportunity to be independent and responsible for themselves, since they have demonstrated that they have good self-controls. Privately, we encourage and reinforce them with specific, positive references to what they did and how they did it, so they'll know to repeat that behavior for continued success.

Rigid procedures that operate by formula (*If this, then that*) and are dependent upon rewards and punishments do not result in student growth in self-control or social capacity. Inflexibility is counterproductive for both teacher and student. The teacher is deprived of the opportunity to act effectively based on specific knowledge of each particular student, and students make little progress toward obtaining the skills needed to avoid the same mistake in the future, or toward understanding the consequences of their mistake for themselves and others. They may learn to comply in order to avoid punishment or get a reward, but they learn little about the value and methods of self-management, especially under challenging circumstances. Further, they and their mentors don't reinforce their relationship as they might have through the opportunity to work together on growth, reflecting as they go.

Children do not develop positive characteristics based on the feelings and subconscious decisions they make as a result of punishment. Where did we ever get the crazy idea that in order to make children do better, first we have to make them feel worse? (Nelsen 1996, 13)

Educational theorist Alfie Kohn states that punishments and rewards are fundamentally similar as they both are used when we want people to do things we believe they would not otherwise freely choose to do. "Moreover, the long-term use of either tactic describes the very same pattern; eventually we will need to raise the stakes and offer more and more treats or threaten more and more sanctions to get people to continue acting the way we want." (1993, 50) Regarding rewards, he consolidates research on their effects to conclude: "(1) the bigger the reward, the easier the task that people choose; (2) when the rewards stop, those who received them earlier continue to prefer to do as little as possible; and (3) easier tasks are selected not only in situations where rewards are offered but by people who are, as a general rule, more reward oriented."(1993, 65)

An approach that provides teachers with flexibility doesn't have a pat answer to the question: "What do you do when a student...?" Although we might wish for a formulaic answer that can be applied to any situation, our answers need to be prefaced with "It depends...." This approach doesn't treat all students the same. The teacher decides what he thinks will best meet that student's needs at that moment.

What *does* support the development of responsible independence?

Every time a student breaks a rule is an opportunity to teach him how to make good choices. In this approach, students form the habits of reflecting on their behavior (independently or with adult help), regaining self-control, and changing their behavior to better support their learning. The approach nudges them toward social competency, and it helps expand the motivation for their actions beyond self-interest. In these ways, the approach develops student motivation to observe the rules as more than manipulation of their behavior.

Pearl and Samuel Oliner interviewed individuals who worked to rescue Jews during WWII. The parents of the rescuers had all presumed error rather than evil in their children when they broke rules. They presumed their children were basically good, but made mistakes sometimes, and engaged in conversations with them designed to help them correct their behavior. The researchers found that these conversations about fixing mistakes led to altruism. (Oliner 1988)

When we make rules together, we begin a conversation. When we reflect together on how well we are abiding by our Social Contract, we continue the conversation. When we introduce our approach to redirection, and teach students how to go through the mental process of changing behavior, we reinforce their developing sense of responsibility. Each redirection and each problem-solving session with students who balk guides them in the right direction. Our mindset, our trust in each other, our assumption of students' positive intentions, our faith in students' capacity for self-control, our casual chats with them to build relationship—all contribute to the conversation.

When people who are being limited understand the reason for limits, they are also more likely to accept them without feeling undermined. [It] may be useful to go beyond just providing a rationale to encourage people to think for themselves about why a task might be useful for them. When they fully understand why something is important they will be more willing to do it autonomously. (Deci 1995, 150)

Chapter 7, about redirecting, and Chapter 8, about problem-solving, include specific conversations to have with students to boost their resolve and capacity to recover from making mistakes. The conversations guide them to adjust their behavior and make choices that increasingly take into consideration more than their own self-interest. The cumulative effect is social competency.

Rigor and integrity

When a student breaks a rule, no matter how minor, we redirect. By interrupting early, we keep our students on the right path, and we stand for the goals each student has made, for the Social Contract we've made together, for increased self-control, and learning. We hold all students accountable for their behavior, all the time, without exception. If a student lacks the self-control to fix his mistake on his own, more teacher assistance is offered. Rule-breaking behavior is never allowed or ignored.

When we interrupt rule-breaking early, long before insults or chairs are hurled, while students are still reachable, the feeling that accompanies each redirect is more positive. When teachers "sweat the small stuff," students experience within themselves—and witness for others—equitable, dignified treatment, reinforcing trust in the community and deeper investment in the school's rules.

Keep teachers teaching and students learning

After a teacher redirects a student for any minor infraction, she moves back to teaching the content of the lesson. Students, therefore, must be taught to refrain from arguing, debating, negotiating, or pleading. Infractions that earn redirection tend to be smaller ones. When the process is well introduced and communicated as nudges back on track rather than punishments, most students go along with it. In our opinion, no infraction or response should be fought over.

If students push back for small redirections, more serious consequences may occur, and the student knows it. It's better to clean up after yourself as you go. The idea is for both teacher and students to proceed calmly. The teacher's mental conversation can be: *When one thing doesn't work, I have others to use, and I will. I know it, and so does the student. I want minimal disruption for everyone, including the rule-breaker.*

For many of us, disciplining students is a necessary, unpleasant chore we need to do regularly to keep our educational house in order. We do the chores of redirection and problem-solving so we can get on with learning. If we live for these chores alone, we're out of balance, obsessed with cleaning house; if we let them go, the mess quickly piles up, and cleaning up takes even more time and effort.

Positive relationships sustained

This approach calls for an allied relationship, not an adversarial one. We are walking beside our students, working with them, gently, firmly, reliably steering them in the right direction. You'll have work to do to convince middle level students of this if the schools they have attended prior to coming to yours have used a coercive approach with punishments and rewards to correct student behavior. Responsible sharing of power may be new territory for many.

Assidere: Latin: to assess—but, more literally, to sit by, and/or watch over, on an ongoing basis. As we observe student behavior, we sit next to them, with a friendly, non-threatening attitude, always ready, consistent, a reliable presence students can trust to operate fairly. We also stand *above* them, watching over them, analyzing their strengths and weaknesses, assessing our own pedagogical decisions, while taking seriously our responsibility for redirecting any behavior that doesn't fit our Social Contract. We're allies, not adversaries, but allies with weight.

*To achieve our goals and support our Social Contract, I have to watch how well you live by the Contract. It's not that I'm out to catch you when you break a rule, but rather that I'm here **for** you, to help you when you make a mistake, so we can all get it right and have a great year together.*

Watching carefully

We must observe our students carefully. Much that they say to us is nonverbal, and it is easy to mistake insecurity for anger, or embarrassment for an "I don't care" attitude. Adolescents often look away from us, not necessarily because they aren't listening or don't agree, but out of awkwardness or avoidance of domination, and sometimes a worry that we think badly of them. It's important in building trust to read them with care. Presume positive intentions unless you are fully convinced otherwise, and don't insist that students always look you in the eye or show you that they care. Especially under pressure, body language can often belie a sincere desire to get help. If you're in doubt, ask them:

Helene, I'm assuming you want to do well in school this year. Your goal was to get better at reading. Is that still what you want?

Social skill growth assessed

We plan for social skill growth, we execute our plans, and we hope for improvement, but often we do not take the time to systematically determine whether or not we have achieved that improvement. To do so is very satisfying, because it provides clear evidence about the efficacy of our actions. Sometimes we fail to track the results simply because it hasn't occurred to us to do so. Other times we can't think of an easy way (and there's no time for complicated ways) to do so. See Appendix B for social climate and skill assessment approaches from teachers.

Consistency from class to class

Students are more likely to endorse our corrections of small infractions and use a teacher's redirect to change behavior when the same responses to misbehavior are used throughout the day and throughout the school. When consistency exists, students understand that the Social Contract and the community that made that contract are an inseparable part of the fabric of school life. Conversely, if some of a student's teachers are holding the line for all rule-breaking while others are not, those using consistent redirections will have to work even harder to gain student acceptance. See Appendix G for more about consistent management beyond the classroom.

Strength to keep it going

Managing adolescent behavior requires us to understand our frames of mind about our students and about teaching in general. At our best, we operate out of the three teacher mindsets mentioned in Chapter 2: we know our students can grow; we take responsibility for empowering growth, and we do it with an open, objective mind. We use our inner powers of analysis, our courage, and our commitment to maintain the integrity of our community's rules by holding students accountable for fixing their mistakes every time, every day, all year long. It's a demanding and crucial part of our work.

Redirecting

We build relationship and community every day so the students can see that they're part of something. I work at my relationships with them. They say that I respect them, and that's one of the reasons why they respect me. I'm consistent; they know I'm going to pick up on everything. I can sweat the small stuff because I have good relationships with them. I used to think I didn't want to take students up on everything because then I'd be nagging at them. I thought I had to pick my battles. But what I've found from sweating the small stuff is that it rarely gets to anything big! If I tell them, for instance, "Right now I need you to sit at your seat or take a break but you can't just wander or stand up," immediately [this student] would sit down. Before, I might have thought, "Well, just give him a minute and he'll come back." I think it works to hold them so tight. Rigor and consistency are part of the mutual respect we have created.

—8th grade language arts teacher, Greenfield MA

When students break the rules, they need redirection to preserve the Social Contract and continuously develop their individual social skills, resilience, and capacity to balance individual and group needs. This chapter presents a variety of redirection options from which we can choose each time we see rule-breaking behavior:

Nonverbal cues

Verbal cues

Loss of Privilege

Fix It on the Spot

Take a Break

Take a Break Out (of the classroom) and Back

Spectrum of misbehavior

Teachers deal with a variety of student missteps, many of which are minor, some of which are potentially destructive. All of the redirection alternatives described in this chapter are used to interrupt behavior and point students in the right direction with minimal teacher assistance and, except for Take a Break Out and Back, little or no disruption to learning. They're appropriate for rule-breaking behaviors when the effect of the mistake is slight, and the student is still enough in self-control to fix her behavior largely on her own.

Students who can't or won't make use of the redirects discussed in this chapter may need additional problem-solving structures that involve greater teacher assistance. Misbehaviors we will not address in this chapter are:

- Repeating patterns of misbehavior: if a student proves unwilling or unable to change her behavior, repeatedly using the same redirects won't work. This student needs direct assistance from an adult (see Chapter 8).

- Very serious transgressions: if a student swears, fights, intentionally damages school property, is defiant, puts down a culture, race, religion, gender, or sexual orientation, or breaks the law, direct adult intervention is required. Chapter 8 offers effective responses for some of these, but others will need to be handled outside of the classroom. Measures for mistakes which occur or require assistance outside the classroom mainly lie beyond the scope of this book, but are briefly discussed in Appendix G.

No rule-breaking is too small to redirect

Rule-breaking that is sometimes dismissed as minor—side-talking, blurting out, a condescending look, rolling the eyes—are all damaging to the social fabric of the learning community. Sometimes they are put-downs, and as such seriously wound the sense of safety each student needs in the community in order to perform well. It is important to respond to the so-called small things, and not ignore them, so that such hurts do not damage the community's safety and confidence in the Social Contract, and so students who make mistakes can get back on track more easily than if things were allowed to escalate—and escalate they will; students who test the limits will push until they are stopped.

Examples of seemingly minor rule infractions that call for redirection include any and every violation of the Social Contract:

- If a student blurts out an answer when the established expectation is to raise hands and wait to be called upon, redirect him.

- If a student engages in a side conversation when the established expectation is to listen attentively to the person who is addressing the large group, redirect her.

- If two students are fooling around, jostling each other and laughing, when the established expectation is focus on learning, redirect them.

- If a student rolls his eyes at another, yet the Social Contract includes the rule "Be respectful," redirect.

- If a student leans back in her chair so far that the chair's two back legs can slide out from under her or damage the floor, yet the Social Contract has a rule that says "Be safe" or "Respect the environment," redirect.

GROWTH THROUGH ADJUSTING BEHAVIOR

In response to redirection, we want an honest effort on the part of the student to change his or her behavior. When the student is successful, she grows. When she begins to internalize what it takes to get back to learning after breaking a rule, she's a bit more resilient, and a bit more prepared and able to control herself next time.

To teach students in a rigorous but friendly way to adjust their own behavior, we must vigilantly watch them so we can redirect whenever their behavior runs contrary to the Social Contract. At the very moment when a student first transgresses the Social Contract and the infraction is still small, he or she has a better chance of changing the behavior than even a few moments later, when the behavior has escalated and/or done more damage. With quick, early redirection, free of heightened emotions and concerns about saving face, the student can learn to stop the rule-breaking behavior. *I'm not in trouble yet, but my teacher has intervened, so I'll stop.* To the extent that you can remain open to seeing students as capable of self-control and positive relationship, you can decrease the chances of escalated exchanges and behaviors that result in disrupted learning and interventions beyond the classroom (see *growth mindset* page 20).

What we are after is incremental skill-building—not retribution, but learning. The objective of redirecting when students still have a fairly good level of self-control is that they will be responsible for fixing their own mistakes, without additional assistance from an adult. For their own sense of autonomy, we want to give them a chance at self-sufficient success.

Adjusting Behavior with Reflection

No matter what specific redirection is used, the Reflective Loop provides a structure to help students get back on track. The *student* moves through the following steps when a teacher redirects him or her.

1. Plan to change behavior

First, the rule-breaker may need to calm down. He might take a few deep breaths, or gaze out the window, or count his teeth with his tongue (with his mouth closed), or do a few finger push-ups. She might think through the words to a favorite song, or visualize herself doing her favorite thing in her favorite place with her favorite people. To prepare for these moments, you might spend some time in the first few days of school having students share, write, or draw about ways they quiet themselves.

Then the student thinks about why the teacher intervened and how he needs to change: *Where did I mess up? What do I need to do to fix my mistake? What am I going to do to stay on track?* This process is done internally and alone and should take no more than a minute or two. Some redirects, such as Take a Break (in or out of the room), require that students move somewhere nearby to get themselves back on track, while other redirects do not. Take a Break Out and Back requires going to a different environment and writing out a plan before returning to the classroom

2. Act

The student goes back to work with a plan, or at least an intention, to stay on track. *I'm fixing it, I'm back; things are OK.*

3. Reflect

In many cases, reflection may be no more than a student's sense of satisfaction or relief that he has navigated himself through the mistake quickly and with minimal embarrassment. Sometimes reflection is done with the teacher (for example, after a break out of the classroom), but with most redirections, students simply experience that things are now working, the problem is gone, no big deal—I'm OK.

This reflection is then part of the student's understanding should he need to adjust his behavior in the future—the Reflective Loop helps students gradually accumulate skill and understanding as they work to live by the rules.

Introducing Students to Adjusting Their Behavior

Before redirection is implemented, introduce students to your approach—the philosophy of redirection and the specific steps you'll want them to take to get back to learning. These introductions provide another way to reinforce the nurturing spirit of this approach to discipline. The students help create the rules. If they can see our benevolent and thoughtful efforts to *teach* them discipline, they will be better able to continue to see themselves as active, able agents in relation to the rules, even when they struggle to follow them.

Insofar as children experience rules as imposed on them from the outside, they remain locked within the bounds of their egocentrism or subjectivity. (Power, Higgins, and Kohlberg 1989, 28)

Beginning the conversation about rule-breaking

In Chapter 3 of this book we discussed ways to establish rules democratically, rules that are based on students' vested interest in improving their own lives. In Chapter 4 there were options for demonstrations, modeling, practicing, planning and reflecting on the rules, and reminding charts and role plays to help students avoid the sticky spots. In this chapter, we continue the conversation about social behavior with suggestions for dealing with the times when students violate the rules: a variety of redirections appropriate to different situations and students, suggestions for introducing each redirection, as well as reflections from teachers and students, research, and some classic character-building stories you can use to deepen student understanding and provide an interesting twist to the conversation.

The early conversations about rule-breaking should

- Teach students how to use the Reflective Loop to respond to the redirections by correcting their behavior
- Establish the reasons and guidelines for redirecting behavior so students understand and endorse the process
- Introduce the different kinds of redirections the teacher will use

When and with whom

Advisory is the ideal time to introduce, contextualize, and practice responding to redirection. Gathering teams together is another approach for disseminating information intended for all students. This way, everyone hears the same information (including teachers), time is saved, and a sense of team unity grows.

If you're implementing this approach alone, without support from the other adults in your building, you may decide to dedicate a portion of several class periods early in the year to laying down a behavior foundation upon which you and your students can build all year long.

Using the Reflective Loop to change your behavior when you break a rule

Begin by explaining that students need to become adept at altering their behavior when that behavior breaks the rules:

Once rules and procedures are in place, we need to live by them, and when we don't, it's my job to get us back on track. To do that, I'll be directing you to change any behavior that breaks our agreements. I'll explain the different ways I can use to redirect you, and we'll talk about why this process is so important, but first let me show you how you can use any of the redirections to adjust your behavior.

In most cases, when you receive a redirect from me or from any adult in the building, you will be held responsible for changing your behavior by yourself. One way you can do that is by thinking your way into an intention to stay on track. You plan your moves, take action, and, later, reflect on how you're doing. It's a Reflective Loop: you plan it; you do it; you review it. Here's an example.

Think-aloud dramatization

Model the steps of adjusting behavior, the Reflective Loop, using a "think-aloud" dramatization. Explain to students that you're about to verbalize a student's thought process. It will be an example of how to think through a mistake when they are redirected.

Start with a quick, simple dramatization. Switch roles with a student. While the student in the teacher role acts as if she's teaching a lesson, tap your pencil on a desk or try to engage a neighbor in a whispered conversation. Have the "teacher" look at you and give you a nonverbal signal for quiet.

Establish the reasons for redirections

It is crucially important that students understand that the purpose for redirections is to teach, not punish. With students gathered in a circle, make your purpose for redirecting behavior clear, along with the non-punitive intention of the practice:

Everyone makes mistakes. [Tell a story about a mistake of your own.] *But in this class, now that we have our Social Contract in place, it's never going to be OK to break a rule, and I'm going to help you develop ways of getting yourself back on track quickly if and when you do.*

Talk with students about fixing mistakes for the sake of growing in autonomy and competence. Impress upon them their power in the face of mistakes. Invite students to reflect in partners or as a group.

Tell about a time when you made a mistake and then corrected yourself or tried to make up for what you did.

The success of our school year is ultimately dependent upon each of you. The degree to which you pay attention, participate, strive for excellence, engage each other in healthy discussion, play, celebrate successes and take care of each other—all of that is up to you. And a big part of our success this year will depend on your willingness to adjust your behavior quickly. You're in control of your behavior; therefore, you're in control of what happens to you in school.

Respectful adult support

I'm not here to punish, humiliate, embarrass, harass, or pick on you. By and large, when you break a rule and get called on it, you are not in trouble; you are learning the skills of responsible independence. If you choose to take my cues and adjust your behavior yourself, you will grow in the adult skill of self-control.

When students refuse to fix their mistakes

On the other hand, if you choose not to abide by our Social Contract, if you choose to ignore me when I call you on rule-breaking, or ignore your responsibility to fix your mistake yourself, then I'll have no choice but to take some power back and manage you.

Clarify responsibilities

Discuss the different roles with students, and take time to answer any questions.

We're going to have to work together on this, but our relationship to the rules (our Social Contract) will be somewhat different. We made them together, but we'll have different jobs when it comes to maintaining them.

Teacher's job: self-management & managing others	Student's job: self-management
1. Maximize teaching/learning time	1. Maximize teaching/learning time
2. Follow rules & notice *all* behavior	2. Follow rules; notice own behavior
3. Redirect self/students whenever a rule is broken	3. Accept any/all redirects
4. Keep it objective	4. Keep it objective
5. Address *all* mistakes, while being fair, consistent	5. Fix own mistakes, while being fair, consistent
6. Keep teaching	6. Keep learning
7. Remain positive: acknowledge success	7. Remain positive; respond to cues

We all make mistakes

Notice that many of the responsibilities in the teacher and student roles are the same or similar. Teachers make mistakes, too, and we all have to deal with our mistakes, sometimes privately, sometimes publicly. If the teacher mistakenly redirects the wrong student, that student still needs to cooperate and follow the redirection, but we need to listen to his complaint and make any appropriate apology or repair at a spare moment later in the class, to clear the air before moving on.

An apology from the teacher helps humanize the classroom. In no way does it diminish the teacher's effectiveness, as long as the rigorous approach to rule-keeping is maintained.

Keep learning

When someone is redirected by the teacher, the rest of the students need to continue learning. Stopping to discuss the situation with the rule-breaker, who may try to negotiate, argue, ask for clarification, etc., distracts everyone else. For this reason, negotiating a redirection is not permitted. The redirected student needs to comply immediately, and later, if they have questions or complaints, they can express those privately to the teacher.

I will listen to your concerns if you think I have been unfair or mistaken in a redirection that I give to you, but not at the moment of redirection. Follow the redirect, and find a moment later to talk with me about it. Our job is to learn, and we cannot afford to hold up that process.

Toward responsible independence

We gain in two crucial ways from this approach to rule-breaking. First, our relationship with rule-breakers remains more positive than if we allow them to escalate and then intervene. A better relationship means more effective teaching. Second, the student is much more likely to be able to adjust his behavior at the time he is first starting to stray than he is in an escalated condition. We help the student construct the habit of self-correction by intervening when she or he is more able to correct.

After being introduced to this constructive approach and taught how to alter behavior after making a slip, once students have been given a redirection, they are in charge of fixing the problem, without additional direct help from an adult. This point needs to be emphasized regularly, especially in the first part of the school year. For many students, cues from adults become less and less necessary, and they are able to catch themselves *before* breaking a rule, and improve their behavior.

When working to follow the rules created together to benefit the good of the community, students are getting direct practice with placing their interests alongside those of the group. Each impulse they have that conflicts with the rules is considered as the student works to align her individual perspective with the group perspective. Review pages 8-9 and 14 for more about how "perspective taking" and constructive interaction with conflict foster social development and an interest in the community good.

Story for Reflection: Resilience

Stories like the one that follows appear throughout Chapters 7 and 8. Their meanings are open-ended, designed to prompt students to reflect on their behavior.

The Farmer and the Donkey

A donkey wandered away from his owner when the farmer wasn't looking, went down a slippery slope, and fell into a ravine. The farmer tried to help him get out, but the donkey was too heavy. Then he had an idea. The farmer got a shovel, and, talking encouragingly to the donkey, began to shovel dirt into the ravine.

Some of the dirt fell on the donkey, who didn't like it very much, and for a moment the donkey even thought the farmer was attempting to punish him by burying him alive! But slowly, as the farmer kept shoveling and kept encouraging the donkey to shake it off and step up on the dirt, the donkey realized that the dirt was rising higher and higher. "Come on, donkey, I know you can do it!" said the farmer, "Shake it off and step up!" After a while, the donkey realized he had made considerable progress in extricating himself from his difficult position. "Come on, keep going, you're almost here! Shake it off and step up, and soon you'll be out of the hole!"

The donkey took his advice, shook off the dirt that fell on him, and stepped up onto the pile until he was able to walk out of the ravine to freedom.

Story discussion

After reading the story, discuss similarities between the story and redirections:

- Donkey made a mistake—students will break rules
- Farmer helped donkey fix mistake—teachers help students fix mistakes
- Farmer's help felt uncomfortable at first—getting a redirection from teacher feels uncomfortable at first
- Farmer encouraged donkey to be resilient—correcting behavior teaches resilience in students
- Shake it off, step up, literally—shake it off, step up, figuratively
- In both cases, caring adults are there to help

When receiving adult guidance, students who shut down (by putting their heads down, by swearing and walking away, by refusing to accept help, by avoiding school work, by glossing over a behavior mistake by hiding behind a joke, etc.) rather than bouncing back need to grow their "resilience muscles." Teachers can use the farmer and donkey story to offer the "Shake it off, step up" model for addressing problems.

NONVERBAL CUES

What surprised me was that when I stopped being defensive, the students stopped taking what I said personally. If the teacher doesn't take it personally, he or she is modeling for the students a way to cleanly address problems. That kind of adult modeling has to come into play. You have to show them how to handle listening to opinions you don't like, things that could set you off, and stay away from knee-jerk reactions. The basic message I try to send is: "You're allowed to have that opinion, but the expectation is that we fix rule-breaking behavior."

My words and my body language have to say that I'm not angry. The message I'm trying to give is: "That's not good. I can't accept that," but all that I'm doing is shrugging my shoulders or putting my finger to my temple to communicate, "Think!"—something I'm always advising students to do.

—High school teacher, Harrisburg PA

A nonverbal signal for silence

We communicate extensively without spoken or written words. Gestures and facial expressions can speak volumes. A person's body language, proximity, or tone of voice can dramatically alter the verbal message she's sending.

Using nonverbal cues to redirect misbehaving students is often the easiest, quickest, least disruptive, and least embarrassing way to interrupt the rule-breaker and initiate her process of getting back on track. We should make it clear to students that we are happy to use nonverbal cues, but students must take them seriously by altering their behavior each time they receive one.

In return, students give *us* nonverbal cues which can help us know how to help students and avoid escalated responses—theirs and ours (review Section III introduction, page 141).

Introducing Nonverbal Redirections

Students are more able and likely to respond positively to nonverbal cues if they are introduced to them and taught how to respond. Hold a discussion session with your class about the uses of appropriate nonverbal communication.

Gather students in a circle, and talk about the fact that a large percentage of what we communicate is done nonverbally, and that young children are able to read and respond to nonverbal communication—and communicate nonverbally themselves—before they can speak. Babies' facial expressions, leg kicking, crying, cooing, etc., are all means of communicating; their quick laughter in response to caretakers' playful hand and facial gestures show their capacity to understand nonverbals.

Brainstorm and record with students a list of positive and negative nonverbal cues.

Positive cues could include high-fives, knuckle-bumping, back-patting, crossing your fingers, pointing a thumb downward while frowning. Model some, or have students model.

To discuss negative nonverbal ask students if they've ever heard or said, "Don't look at me that way," or "S/he's staring at me!" Include the effect disrespectful looks and gestures have: the cut-off "talk to the hand" gesture, or the "you're crazy" finger movement.

These discussions heighten awareness of the power of body language and will serve as handy referents when students respond to a redirect by saying things like, "I didn't say anything!" We can point out that although their mouths said nothing, their expressions said a lot, and it wasn't positive: "Remember our discussion of nonverbal communication?"

Teach your nonverbal cues

Introduce the nonverbal cues you will use to help students keep their behavior on track. Here are some possibilities:

- Raise a hand as a signal for silence
- Cup a hand to an ear to ask a speaker to raise his/her voice
- Mime opening or closing a book to direct students to do the same
- Make eye contact with a student to remind him/her to focus
- Shake your head to tell a student to stop a small rule-breaking behavior
- Point to a different seat in the room to direct a move to that seat
- Nod or point towards the Take a Break spot to signal someone to take a break and re-center (see page 170 for more about Take a Break)

Some of these cues require introductory modeling and practicing because they are subtle or require practice. For example, catching a student's eye can be read in multiple ways. Clarify what you mean when you catch someone's eye so students know how to respond.

Impress upon students how important it will be for them to read and respond to your nonverbal cues quickly, quietly, and without discussion. Remind them to use the Reflective Loop, a quick internal conversation to help them refocus on learning.

It's like a second language I'll use to communicate with you. But it is not the beginning of a conversation—just a signal for action. Remember, no negotiating a redirection at the time, but I'm open to discussing it with you later. It's usually no big deal—just a small mistake you can fix and move on.

Keep it minimal and quiet

Be sure students understand that these nonverbal cues are used to redirect them away from undesirable behaviors by means of body language instead of words. We use quiet communication to minimize distraction from learning and maximize student independence.

Once students have been introduced to the nonverbal cues, use the ones that don't require further explanation. Save the Take a Break and Take a Break Out and Back cues for later (see pages 170 and 179 for more information about these practices).

Now let's try using them. When I use a nonverbal cue with you, remember: you're not in trouble, but you are responsible for reading the cue accurately and changing your behavior so you're back on the right track as soon as possible. You'll do this yourself, with no further help from me. Just fix it quietly and quickly.

Give verbal redirections to students who do not respond quickly and appropriately to nonverbal redirections (see Verbal Cues below, page 157). Point out to them that if they respond to the nonverbals, there is less fuss and less attention on the error. Later, give them another chance to respond to nonverbal cues.

Checking in: assess, remind, and adjust

Remember to check in with students regularly to assess what's working and what isn't. Chances are you'll need to revisit these discussion points periodically to maintain the integrity of the approach. Ask questions like these after the first day of using them and whenever this type of review is necessary:

How are we doing with our nonverbal cues?

Who can remind us what your job is after you receive a nonverbal cue?

How can I make the cues more clear?

What's working and what's not with our nonverbal cues?

Example: Nonverbal cue for lesson interruptions

In addition to the more familiar classroom signals, here's an example of a cue you might develop for a behavior issue that occurs frequently.

Problem scenario: You are interrupted during a whole-group lesson by a student who makes an irrelevant statement like, "May I use the rest room?" or "You can't give us a test this Friday; we haven't had enough time to learn this," deflating energy and momentum.

Before such interruptions occur, proactively talk about the difference between participating appropriately in group discussions and interrupting inappropriately. Appropriate participation requires waiting for the right moment to contribute—patience and timing. Exchange roles with a student and model waiting attentively until a question is asked before raising your hand; then wait to be called on to answer it. See more about role play on page 99.

Next, teach the class a nonverbal cue you'll use with students who raise their hands to ask questions at inappropriate times. A simple nod of the head indicates "I see you, but right now we're in the middle of something that can't be interrupted, so please put your hand down and remain focused on the topic." Model it, and practice it with students before instituting it. Make sure they notice the details:

- the student's hand went up at a time that wasn't appropriate (bad timing)

- what the nonverbal cue looks like
- the student put his hand down and paid attention to the discussion, without being upset by the redirect
- the teacher *remembered* to get back to the student as soon possible
- the student asked the question after the teacher invited him to speak

Tell students that you expect them to read and respond positively to the new cue, and that inappropriate interruptions are not acceptable.

VERBAL CUES

Most redirections are cued with words. Many times, that's all a student needs to change behavior—a word or short phrase from the teacher that interrupts the behavior and calls for a change on the spot. *Gloria, focus. Marcus, wait your turn. Danielle, you and Frances need to work separately today.* Some verbal cues call for an interruption in behavior by having the student cease work for a few minutes to calm himself. Take a Break is such a verbal cue, and often Loss of Privilege is, too. Both are discussed in the next section. Many other cues are designed for an immediate shift in behavior in response to the spoken cue. Much of the time the desired shift occurs quickly, and everyone can move on.

What to Say and How to Say It

What we say to students when we redirect them can make or break a student's chances of learning from her mistakes; *how* we say it may be even more important. The power of our words and our tone of voice cannot be overstated. Daniel Goleman cites a German study in which employees preferred negative comments made in a positive tone by supervisors over positive comments made in a negative tone (*Social Intelligence*, 2006).

The focus remains on the lesson when quick verbal cues are consistently delivered by teachers and followed by students

When we talk, our mindset is consciously or unconsciously communicated to listeners. Although we may not speak directly about our values, students tend to accurately understand what is important to us. Conversely, if we tell our students one thing but present ourselves to them in a contradictory way, they quickly figure out that we don't seem to mean what we say or say what we truly feel.

I think of teacher language for discipline this way: we're simply providing a verbal mirror for the kids, so their own behavior gets reflected back to them. Mirrors never judge. They simply reflect what's in front of them.

—Middle level teacher and *Developmental Designs* consultant

Keep a neutral tone

In redirecting, we need to avoid extremes—no raised voice, but not overly friendly, either. For maximum consistency, we use our authentic voices, the same pitch and tempo we use when teaching academics. We keep our emotions out of the communication. We strive for neutrality and objectivity.

Preserve relationship

Show students that you know and accept them as individuals. Doing so demonstrates that you care, and you can be trusted because you pay attention to what they need. Remind them in a phrase or sentence that you're in relationship with them, then give the redirection.

I know you like to participate and are always prepared with an answer, Patrick, but you need to stop blurting answers so others have a chance, too.

Rachel, I know it's hard to stop when you're on a roll, but I gave the clean-up signal a minute ago and you haven't started to put your things away yet. You need to stop working and get going on that.

Express your faith in their ability to change and grow

You've done this correctly before, Kallie, so I know you can do it again. Stay focused.

Take a break so you don't waste any more time, Vera. I know you can make better choices about how to use your time.

We've used some of our redirection tools today. Let's take a moment to notice that everyone is on task right now, working hard. Those who were redirected have fixed their mistakes. I did my job, and you've done yours. Thanks!

Use your authority carefully

The teacher is in control. We avoid being bossy, but we don't leave the door open to refusal by sounding wishy-washy. Redirect, then look away or walk away to avoid power struggles. The teacher needs to be clear and certain, neither weak nor bossy

Pose the redirect as a direction, not a request

Tell the student what s/he needs to do. Don't delay or ask a question that won't help the situation ("Why didn't you do what you were told?"). Don't be manipulative or indirect—say exactly what you want the student to do. Use the name of the student you are addressing to avoid confusion and increase clarity.

Douglas, I know you love to read, but put your book down and come to the circle, Roy. You need to be with us.

Turn around and face your partner, Olivia.

Keep all four legs of your chair on the floor, Nancy.

Frannie, move to the empty seat next to Keesha.

Be brief
Avoid lectures and interrogations.

Participation by everyone helps us build our community, Lola; join us.

Talk straight
Don't be sarcastic or witty. Don't beg or appeal to a student's affective side, because this lessons objectivity and neutrality. And redirecting is not the time for jokes. Jokes usually get in the way of problem-solving and can create confusion and distrust.

Describe the desired behavior, or what's wrong, or both
Be descriptive, not judgmental, and encouraging. Give information.

You're not following our Social Contract, Jackson. We agreed to do our best, and you're not putting forth enough effort. Get back on the right track.

When you take a break, your job is to change your behavior, Grace. You came back too soon, and you broke the same rule right away. Take a break again, but take it seriously this time. I know you can do it.

The assignment is past due, Ella. Now we have to figure out another plan for you. Write a proposed plan and give it to me by the end of the day.

Sit up, Andrew, and pay attention. I know you're tired, but you can learn now and rest later.

Remind them that they're not in trouble and are still in control of their destiny

Ollie, you're not in trouble, but you need to fix that. Move to the empty seat next to the globe.

You're responsible for getting back on the right track, Chris, and taking action on your plan.

You're still free to choose, Zev, but if you don't take advantage of this opportunity to change your behavior, I'll have to take over and send you to the office.

Make verbal redirections relevant to infractions
Make sure the redirection is related to the mistaken action. If two students are chatting instead of working, redirect one of them to take a different seat. If someone pushes his way past another to get materials, have the pusher return to his seat and get his materials after everyone else. Detention makes no sense to a student (or to anyone) as

a consequence for blurting out repeatedly instead of raising a hand to speak; instead, redirect the blurter to be exclusively a listener for the rest of the discussion time. Take away the privilege that is being abused rather than one not related to the specific misbehavior, and you will preserve students' perception that your redirections are fair and meant to correct, not to punish.

Introducing Verbal Cues

Tell everyone the things you might say to redirect. Their response needs to be quick compliance, with questions afterwards, if they have any.

Example

Hassan refuses to listen to his group-mates' opinions about how to solve a math problem. He insists the others' methods are wrong and will not hear them out. Some laugh off his stubbornness, but some are irritated.

Teacher: *Hassan, we agreed to be respectful and open-minded in this school. You need to accept everyone's right to share their opinions, even if you disagree. I know you can do it: start right now!*

Hassan stops his arguing and is silent for a while. Then he mumbles "Sorry," and does more listening than talking thereafter. His tone is more respectful. The verbal redirect called his attention to how he was treating his classmates, reminded him that his behavior broke their agreements about how to behave, and was enough to point him in a better direction.

Challenges of Verbal and Nonverbal Cues

Q. *What if I get a lot of pushback to my verbal or nonverbal redirections?*

It depends on the student, your relationship with him or her, what's happened prior to the need for redirection, and other factors. Addressed below are some of the issues specific to verbal and nonverbal redirections. See page 183 for more about choosing the right redirection in general and when more teacher assistance is called for.

Proactive measures that can help the next time

Some endorsement work may be in order. When you reflect on redirections that require students to change their behavior, one factor to consider is whether you have adequately introduced students to their responsibilities in the redirection procedure. Revisiting the "Farmer and the Donkey" story (page 152) and students' and teacher's roles (page 150) may help, as may a discussion about the payoffs for the student of learning to adjust her mistakes (page 148).

Your relationship with the student may need a boost for him or her to perceive your good will and partnership. Infusing encouragement in your redirections can be the ticket to shifting students into willing acceptance of your redirections. (See Celebrating Success below, page 187).

Always notice positive behavior, and comment on it from time to time. Proactive encouragement is effective even when you are reacting to rule-breaking. After setting a behavior norm by modeling and practicing it, it's just as important to tell the class when you see them following the model well as it is to correct them when they are not. We build good will and awareness when we invite students themselves to notice and name the good things they see.

Vary your redirections

Maybe you are relying on certain redirections too much. If you consider yourself better at nonverbal redirects than verbal, for example, and have therefore been avoiding giving verbal ones, students may have figured out that they can ignore you and you'll just let it go. In this case, a student may need a stronger redirect that gives him time out to think or that takes away a privilege for a while. And you need to bring all of your redirecting skills up to speed, so everyone knows and trusts that you will handle your job well in difficult situations. (See below, pages 183-185.)

Bolster your teacher mindset

Revisit Chapter 2 to reflect further on the mindsets that support effective behavior management. For example, students may test you to see if you really will hold them accountable. Your strong, clear *action mindset*—your commitment to act on behalf of their well-being—will bring you through such a test so that everyone knows you say what you mean and mean what you say.

Communicate skillfully

Finally, the way you redirect—tone, manner, body language—may be an issue for a student who is pushing back. See page 185 to help you think about the tone and mood most effective for imposing redirections.

LOSS OF PRIVILEGE

Loss of privilege is appropriate when someone abuses the privilege of working in a group or sitting where he chooses or using a piece of equipment. It is not meant to punish, but to stop the abuse. Later, the student will be given another opportunity to handle it responsibly, but for now, no.

Sometimes when I tell a student to change his seat or leave his group or sit out for a while because he's not following our rules, what I hear back is, "Can I have one more chance?!" I reply "No. If I did that, it could grow into a big issue for our community." Either we mean what we say about the standards we've set or we don't, and letting one person continue to do something badly shows that we are not, at that moment, living up to our community agreements.

—High school teacher, Harrisburg PA

The logic and relevance of Loss of Privilege are clear. We redirect students by taking away a privilege if they demonstrate they are unwilling or unable to exercise that privilege responsibly at the time. When we believe a student is ready and the opportunity arises, we restore the privilege, so she has an opportunity to demonstrate growth by changing her behavior. Without regular opportunities to practice and to demonstrate improvement, little growth is possible. Like other elements of this constructivist approach to discipline, the Loss of Privilege process teaches social skills and aims far beyond compliance, for internalized motivations for positive behavior. What we wish for students is that they be motivated to do what they do because it is the right and best thing—what Kohlberg identifies as the highest level of moral development wherein actions are governed by "Universal Principles" (page 8).

Relevance is crucial

When using Loss of Privilege, make sure that the consequence is relevant to the misbehavior. Take away the privilege that is being abused. If a student abuses a material, remove the privilege of using that material for a time (not the privilege of recess, unless he needs to use his recess to clean up a mess). Then, after reviewing with him the proper use of the material and expressing your confidence in the student's ability to change, restore the privilege.

Relevant consequences can make the difference between confidence in the teacher-student relationship and the student's feeling the consequence is merely punishment or, worse yet, getting even.

It isn't relevant to remove lunch privileges from a student who slams a book against his locker. Instead, consider removing the privilege of using his locker for the rest of the day. A student who is frequently late for class may not learn much from losing recess privileges because of his tardiness. Instead, figure out what's making him late. If it's something he can control, remove the privilege of being in the halls before class for a few mornings; have him report directly to his first-period class upon arrival.

Consequences of transgressing [limits] are not the same thing as punishments. Punishments are a means of controlling people, but limit-setting is not about control. It is about encouraging responsibility. If people set appropriate limits and communicate fair consequences, then they can leave it to the student...to decide whether to stay within the limits, or to transgress them. It is the person's choice, and if the limit setters are not willing to let him or her make the choice, they are not being truly autonomy supportive. (Deci 1995, 151)

Adults determine students' rights and privileges

Before the start of the school year, the school staff should determine what rights students have at school, and distinguish these rights from the privileges they'll be offered.

Rights are broad. We are responsible for providing them to everyone. A team of adults may declare such rights as:

- a quality education, including knowledge and academic and social-skill development
- a safe and productive learning environment, including basic human needs being met (e.g., food, shelter, use of bathrooms); healthy relationships with staff and students; opportunities for developmental growth

Privileges are narrower. They are earned, and they may be take away if students abuse them. Privileges may include

- Participation in daily academic and social routines
- Use of materials
- Use of facilities (locker, gymnasium, lunch room, media center, etc.)
- Access to various areas of school at certain times
- Movement within a classroom
- Choices (of seats, whom one sits beside, materials, work partners, when one comes and goes)
- Use of redirections with little teacher assistance (e.g., nonverbal cues)

Redirects are privileges

It is a privilege to attend a school where teachers understand that growing self-control and resilience requires thinking and practice, show faith in students' ability to grow, and are neither autocratic nor permissive. When a student breaks a rule and is interrupted and required to change behavior and get back on track as soon as possible, that student is experiencing a privilege. She is learning from the mistakes she made rather than being punished or allowed to repeat the same mistake over and over. She is growing in her capacity for self-control, problem-solving, and resilience.

Because redirects are privileges, they may be lost temporarily if abused.

Privileges that may be taken away for a time

- A student who does not respond quickly and positively to nonverbal cues needs his teacher to use other redirects, removing the privilege of nonverbals for a time. A conference with the student may help identify the reason why nonverbal cues aren't working, and the teacher and student may create a plan to solve the problem. (See page 194 in Chapter 8 for more information about conferencing with students.)
- If a student repeatedly gets out of control seated in a certain place, she temporarily loses the privilege of choosing where to sit.

- If a student disrupts class on Monday, he may lose the privilege of being in class on Tuesday.
- If a student breaks the rules during Wednesday's community-building activity, she may be required to sit out of Thursday's activity.
- If a student uses a computer in the computer lab inappropriately, he may lose the privilege of being in the lab for a period of time.
- If a group of students has chosen to work together on a project but is doing so ineffectively, those students may be told to work alone instead.

Introducing Loss of Privilege

Share privileges and the misbehaviors that result in privileges lost

After adults determine students' rights and privileges, share the results with students. Include what privileges may be lost, and what misbehaviors would potentially result in losing them. When we share this information with them, we honor their need to be informed.

Here are some possible privileges along with specific scenarios in which privileges will be lost.

Bathroom passes: the privilege is revoked when a student asks too often for a pass or is gone too long. He must take care of his restroom needs during the passing period.

Hallway use: the privilege is revoked when a student behaves inappropriately during passing time or is habitually late for class. For a day or two, she must carry more materials with her so she doesn't need to visit her locker. Teachers work together to hold the student in classrooms during passing times and send her to her next class only after the hallways have cleared.

Choice of seat: if two friends sitting next to each other have trouble following the rules, they must move to different seats in the room.

Choice of learning partner/group: if a student can't stay focused with the classmates she's chosen to work with, she may lose the privilege of choosing her work partner(s) for a time.

Choice or use of learning material: a student who uses a piece of equipment or a supply inappropriately may lose the privilege of using it for a time.

Bus (where you sit, and whether you're allowed to ride): if a student bullies or harasses others or refuses to stay in his seat, that student may either lose the privilege of choosing his seat or lose the privilege of riding the bus altogether for a time.

Community-building activities: if a student disrupts an activity or subverts the success of a daily greeting, that student may lose the privilege of participating in the next day's activity or greeting.

Participating in a learning activity: While students have a right to a quality, equitable education, that does not mean they must be allowed to remain in class all the time, regardless of behavior. If a student is disruptive, the privilege of being with the rest of the group may be lost for a time. See Take a Break below for a structure which removes students from the group temporarily to collect themselves before they regain the privilege of participation.

Restoring the privilege

Explain that you will restore the privilege as soon as you think the student is ready to follow the rules. The student needs to demonstrate that he can handle the privilege in order to get it back.

The chance to try again and improve is available after the privilege is restored. If a student who intentionally breaks his pencil in class is forbidden to use pencils forever, there is no room for resilience and growth. Do a quick check-in with a student who is about to regain a privilege.

I know you can use the bathroom pass privilege and follow the rules, Andy. Now that you've had time to think about it, try it again. Take the pass. Be back in three minutes.

Teacher: *You're about to return to the hallways during passing time, Rita. Remember the agreement you've made about using the hallway?*
Student: *Yes.*
Teacher: *What did we agree you'd do?*
Student: *I'm going to walk quickly to my locker, drop off and pick up the right materials, and walk quickly to my next class. Talking to friends is OK, as long as we're moving quickly as we talk.*
Teacher: *All right! Sounds like you're set. Let's make sure you remember your plan today. I'll find you at lunch to see how you're doing, and I'll ask Ms. Forester to check in with you as well.*

Using Loss of Privilege for a Group

Start by doing everything you can to avoid needing to use Loss of Privilege with the entire group. Use your *withitness* (page 33) to notice and respond quickly to any and all rule-breaking by redirecting students as soon as they break a rule. Explaining to students how "a redirect for one student is a reminder to all" helps keep them alert to their own behavior and its relationship to the Social Contract.

When several students are losing control or the large number of rule-breakers indicates that some withdrawal of privilege is necessary, use group Loss of Privilege, but try not to use it abruptly. First, interrupt the inappropriate behavior. Remodel your expectations, or ask students to remind everyone of their responsibilities. You may decide to use an "If... then..." statement to clarify the importance of changing behavior now, before loss of privilege:

If as a class you aren't able to keep your voice levels down while you're working in groups, then you'll all have to work in silence, independently.

There's way too much blurting happening. If you can't control that urge, then we're going to end this discussion, and you'll have to learn the material alone.

If you can't neaten the room at the end of the class period, then you'll have to do it during passing period.

If we can't sit in the cafeteria and eat lunch peacefully, then we'll have to eat in our home-room, and we will do so silently.

If you still see the need to use group Loss of Privilege, be prepared to follow through, and state what the group needs to do to have the privilege restored. Model and practice the correct way of doing things before you restore the privilege, and express your belief in the group's ability to change for the better.

Before you restore the privilege

After taking away a group privilege, you may have additional work to do before restoring the privilege. A version of a class problem-solving meeting may be in order, or a social conference or role play. See Chapter 8 for these interventions. Additionally, relationships may be weak, requiring you to back up and do some team- or trust-building activities (see www.originsonline.org for activity descriptions).

Use with caution and sparingly

Use caution when considering removing a privilege from the whole group. If it seems to the group that you're withdrawing a privilege from everyone arbitrarily, without warning, or unfairly, it will feel like a punishment, and confusion, hurt feelings, loss of confidence and relationship, and even some rebellion can result.

The biggest disadvantage to using group Loss of Privilege is that students who are behaving according to the Social Contract lose the privilege, too. These students may say, "Why should we lose the privilege? We weren't doing anything wrong!" Another big risk here is definition and alienation of groups—the "good" and "bad" kids. To address these issues, acknowledge the inherent inequity of removing a privilege from an entire group, and explain why it's necessary:

When several people disregard our Social Contract, I have to stop and get us back on track. It won't be fair to everyone, but it's my job: I'll never allow rule-breaking to block learning. I'll always stop that type of behavior. When we have time and everyone is back in control, we'll try to sort out what went wrong and how to fix it for next time.

When used sparingly and after doing all you can to avoid using it, group Loss of Privilege can work well. Students may exert positive peer pressure on their rule-breaking peers to straighten out their behavior. Role play (page 212) may be used to teach students how to respectfully assert themselves by guiding their peers to better behavior. Following group Loss of Privilege with a problem-solving meeting (page 205) can help solve the problem, and may shed light on other things that need improvement.

Effective teacher mindset leverages success

Using group Loss of Privilege requires an *objective mindset*. If students don't control themselves during work time, it may be because you forgot to create and review the rules for work time, or because the tool they're using for the first time wasn't explored properly ahead of time, or you didn't take care to connect students to their learning. Do not take the failure personally: the lesson failed, not you. You'll fix it, and it will be better next time. Like everyone else, we make mistakes.

To fix it, a *growth mindset* is needed. Assess what went wrong: Did I misjudge student competencies (for example, did I assume they'd be able to handle something they proved unable to handle)? What do I need to teach or reteach in order to make next time better? How can I address the issue so we get it right next time? What problem-solving tool should I deploy to fix it?

At all costs, avoid blaming the students. The minute we say to ourselves something like, "These kids just don't get it," or "These kids can't," or " I can't reach them," our chances of ultimate success plummet. Our *commitment* to our young learners, our belief in the possibility of their success, and our determination to help them learn are our best allies—and theirs.

Challenges of Loss of Privilege

Q. *What if a student takes a loss of privilege personally and is resentful and resistant?*
Some students may not respond well to a redirection, and Loss of Privilege carries with it a consequence which a student may dislike. Make sure the consequence fits the infraction so that it makes sense that he is denied a privilege when he has demonstrated some irresponsibility with that very privilege. Be sure the student knows that the deprivation is temporary. Remind him of the confidence you have in him that he can and will use the privilege appropriately once it is restored. Remind him of the farmer and the donkey; this is an opportunity to shake it off and step up (see the story on page 152). You may want to review some things you said as you introduced redirections:

To be part of our class discussion, Dante, you need to follow our rules about participation. Standing on the sidelines for a while can help you focus on why our group needs you to use your self-controls. If you feel that you're ready tomorrow, you'll be back in the discussion.

You might feel that a talk with the student to determine why Loss of Privilege isn't working would be useful (see social conferences, page 194). Perhaps for this student, other redirects will work better until he's ready to comply with Loss of Privilege to help him follow the rules, making it clear that one way or another he must change his behavior:

Oscar, I see Loss of Privilege hasn't worked for you. Whenever you or anyone else misbehaves, my goal is to get you to quickly fix what's off and move ahead; so what can we do to get you to do this? Should we not use Loss of Privilege for a while? If we set it aside, what redirect will work for you?

It's also possible that your relationship with this student needs some work. Response to redirects is closely associated with how much the student trusts that you have his best interests in mind. You may gain a lot of influence with him by having a brief, friendly talk outside of class or as students enter the room, not about his rule-breaking, but about his life. A call home to fill in the gaps—not to criticize the student—may also help you be more effective when redirecting the student. Although Loss of Privilege is an effective and reasonable redirection, the variety of human nature tells us there will always be exceptions. There are many options in disciplining because there are many personalities to deal with, and one size never fits all—it always depends.

Q. *After I restore a privilege to a student, what can I do to help her use it wisely?*

Before you restore it, consider talking with her briefly to tie up any loose ends and express your belief in her ability to exercise the privilege well.

You're about to regain the privilege of using our computers, Rochelle. I know you can handle it. Before you start, tell me how you'll use the computer from now on.

As she begins to exercise the restored privilege, reinforce positive things you notice about how she's doing, and help her plan how she'll avoid repeating her mistake.

You're visiting the correct site, and I can see you're staying out of I Tunes. Thanks, and keep it up, even if you get a little bored. What will you do if you're tempted to move off your task and use the computer in ways that are not within our guidelines?

You are using the Reflective Loop to help her plan appropriate behavior. At the end of her session, reflect with her on what she did to stay within the guidelines.

Finished, Rochelle? How was it? What did you do to keep yourself focused?

Story for Reflection: Loss of Privilege

Tell this story to prompt student reflection on their behavior.

Long ago, kites and swans had the privilege of song. Each had many beautiful songs to sing, and they filled the air with melodies as they soared. But one day, they heard the neigh of a horse, and they were so intrigued with the sound that they spent hours trying to imitate it. After a day of straining their voices with loud, guttural neighing, they had lost the gift of singing.

Moral: The desire for imaginary benefits often involves the loss of present blessings.

—"The Kites and the Swans," Aesop's Fables

FIX IT ON THE SPOT

Sometimes the mistake a student makes is immediately repairable. If a mess is made, it can be cleaned up. If someone's work is spoiled, the spoiler can help the person do it over. If people are pushing and grabbing, they can stop and figure out an orderly way for everyone to get what s/he needs. The focus is on reparations—making whole something that is broken. This is a consequence of rule-breaking that is easy for most students to accept because it is directly relevant to the infraction, and it is respectful and realistic to expect that if you broke it you will fix it.

Sometimes when a student misuses something, the privilege of using it is removed temporarily (Loss of Privilege). When there has been damage to materials, repair may be required before the privilege is restored. If a student damages a textbook, for example, she may be required to replace it, restore it, or, if these options aren't realistic, do service in the school to earn the privilege back. Before deciding what course of action to take, ask yourself, "Is it realistic to expect her to replace or repair the damaged item?" If not, service to the school, which will have to purchase a replacement, would be relevant and appropriate.

Fix It on the Spot is a strategy for rule-breaking that is often attached to other redirections. In addition to a link between removing the privilege for a while and fixing what you damaged, we may ask a student who has violated a rule to take a break and think about how she can fix what has been damaged. We may use a simple verbal redirection: "Clean up the scraps on the floor before you leave class, girls." Or we may sometimes just point at a messed-up bookshelf after a student has grabbed a book from the bottom of a pile, and that may be enough for him to understand the repair that is needed.

Damages that require problem-solving

When what is damaged is a person, because feelings or reputations are negatively affected, students may have to think hard about how to repair the damage. Chapter 8, page 221, describes the act of apology process, a structure useful for going beyond a verbal apology to an action from which both the injured party and the person responsible may benefit.

An 8th grader takes a moment to clean up after a mistake

TAKE A BREAK

Take a Break is part of the classroom atmosphere that I want to have—that it's OK to make mistakes. Because of where they are developmentally, I expect my students to challenge and push back. They need support for the many things that trigger high emotions in them. You have to have a structure for students to learn to fix their mistakes. They need a tool that allows them to pull themselves back together while the rest of the class continues learning. In the Take a Break spot, I see students get it back together after being upset about something. They go there and maybe read a little bit and then come right back in. I don't have to say anything; it's about them. It's about them gaining control over their actions to get where they want to go.

—Middle school teacher, Wheeling IL

Take a Break (TAB) involves moving a rule-breaker to a different part of the room, away from where his inappropriate behavior happened. It is useful when moving to a new setting is likely to help a student create a plan to fix an error. Like all people, adolescents sometimes need a change of scenery to help them settle down. Take a Break affords students an early opportunity to self-regulate and gives guided practice in problem-solving. Early in the year, a process to use Take a Break effectively is taught and practiced, and notes are posted. Students don't perceive Take a Break as punishment when it's introduced and used effectively. Rather, they come to consider it as think time that allows them to regain self-control with dignity and independence. This practice builds resilience and helps students develop the capacity to internally adjust *before* misbehavior occurs.

Breaks help students quickly refocus and return to learning

A middle schooler explains that there are times when she and her classmates are self-aware enough to understand that they need to collect themselves. "Sometimes teachers don't send you to take a break. You go there on your own. Sometimes you're going through hard times, and you might just need to take some breaths, and that's all right."

An 8th grader notes that taking breaks has helped teach students at his school to manage their own behavior. "We try to stop and control ourselves; there are times when we take a few minutes and put our heads down or something like that." Students are permitted to take a short mental break at their desk if they feel they need one.

—Middle school students, New York NY

Steps of Take a Break

When a student is told to Take a Break, she stops what she's doing and moves to the Take a Break spot. Then she uses the Reflective Loop to adjust her behavior:

Plan to change behavior: Center herself, identify her mistake, and figure out how she will change her behavior

Act: Return to the regular flow of class and put effort into behaving differently

Reflect: Noticing the difference, she sees that she can manage herself

The process is almost identical to when a student receives any other verbal or nonverbal redirect. The only difference is that taking a break requires getting up and moving to a different spot and having a few minutes to think in a slightly different environment. Sometimes the walk itself settles the student down.

Effective use of Take a Break

When and for whom to use it

We sweat the small stuff. Even students with good self-control need to take a break sometimes. A break of half a minute to two minutes is about right, because it provides enough time for calming down and thinking but doesn't allow students to stray from learning for longer than necessary.

It may be used *after* trying other redirects. Students may receive a verbal or nonverbal redirect or be asked to move to a different seat. If they can't or won't fix the problem after receiving such cues, taking a break may give them the space they need to be more successful.

It may be used *before* trying other redirects. Some students continue to misbehave until the teacher uses a consequence they "feel." For these students, waiting to use Take a Break until you've used other redirects first renders these first efforts meaningless. Students may consider them hollow threats, or merely the preamble to getting a break. It usually is not effective to warn students that if they continue doing something they will need to take a break. Likewise, warnings are not effective in general: students come to expect them and will say, "But you never gave me a warning!"

Its use is discretionary and variable. Like all discipline strategies in a relationship-based approach, there are patterns but no formula for the application. A student may receive more than one direction to take a break in a class period. Two or three breaks in one class period should be fine, as long as the student truly puts effort into fixing what he damaged. On the other hand, a student who's perfectly capable of controlling herself but chooses to abuse her break by exceeding the time limit, or returns immediately without thinking or altering behavior, a student who talks while he's in the break chair—any of these students may need to be sent to another classroom to take a break (See Take a Break Out and Back on page 179) or to the office for follow-up rather than being given another chance at taking a break in the classroom.

Its use is fair, but not always uniform. Teachers may use Take a Break more with some students, less with others. Our goal is to teach students self-control and resilience. To that end, we may use it more frequently with Paul than with Mark because Paul responds really well to it while Mark responds far better to nonverbal redirection. A teacher may choose to redirect one person to the break spot and use a different redirect for the same rule-breaking behavior for another student.

Our commitment is to consistently redirect misbehavior, but we may use any re-direction tool with any particular student at any particular time. Telling this to our students is important. We can use the tools differently and still be fair because we measure fairness by what is best for each student. Adolescents understand when we explain that one size never fits all: each of them is an individual, and they need different structures to succeed. We are committed to working with each to find the pathways to success in school:

I promise to work with each of you to help you meet your needs and work your way toward success in school. That probably means different approaches for different people at different times. We'll work together to figure out what helps you keep aligned with our Social Contract.

Use a firm and encouraging tone

It's not negotiable. When they are redirected, students respond quickly and appropriately. Arguing, bargaining, negotiating, postponing, asking for another chance, etc., isn't allowed. If the student takes issue with a teacher's decision to use Take a Break with her, she may discuss the matter later—during passing period, at lunch, or after school.

It's not punishment. None of the redirections in this chapter are punitive. The message is:

We're working together to support the Social Contract and the rules we made, and our approach is firm, our expectations high. Because of this, we're catching small problems before they become big ones. You adjust your behavior, and we move on.

Share control

Students are responsible for fixing the problem. After being redirected, the student pulls himself together independently before returning to the regular flow of class on his own.

Timing of the return from a break can be either a student or teacher choice. Generally, the control lies with the student. She can self-assess whether she is ready to return to the group with changed behavior, as long as she doesn't take too long to do so. The teacher may need to take control when the student returns if the student hasn't used the break well. The student may be told to wait in the break area until the teacher can have a short talk with him to determine the student's readiness for return to the class. It is best not to exercise this option if you know it will be a long time before you can talk with the student. Use Take a Break Out and Back instead (see page 179).

To introduce Take a Break, we talk about the process and how to create the TAB spot as a quiet place. We read the picture book *A Quiet Place*, and then students establish through drawing or painting what their quiet place is. These images are kept in the TAB spot. We figure out where we want to set it up and create the spot together as much as possible. At first, they go through a lot of experimentation as they test whether I mean what I say. I'm clear about when they are abusing the process and about how to move to TAB no matter what. If the space is taken, I know how to move students to different spaces in different situations. They can push their chairs out of the circle or next to a computer. TAB is not only a place, but an idea. This is especially important to convey in the middle grades, when students move around a lot. It helps them be successful in any working space.

—Middle school teacher, Wheeling IL

Create the break spot together. Usually teachers determine where it will be, but students might have some input. Students are made aware of the spot and are taught how to use it correctly before TAB is implemented. The spot should be in plain view, a few feet away from the action, and easily reachable from anywhere in the space. You may choose to have two break spots available, and in a pinch, if spots are occupied, a chair slightly removed from the group will do. The idea isn't to isolate the rule-breaker, just to move him to a new spot a few feet from activity.

Many teachers invite students to give a name to the break spot. The Bahamas, Vacation Station, R & R, the Chill Chair, Collect Your Thoughts Place, and the TAB chair have all been used. Instead of saying "Take a Break," the teacher might say "Go to the Bahamas," or "You need a vacation." The light touch, and the fact that the students named it themselves, adds to their endorsement and acceptance of the process.

You may choose to decorate your spot with images, objects, or signs that might assist the break-taker in centering herself. A picture of a serene beach, an inspiring quote, or a rock to examine might help students center themselves. One school set up a way for students to electronically monitor their degree of calmness while taking a break by taking a computer reading of their heart rate!

Importance of teacher teamwork

Introduce and implement Take a Break on the same day your colleagues do to ensure consistency. Students will probably test the system, and you'll need each other's support to be consistent, clear, and firm with all students. Also, a united approach will help teachers who struggle with discipline to become more assertive, and will keep teachers with authoritarian tendencies from using TAB punitively or as a way of dominating students.

Two different break spots; Take a Break can happen anywhere

Introducing Take a Break to Students

It is crucial to distinguish Take a Break from all of the punitive uses of "time out" that have been part of many students' experience. Express your sincere intention and commitment that this structure will be a way that students can independently and with dignity adjust their behavior.

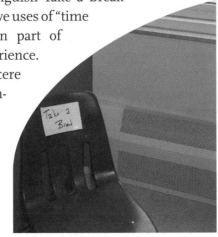

Meet as a class in a circle or as a team in a large group so all students in the team get the same information at the same time. Have chart paper ready for note-taking.

1. Introduce the purpose and parameters of TAB

Make clear to students why you will be asking them to take a break.

Whenever you make a mistake that breaks a rule, I am committed to helping you get back on track. One of the ways I'll do this will be to use Take a Break.

Take a Break is designed to quickly get you back in the right groove. If I tell you to take a break, the entire process should last just 30 seconds to two minutes: long enough to stop and think, and short enough to not waste time. The goal is to get back to learning as soon as you are ready.

I'll use Take a Break, or TAB, for small mistakes. We redirect you for these in a variety of ways, and TAB is one of them. We'll do this so big mistakes are less likely to happen and so you can practice regaining self-control and getting back to learning.

Why change your seat for a few minutes? To help you make a shift. The process of quietly thinking about your behavior and planning to change it can give you the power to turn bad moments around, not only in school but in all your life. You're in control of the process. You handle your own problems. If you don't use TAB successfully to help you fix your behavior, adults will need to intervene. So if you want to be more in control, take TAB seriously.

Whenever I tell a student to take a break, it's because that student's behavior is outside of our guidelines. It's nothing personal. I'm saying, 'Your behavior right now is not acceptable. Take a break and fix it.' You'll see me calmly and quickly asking students to take breaks, probably every day.

Think of it this way: it's a chance to grow on your own when your teacher tells you to take a break. It's not punishment, it's not a detention, it's not a phone call to your parent, it's not suspension. You're really receiving a privilege: I believe in you, and trust you with the responsibility to fix your own behavior when you get off track.

TAB is not a punishment

This point may need to be revisited many times before it sinks in; many students are used to a more punitive approach to behavior management.

Take a Break is for everyone, because we all make mistakes. We'll all use it. It's the way we nip small problems in the bud, before they get big. As your teacher, I can't ignore it when a rule is broken. I'll deal with it, and think at least as highly of you after TAB as before. Anyone who understands TAB will admire your ability to handle yourself when we see you adjusting your behavior. That is a life-long skill. Sometimes I may need a break, so you'll see me sit in the break chair. Everyone in this room will need it at some time.

2. Explain your expectations

Students need to know what they'll be accountable for when Take a Break is used. Tell them what you expect of them.

With power and control comes responsibility. When you break a rule and we tell you to take a break, you are to stop the rule-breaking behavior and move to the Take a Break spot quickly. Then use the Reflective Loop to help you get back to learning:

Plan to change behavior: *Center yourself, identify your mistake, and plan to change the behavior.*

Act: *Return to the regular flow of class as soon as you're ready, and make an effort to get on track.*

Reflect: *Think about how you are staying on track; notice that things are better now.*

You must put effort into getting back on track rather than just going through the motions. Your behavior after returning from taking a break is the evidence of whether you used the break as it was intended.

Most of the time, you decide when you are ready to return and follow the rules. But remember, your time away has to be somewhere between 30 seconds and two minutes. Occasionally, I may decide to be the one who invites you back after we talk briefly. In these cases, I'll work to make the break time short.

If someone breaks a rule more than once in a class period, I will decide whether to tell him to try TAB again, or try something else.

If I tell you to take a break, you are to do so immediately, without arguing, asking for another chance, trying to negotiate, asking why, or anything else. Just go. If you feel you really did nothing wrong, return to us in 30 seconds and get back to work. Later, when I'm available to talk with you, please come to me if you have any questions about why you were sent to TAB, or if you feel I made a mistake in sending you. We're all in this together, and I may indeed redirect the wrong person occasionally. If I do, I want to hear about it, but tell me when we can discuss it without holding up the class.

3. Show students where your TAB spot(s) is (are)

Here is where students can have some input. They might help decide between two locations, or they might give the spot a name, or suggest ways to make it more comfortable.

4. Model and practice the steps of TAB

Use modeling (page 88) to demonstrate for students how taking a break should look, sound, and feel. Ask a student (or several) to model it. Be sure they model it exactly the way you did.

Take students through a "think-aloud" dramatization to provide an example of the thought process behind adjusting behavior. Invite students to watch carefully, as you'll be debriefing afterwards.

Think-aloud example

Teacher plays the role of Bob, a student being redirected. A student plays the role of the teacher giving the redirect.

> **Scenario:** Bob turns to talk to a neighbor while teacher is leading a lesson.
>
> **Teacher:** *Take a break, Bob.* (Bob stops talking, stands up, and moves quickly and quietly to the break spot.)
>
> **Bob (seated, thinking aloud):** *What?! Embarrassing, getting called out like that. Barely did anything wrong.* (Takes a deep breath to center himself.)
>
> **Plan to change behavior:** OK. What did I do? Well...hmmm... I was sitting, I was quiet, I was following along pretty well... but then I tried to ask Benny what he was planning to do after school—sidetalking when the teacher was talking. OK, that's against the rules. What am I going to do now? I'm going to return to my seat and get back on track by listening to the teacher. I'll wait until after class to talk to Benny about the weekend.
>
> **Act:** Bob returns to seat and does not side talk.
>
> **Reflect:** *Here we go. I'm sitting here, listening. It's 5 minutes to the bell and then I can ask Benny.*

5. Clarify when TAB will be used

With the students, generate a list of common rule-breaking behaviors for which you may use Take a Break. Post the list for future reference. Over time you may add to the list. The list may include:

- side-talking or off-task talking during group work
- blurting an answer when hand-raising is expected
- leaning back in chair
- eye-rolling
- tapping pencil or foot, or other noisemaking
- responding too slowly to the signal for quiet
- daydreaming
- passing a note
- mistreatment of materials
- hands on other people's stuff
- getting out of seat without permission
- resting head on desk
- saying something that might be inappropriate or hurtful
- doing something that gets in the way of others' learning

6. Explain how Take a Break fits with other redirects

We'll mix Take a Break in with our other redirects the same way a good baseball pitcher mixes up his pitches. Sometimes we'll direct you to take a break as soon as you break a rule, and at other times we'll use it after trying other redirects first. If someone is unwilling or unable to use TAB to fix a problem, we may stop using it with that student for a time. But there will always be some form of redirection, because that's part of our job. Standing up for our Social Contract helps ensure that everyone has a good school year.

7. Implement

Check for understanding. Use Take a Break for a short amount of time and then debrief with students. Together, you can assess what's working well so far and what adjustments need to be made. When you are sure that the steps are understood and changes incorporated, implement Take a Break daily and for everyone.

We have a rule to use respectful language in the classroom. There was a girl who was struggling behaviorally, especially with using inappropriate language. When she used bad language in my classroom, I asked her to take a break. Initially, she gave me some pushback. She'd say "Come on, Mr. B.," and she'd question why. Without raising my voice, I briefly and respectfully told her this is the way it is. So she went over and took her break.

After the break, her behavior didn't change. She came back and used inappropriate language again, and I said, "This is the second time—take a break." So she went back again and sat for a while. I let her know that this time I would invite her back. We were playing an activity at the time that she wanted to be a part of. She could see that she was missing out on it. I gave her a few minutes to sit, but didn't let her miss the entire thing; I brought her back before the end. At that point her behavior completely changed. She was much more involved in the activity, less withdrawn. She used appropriate language. Now I don't have to focus on her behavior, so I can focus on her academics.

I have had fewer problems with her than some of my colleagues have, because of TAB. In my classroom, she's given an opportunity. You can make a mistake, but you can pull it back together again. It's a simple way teachers can show faith that students can overcome their mistakes.

—High school teacher, Cambridge MA

Challenges of Take a Break

Q. *What if some of my students resist, saying that Take a Break is for little kids?*

Adults take breaks when they lose focus. Learning to judge when and how you need to stop and refocus is a skill effective people use regularly. Have students poll family members or other adults about how they self-control, how they get themselves back on track. Share your own struggles and your own use of breaks to regroup, and remind them to use your nonverbal cues to straighten up when they slip so they will rarely need to take a break.

Q. *My students still see Take a Break as a punishment, even though I tell them it's to help them focus and succeed in school. How can I get rid of that feeling that they're being punished?*

Some students and teachers may have a more difficult transition to using Take a Break because it looks from the outside a lot like "timeout," the commonly used and usually punitive behavior-management tool of choice in many homes and schools. Here's how to distinguish it:

- Stress in your introduction that the purpose of TAB is to take space and time to independently adjust your behavior, not to punish students.

- Make sure that elements of punishment like an angry tone of voice are not present at all.

- Use TAB for everyone, for small infractions. It is a useful method for regaining self-control before behavior has escalated and it is too late for a stop-and-think to help.

Q. *What if a student goes through the motions without changing his behavior?*

Like any other redirect, TAB may not be used appropriately by all students all the time. We lay out their responsibilities when they receive any redirect, telling them that our purpose is to teach them to independently fix their own behavior, but sometimes they forget. Review, re-model, and assess how you're doing at regular intervals, and especially after long weekends or vacations. Keep it fresh.

If a student fails to use TAB effectively, in spite of your best efforts to keep it fresh, either have a social conference with that student (see page 194) or consider using other redirects with her for a time. Remember, your job is to coach behavior change. This takes much practice and patience, much like teaching someone to sip his tea after years of slurping. It often takes frequent reminders and redirections to change a habit.

Q. *What if the student taking a break is noisy or doesn't follow expectations in some other way while in the TAB chair?*

Remind the student of the expectations and that this is her chance to fix her mistake on her own. If she lacks the self-control at the moment to do this, provide more assistance by directing her to the Take a Break Out room (page 181). There, she will have a change of environment for a short while and have the support of a plan sheet and a quick conference to think through how to get back on track.

Q. *How do I support students when they return from TAB?*

As a rule, don't say anything at all as a student returns. The purpose of the tool is to give students practice in solving problems on their own. Maintain an attitude of respect and confidence that the student has handled this well himself. If a student is successful after a few failures, you might want to approach the student later and acknowledge him for his success: *Lionel, you were having a little trouble focusing, you took a break, and I notice you've been getting a lot accomplished since you returned. You took care of yourself without any help from anyone else. Keep it up!*

What I use most is Take a Break and quick conferences—they go hand in hand. I say, "When you're ready to come back—you know what that feels like—come on back." There's no need to make the student feel bad, and no need to say things like "Good job!" when a student is doing the right thing. We have a no-hat rule, and when I see a student who sometimes breaks that rule complying with it, I say, "I notice there's no hat on your head." Then we silently shake hands. I do a strong grip with the gentlemen, and touch fists with the ladies. It's a quiet recognition that the kids are getting stronger.

—High school teacher, Harrisburg PA

TAKE A BREAK OUT AND BACK

A student who has not responded positively to your in-class redirects might need some time away from his regular environment and the opportunity to make a written plan to get back on the right track. When you've tried several redirection options, when multiple attempts to guide students to improve their own behavior prove ineffective, or when a student's rule-breaking behavior is no longer minor, a brief trip outside of the classroom may be necessary. Stepping away from the heat of the moment or the tense atmosphere created by rule-breaking behavior is sometimes just what a student needs to regain perspective and self-control. Here is the last redirection where in we rely largely on the students to adjust their behavior.

Steps of TAB Out and Back

The teacher tells a student to go to TAB Out and Back. He stops the negative behavior and goes to the TAB Out space, alone or escorted, as appropriate. (TAB Out space for a classroom is next door or just across the hall.) The teacher makes sure he arrives at the designated room. Upon entering the TAB Out space, the student quietly stands near the door until the TAB Out monitor (the teacher or other adult in the room) signals him to be seated in the pre-planned spot. (The TAB Out spot is separate from this classroom's Take a Break spot and is removed from the regular flow of the room, preferably near the door.) The monitor returns to her teaching or other duties. Students do not interact with the visiting student in any way.

Plan to change behavior

The student uses the pencil and reflection form provided as a guide to identify his mistake and think about how he will change his behavior. (See page 281 in Appendix F for a sample reflection form.) The form must be filled in completely. It will be his exit pass when he is ready to return to his classroom; the TAB Out monitor teacher will go over it with him to make sure he has done it well.

He tries to center himself. He takes a few deep breaths to clear his mind and get over or set aside any embarrassment, anger, frustration or other emotion that could cloud his thinking. Using the reflection questions as a guide, he identifies the problem.

He thinks some more. What will he do to fix his behavior? How will he stay on track when he returns? Answers to these questions are written on the reflection form. When the student has completed his reflection, he raises his hand to indicate he's ready to check in with the monitor.

As soon as she's able, the TAB Out monitor reviews the form with him. (It may take the monitor a few minutes to get to the student. Her first job is to tend to her own

students' needs, and if she's giving a mini-lesson to the whole group, for example, that comes first.) The monitor checks that the student is emotionally ready to return to his own room, and has reflected thoughtfully about how he will improve his behavior. When she is satisfied of both, the TAB Out monitor sends or escorts him back to his classroom.

Act

The student enters his own classroom and stands quietly by the door. Other students do not interact with him at all. Again, a wait may be necessary. The teacher reviews the reflection form and talks to the student briefly to ask questions or suggest changes if necessary and to confirm the seriousness of his intention to change his behavior. She may decide to keep the form to remind the student when he returns the next day how he resolved to behave. If an apology to classmates seems important, it should be made at an appropriate time.

The student returns to work, changing his behavior as planned. He puts effort into staying on track.

Reflect

Now the student needs to notice how well he is doing in following his declared intentions. He still is in control of his situation. Like everyone, he will continue to be redirected if he breaks rules, but he and his teacher hope he is now able to take a break successfully in his classroom. If not, he may have to go through another TAB Out and Back process. If the redirections do not result in improved behavior, he will then need adult management for problem-solving his behavior issues (see problem-solving structures described in Chapter 8).

I was observing a classroom as a behavior coach. The teacher sent a student who was out of control in the break chair to her TAB Out partnering teacher. When this happened, the student stood up and loudly declared "and I won't be coming back!" She was back and in control in ten minutes. It may have been the draw of the community of students that helped her return after making a big scene about not coming back. The power of a positive student community can go a long way to support students in following the rules.

—*Developmental Designs* consultant

A quick, supportive check-in between teacher and student is the last step of TAB Out and Back before returning to class

Setting Up and Introducing Take a Break Out and Back

Plan ahead with a partnering teacher

Find a teacher or other adult staff to partner with you throughout the year as your Take a Break Out monitor. Your partner should be someone

- nearby – either next door or right across the hall
- who shares your commitment to TAB Out and Back
- who may use your room as his/her TAB Out space

If your Take a Break Out monitor is a teacher or someone else who regularly works with students, offer to receive her TAB Out students. A reciprocal relationship often works best.

Prepare the TAB Out space and reflection form

The student will need a desk situated a few feet away from any other student in the room. It remains unoccupied and clear, ready for use at any time.

Create a reflection form to guide the student's thinking (see an example on page 281). Place copies of it in the TAB Out space, along with pencils. Arrange the TAB Out desk and chair to face away from the classroom activity, so the student can focus on the task at hand: changing behavior.

Introduce students to the space and the form

Introduce your students to your TAB Out space early in the school year by taking a quick "field trip" with your classes. It will take just a minute or two, and they'll benefit from knowing exactly where to go and what the TAB Out monitor's expectations are. Model the process, from the moment a student is told to take a TAB Out until s/he is welcomed back. Demonstrate with a think-aloud filling out the form. Check for understanding of the entire process.

Let students know that in TAB Out and Back, their job is to plan how to change their behavior, act, and reflect on how they are doing, just as they need to do after any other redirection. The only difference here is that the form and two adults give a little external guidance.

Make sure students understand that the TAB Out space is mostly reserved for students who have not succeeded using other redirections and need more help restoring self-control. The hope of the TAB Out and Back process is that being in a different space with time and a little structure to think will help provide a different perspective. Make clear to them that TAB Out and Back is the last of the tools you'll use that allow students to change their behavior on their own. If they can't fix things independently with TAB Out and Back, you and other adults will get more involved, which could include both administrative and family intervention.

Challenges of TAB Out and Back

Q. *What if the student refuses to fill out the reflection form or does so in an inappropriate way, refusing to take responsibility for her mistakes?*

In response to this resistance, the TAB Out monitor reinforces for the student the connection between working on changing your behavior and maintaining independence.

Jane, if you want to be in control of your situation, you have to take responsibility for your behavior. If you refuse to take responsibility, adults will have to take over. Either way, you must change your behavior. You decide who's going to be the boss of you—you or the adults around you. Your path back to your class demands that you have a clear plan for change. Right now, you're not in trouble. So make the independent choice: use the form to plan how you change your behavior, and come see me when you're finished so we can go over it together and get you back to your class.

Thomas, you've already wasted more than one opportunity to solve your own problem. You have this one last chance to regain control of yourself. You need to fill in the reflection form completely and appropriately, and when you go back to class, you need to act out your plan. You have three minutes and twenty-six seconds. I know you can do it. Get to work.

Make certain that you have done all you can to present TAB Out and Back as another means for students to independently change their behavior. You may want to review the rationale and the procedure.

Q. *What if the student refuses to go to the TAB Out space?*

Call the office and request administrative support. If possible, continue with the lesson after doing so. When someone arrives to assist you, have that person escort the student to the office for follow-up. Don't have the escort take him to the TAB Out space: he's not in enough control to make use of it.

Q. *What if I don't have a partnering teacher for a TAB Out spot?*

Your TAB Out partner need not be a teacher. Any adult nearby on whom you can count to be in a fixed space can receive a visiting student. Many schools create and staff a designated TAB Out room.

Q. *Doesn't TAB Out monitoring take too much time away from the partnering teacher's or my own instruction?*

No. It takes only a signal to admit the student to the TAB Out spot, and just a minute to check with the student when he's ready to return, to make sure the plan is workable.

EFFECTIVE REDIRECTING

Nonverbal and verbal cues, Loss of Privilege, Fix It on the Spot, Take a Break , and Take a Break Out and Back: day by day, we use this array of redirections to keep students on track.

Equity in redirection

Since everyone makes mistakes, everyone needs redirection. A common flaw in behavior management is that chronic offenders get most of our attention, and they get almost all of the redirection. If we ignore the mistakes made infrequently by the other students, instead of using redirections for everyone in the room for even small mistakes, then this approach has no credibility or efficacy. Equity is what makes a relationship-based approach to behavior management work, and it means everything to adolescents. It is the foundation of the Social Contract. We must use all our withitness and all our commitment to see everything and respond with a redirect to every slip, including slips by students who usually follow the guidelines.

Rigor from the start

Be sure students are clear that you will uphold the Social Contract for everyone, every time; you will not overlook any rule-breaking. Each time you intervene, taking future action becomes easier: we get the hang of it, and so do our students, who respond by reducing the amount of pushing back they do. Habits start forming the minute students enter the classroom on Day One. The frontal cortex (the area of conscious decision-making) experiences the message, and the pattern of compliance begins to form. As the new patterns become familiar, they move to storage in the lower brain stem (unconscious decision-making). There, the rule-following becomes habitual. Bad habits are hard to change for the same reason: once the rule-breaking pattern becomes familiar, it goes to the lower brain and is much more difficult to change.

At the end of each week, assess your progress. Is taking action each time a student breaks a rule getting easier? What are you gaining by taking action? Recommit to rigorous intervention next week, and so on, week by week. Before long, it becomes second nature for you to intervene, and for most students to comply.

Choosing the Right Redirection

Choosing the right redirect for a situation is a skill that develops over time. A quick decision is required every time, since redirecting happens in the midst of teaching. Considering the following questions can help build a broader general understanding of the forces at work when you are faced with choosing a redirection.

Can the student probably fix this on her own?

Can she calm down and solve her problem without guidance? If so, a nonverbal or verbal cue that may include fixing something on the spot or a loss of privilege or just some time to think (Take a Break) should work well. If not, she may need to leave the room temporarily, calm down, and think about how to change her behavior with the help of a reflection form and a quick review with an adult. If TAB Out and Back doesn't help, or if she needs to use it or other redirects too frequently, then further teacher assistance may be needed—a social conference or other adult intervention (see Chapter 8). The redirections in this chapter are for early intervention, before escalation, to help the student learn to think her way back to self-control quickly.

Does he habitually misbehave to gain attention?

If this is the case, he needs to gain as little attention for his behavior as possible. A quick, simple nonverbal or verbal cue will minimize interruption of the class.

Which redirects have worked before?

Use the redirects that have worked for a student in the past. For example, if Take a Break usually works for Ben, use it. If it doesn't, don't use TAB with Ben until you have a conversation with him about why it doesn't. If TAB worked for Ben in the past but seems to have lost its effectiveness, switch to another redirect.

Have I overused one type of redirect?

Vary your redirects to keep students alert, and to continuously learn which ones are effective for which students. See page 183 for how to choose between remodeling and role play when students are consistently not following the procedures you have modeled with them.

Is this student expecting me to use a specific redirect?

If a student appears to want you to use a particular redirection (perhaps to make a power grab or subvert the learning process), use a different one.

Do I need to verbally express my faith in her ability to fix mistakes?

The less positive your relationship with the offending student is, the more she might need to hear that you have confidence in her. See page 157 for more about infusing relationship-building into your verbal redirections.

You need to take a break and change your behavior, Martha. I know you can do it.

How much help does this student need to identify the problem?

If students do not know why you're redirecting them, their chances of fixing the problem are slight, and frustration—a lower sense of competence—can result. Most of the time, most students know what they did to break a rule without being told. Teach students that naming the infraction and discussing it will not be done right away, and they can come to you later. Rarely does anyone actually do that, but if you are working with a student who is genuinely confused about the nature of his mistake, you may have to make a special arrangement with him that will be an exception to the "not-now, later" policy.

Am I making the right move at the right time?

You have only seconds to make a redirection decision. We never know beyond a doubt that a move we make with a student is the right one at the right time, but we do our best.

What we are doing at these moments is what Malcolm Gladwell (2005) in his book *Blink* describes as taking a "thin slice," a cross section of the moment that includes what's going on in class, what the student is doing, and the pattern of your past interactions with him. You do not think through all of this methodically in that second or two in which you are deciding; you look at a small piece of all of it and make your decision. According to Gladwell, that decision has an excellent chance of being a good one, as do many of our decisions made in the blink of an eye.

There are moments, in times of stress, when haste does not make waste, when our snap judgments and first impressions offer a much better means of making sense of the world. (Gladwell 2005, 14)

The Right Mindset for Effective Discipline

A hazard of redirecting is that our decisions can be affected by our moods or our pre-judgments of students—by our mindset at the moment. Here is where our habit of reflection pays off. We increase the odds that our quick decisions will be effective and good when we habitually reflect on our mindsets with regard to:

- Perceiving each student as engaged in growth towards potential success in school (Growth Mindset)

- Perceiving yourself as cause in the matter of that growth, accepting the moral imperative to act on behalf of that growth (Action Mindset)

- Perceiving yourself as nurturing both objectivity and personal connection with students so you are able to act on behalf of their growth without pre-judgments (Objective Mindset)

Habitual reflection in these areas helps us become aware of and overcome barriers to effective discipline (and teaching), and increases the likelihood that we will make good decisions.

A group of middle level teachers at a workshop noticed that their principal returned from a break late. The guidelines for the workshop had been democratically created by the group, and returning on time was part of their agreement. They asked the group facilitator what she intended to do about the fact that the principal was late. Her response was to engage the principal in a conversation about what it would take for him to follow the rule about returning on time after the next break. What did he need to do at lunch break to ensure his timely return? They agreed on a plan, and thereafter he returned from lunch on time.

The group's response was, "Is that all you're going to do?" A conversation followed about what was right and fair, and that people who broke the rules should have to pay a price (retribution). The facilitator pointed out that what actually happened was that the principal became much more conscious of his behavior on break and was now following the guidelines (reformation).

—*Developmental Designs* workshop facilitator

Why does bad behavior aggravate us? Why do we want retribution? What is really the goal of our behavior management? These questions are worthy of serious reflection by all educators.

To do the difficult work of consistently maintaining the Social Contract and helping students grow in social competency, we must constantly call upon our powers of commitment, courage, and emotional objectivity. Keeping a cool head in the face of a student's anger, even abuse, is very difficult. Insisting that students who break the rules over and over can learn to follow them requires an extraordinary belief in every student's capacity to grow.

Doing what may not come naturally

Responding to student misbehavior is a risk: we never know how the student will react. For some teachers, this uncertainty creates a fear: *What if I tell him to move to another seat and he refuses? Then I'll have a mess on my hands.* If a situation calls for moving someone to another seat but the teacher opts to ignore the problem or to respond in some other, less appropriate way, she is creating bigger problems for herself and for the rest of the school community.

Treat students well by responding to their misbehavior with the tool that is most likely to work, whether it comes naturally to you or not. Both you and the student will grow. Rather than allowing fear of the unknown to keep you from doing right by a student, take the risk. Sometimes you just have to jump off the cliff.

It's not personal

Remember that it's not about the student, it's about the *behavior*. You aren't passing judgment about the student; her behavior disregards the Social Contract, and your job is to respond to it. Likewise, the student's behavior is not about you. See page 27 for more about the need to take emotional distance.

By keeping the focus on what will best meet the needs of the student, we can consistently take actions that work for him or her. *It's not about my natural tendencies (who I am), but about what I must do to meet the needs of the student.* Having no choice but to take action, no matter how we feel or what we might wish for, makes discipline easier.

The reflective mode can help us. We decide if we've made a good redirect when we can see good results. If students seem to settle down and do some productive work after changing course from a redirection, we move on. If they do not, we try again. And if we see that we're still not getting it right with that student, we move to problem-solving. The next chapter offers assistance in that process.

Story for Mindset Development

Reflection on this story can come to your aid following challenges from or high-emotion exchanges with students.

Two monks saw a woman standing in front of a puddle, unwilling to cross through because doing so would spoil her silken robes. Her attendants were loaded with things she had bought, so they could not help her. She angrily scolded them as if they were not doing all they could. The young monk saw all this and passed by without speaking. The older monk picked up the young woman and carried her to the other side of the puddle. Without thanking him, she pushed him out of her way and continued on.

Several hours later, after the two monks had walked on without speaking, the young monk said, "Why did you help that woman? She was rude and ungrateful, but you picked her up and carried her anyway. I wouldn't have rewarded such a person. She doesn't deserve kindness for her bad behavior." The older monk replied, "I carried her hours ago, but I see that you are still carrying her. Why?"

—Centuries-old story from Zen Buddhist literature

Celebrating Success

Try using an approach to rules maintenance that both redirects students whenever they break rules and *celebrates* successful living by the rules—in the moment and at the end of class periods. Positive reinforcement helps forward both appropriate school behavior and the moral development of students.

Teachers who help their students feel good about learning through classroom successes, friendships, and celebrations are doing the very things the student brain craves. (Jensen 2005, 77)

Comment on what you see

Talk about the behaviors you see—those that support the rules as well as those that break them. Connect specific helpful actions to the rules they support. Students need to see the connections. Make connections verbally, when you notice them. They provide students with immediate feedback they need for steady growth.

Examples of in-the-moment affirmations

When things are going well, mention it (especially important in the first two months of school), and name the relevant rule or modeled procedure:

I notice all the small groups are on task and holding lively discussions. You're being respectful and responsible, and you're doing your best! We'll get a lot of learning done this year.

I notice everyone is listening the way we modeled it. That's going to help us learn a lot.

Almost everyone had an answer ready when I called on him/her during discussion time.

You may also mention successes at the beginning and end of class periods. If you have created charts to add specificity to what the rules look, sound, and feel like (page 97), you or a student may add the positive behaviors you are noticing now to the ever-growing list of things you do as a class to support the rules.

Assess behavior with students

Have the students assess on a regular basis how well they're living by the rules. This uses the power of the Reflective Loop.

Reflective Loop assessment example

- **Plan.** You did this at the beginning of class when you prepared students for the work to be done that day and the *way* that work should be done.

- **Work**. Do the work you have planned, the way you have planned it. At the end of class, or just before you switch to a different lesson,

- **Reflect.**
  Teacher: *Let's take a moment to have a look at our rules. Mary, could you read them for us?*
  Student: *They are...Respect each other, Do your best, and Be responsible.*
  Teacher: *Thanks, Mary. Let's start with respect: how respectful were we during work time? Show us by using 'thumbs up, thumbs sideways, or thumbs down. Ready, go.*
  After thumbs: *What's your evidence?* [Students assess]

- **Plan for next time**
  Teacher: *What's one thing we can do next time to make things better?* [Students share an idea or two]

We show in our actions and conversations that the rules are for everyone, that every break in them is important, and that we are committed to noticing the good and redirecting the mistakes, including, especially, little things. Moment by moment, good behavior habits are formed, and students move down the path to responsible independence.

REDIRECTING: Getting in Gear for Responsible Independence

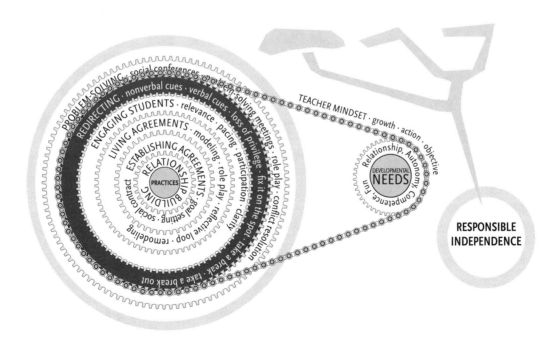

Problem-solving

When I'm working with a student who is pushing back hard, I listen very carefully to her language. If it's aggressive, with a lot of profanity, I ask, "What are you trying to say?" And then I re-phrase: "Do you want me to give you some space right now?" If she says yes, then I say, "Why don't you just say that?" I want her to see that I could listen better if she spoke differently. She begins to get it.

For me the question is: How can I get students to realize that often, what happens to them in school is in response to the things they do and say? The beginning of freedom and power for them comes when they understand that they are not always victims of what happens; *they* have power and influence; what they say and how they behave makes a difference in a conversation. Sometimes I sit with kids and guide them in a step-by-step review of their actions and speech in a situation, and point out where their words and/or actions moved the situation toward a consequence they didn't want.

I ask, "What issue did you have that kept you in the hall? Didn't you feel like going to class? Do you see that's disrespectful? I want you to analyze what happened." I try to make things transparent to the kids. In the end, they usually accept the consequence and even leave the conference with a smile sometimes. What they're learning is that it's *you*—it's the actions *you* take that get you where you are.

—High school teacher, Harrisburg PA

Sometimes the most important thing we can do with students is talk to them or have them talk to each other face to face, seriously, about their rule-breaking behavior. Even after we carefully prepare them to follow the rules and teach them how to take responsibility for changing rule-breaking behavior, some students will still struggle.

Consider three types of adolescents:

1. Some will do it your way. They are willing to follow adult instructions, and they have the self-control to do so.

2. Some are on the fence, but are willing to give it a try because you have effectively presented the case for doing it, and they endorse it. This initial endorsement will grow in strength for many, and although some may begin to push back, consistent redirections for small things and for everyone will keep those students engaged so that learning can be continuous.

3. Some will continue to push limits and test boundaries. These adolescents may appear to be in step with you at first as you model and practice the routines and present your case for how and why you handle behavior issues the way you do, only to challenge your authority as soon as you require that the rules be implemented by them as well as everyone else. They may be determined to push back, or they may suddenly become rebellious after a period of rule-following. Although resistance and rebellion are developmentally typical, they must be addressed, or the work of school will not get done.

When redirections are not sufficient

Don't lose confidence when the redirections presented in Chapter 7 aren't sufficient for every student. Remember, *we're still on track, we're still doing a lot of things right.* We're building positive relationships, we're creating lessons that engage, our behavior-management approach is strongly proactive, and we're paying attention to all misbehaviors, great and small. Our work to build social competency has had good effect, even on the most disruptive. It's just that for some, more is necessary. If we hadn't done what we've already done, constantly and incrementally building the base for responsible self-management, rule-breakers would be more numerous and more disruptive.

Teachers are faced with students who aren't willing or able to fix behavior problems by themselves. Some adolescents need extra help managing their behavior, just as some need extra help in math or science. When our reinforcing, reminding, and redirecting interventions aren't sufficient to keep some students on a positive path, we assist them in other ways. We believe in their capacity for growth, but we need additional tools to help them solve their problems.

Problem-solving structures

This chapter presents problem-solving tools that can be used in the classroom:

Problem-solving social conferences (teacher-student conversations)

Problem-solving meetings (whole group teacher-student meetings)

Role plays (group enactments of problem scenarios and solutions)

Conflict resolution (student-to-student meetings)

Act of apology (student/teacher-to-student address of damage done)

All follow this 5-step format:

1. *Identify* the problem

2. *Brainstorm* solutions

3. *Choose* a solution to try

4. *Act* on it

5. *Check in* to reflect on the effectiveness of the solution

Other tools are available through other professionals: psychologists, counselors, social workers, nurses, administrators, and behavior specialists all have specialized skills in settings other than the classroom. The tools described in this chapter are for use during class before turning to other professionals to assist our students.

Introducing problem-solving structures to students

In general, the best way to introduce a problem-solving structure to students is to demonstrate by actually using the structure to solve a problem, commenting as appropriate, before, after, and sometimes as you go, about how the structures work to help us find our way to good social solutions. With social conferencing, the teacher is always present, guiding the process, so students need only follow that guidance each time. Similarly, when you do your first role play with students, you can introduce it by explaining what it's for, but learning the process occurs in the experience of it, and the process is always mediated by the teacher.

Conflict resolution and act of apology, however, are designed to be handled independently, at least at times, without the guidance of the teacher in every step. Introduce these two structures by explaining how useful they can be to students, and provide a sample conflict resolution and talk students through the process of an act of apology. The best place to teach the two processes is during advisory, and then students can use the processes, with permission from classroom teachers, as needed.

PROBLEM-SOLVING SOCIAL CONFERENCES

A problem-solving conference is needed when a student is unable or unwilling to self-direct her shift away from rule-breaking. The conference provides more help from the teacher and presents opportunities to both set the student back on the right track and strengthen your relationship with her.

Taking time to problem-solve with a chronically disruptive or disengaged student can help everyone, the sooner the better. When a student is left adrift—is allowed to behave repeatedly in a manner outside the framework of the Social Contract—everyone suffers. Left unchecked, the consistent rule-breaker typically ends up in the office for disciplinary action. Perhaps even worse, students lose confidence in the Social Contract, and your relationships with students suffer, as does the efficacy of the redirection tools, being used over and over to no effect.

The best results come from using intervention conversations before a student gets stuck in a rule-breaking rut. Outlined here is a problem-solving conference that is quick enough to be used during the class hour or at the door before a student leaves.

Martin came to my class with a history of throwing chairs when he became angry. I headed trouble off at the pass by talking with him right away. "I want you to know that in this class we get mad sometimes, but we don't throw things. You don't have to live *down* to your reputation here. We can help you build a new, positive reputation for you to live *up* to!" During this conversation, we came up with a way to deal with his anger that was safe and not disruptive: when he became angry, he would take a break to cool off, and return when he was ready. Sometimes he would walk down the hall to the restroom, and he knew that during this cooling-off time he was to settle down and do nothing else—no wandering around, no disrupting other classes. We agreed that he could give me a signal that he needed to go cool off, or he might just go to the break spot on his own. He didn't abuse our agreement; he came back quickly and rejoined the group, ready to work. Martin never threw a chair in my class.

—5th grade teacher, St. Paul MN

Steps of a Quick Problem-solving Social Conference

As other students begin working on an assignment, ask the student to step to the doorway.

1. Identify the problem

Describe the student's rule-breaking behavior and the rule that was broken.

Darian, hi. I noticed today when you sat down you put your head down on your desk and stayed that way while I was getting things started and giving instructions. I've noticed that you spend a lot of time these days with your head down, and when I tell you to pay attention, you say you are, and keep your head down. Do you realize that you're not getting your work done and falling pretty far behind?

Do you see that this way of behaving is breaking our agreement that everyone will put effort into achieving his or her goals? I won't overlook breaking that rule, because it sets all of us back when someone is clearly not making an effort.

2. Brainstorm solutions

Ask what is needed from the student to avoid rule-breaking and offer suggestions if needed.

What do you need to do to keep yourself focused and working in here, Darian? You said you wanted to pass every subject this year. What can you do to make that happen?

Would it help if I gave you a starter question as soon as you come into class? Do you need to talk to an adult about anything going on in your life? I could arrange that for you.

3. Select a solution

Define a plan with the student. Writing a note to yourself about the solution selected can help you remember the plan when you later check in with the student.

OK, I'll have a question of the day ready on an index card for a few days. You will have three minutes to answer the question and hand it in. They will be just fun questions but they will get you started thinking and writing. Let's see how that works.

4. Take action

Send student off, clarifying the plan. In this conversation, you establish four things:

- You care about him and are committed to his success.
- He's breaking a rule with his behavior, and that's not acceptable.
- He can and must fix it, and you will help him.
- He needs to reflect daily on how he has behaved in class.

Let's take action on this. Reflect on how you're doing every day, because that will make you very conscious of your behavior. I'll check in with you at the beginning of class for a few days, and if things don't seem better, I'll give your mom a call and maybe set up something with the social worker. I know you can do a good job in our class, Darian, and I want to hear your ideas about the coming-of-age stories we're reading.

Every social conference is based in relationship. The success of the conversation depends on the perception the student has that you notice him, care about him, and have the power and the will to help him. You aren't going to just go away, and neither is the problem, unless he, with your help, does something about it. You are allies, not adversaries, both after the same thing—that he be happy and successful.

5. Check in

The next day, check in with the student as he arrives in class to complete the Reflective Loop. You have planned, taken action, and now you meet to reflect together on how it's going. You will make any adjustments to the plan that you think will help it work better.

No social conference with a student will bear fruit unless we follow through and do exactly what we told the student we would do. We must check in with her the next day as we said we would, and we must contact the parent if we said we would. We must set up something with the social worker if we promised that would happen if things didn't improve and they haven't. The integrity of the process, the seriousness with which the student views it, depend on whether we follow through on our words. We take action, because the success and happiness of the student depend on our doing what we say, and because we care very much about the student.

The students are true to the commitments they make in their social conferences with me. I write on a sticky note that they had a social conference and what they agreed to do. They follow the plan. They've learned that I'll follow through, even if they don't. I think in the beginning they thought something like "Maybe she'll forget," but now they know I'm not going to.

—8th grade language arts teacher, Greenfield MA

Careful Listening and Speaking

I keep the conferencing language in front of me, in my planner. It's becoming second nature to me. I can use it and go through the steps and have dialogue with students. I've practiced not getting frustrated, listening, having patience, trying to figure it out—all these qualities are vital to social conferencing. Once students realize that you are there to help figure things out and you're not going to speak with sarcasm, raise your voice, or leave the room frustrated, they finally see that this is different; this is going to be a different experience. I build the trust so they do eventually tell me what's going on and we can start to find a solution.

—8th grade teacher, Wheeling IL

Listen carefully

Even in social conferences in which the teacher does most of the talking (which is often the case), the teacher's *listening* can determine the success of the exchange. When we listen with attention to details, nuance, and nonverbal signs, we can learn valuable things about the student and about ourselves. It's not easy to listen carefully when you are struggling with a student's behavior, especially if the message is sarcastic, critical, or hopeless. Nonetheless, the message may contain valuable insights into ways that you may be unknowingly thwarting your own success with adolescents. It takes every ounce of commitment you have to listen for such insights.

The conversation may shine a light on

things you could improve in your practice—maybe in lesson-planning or behavior management or relationship-building. As we train ourselves to listen attentively to what a student says, sometimes we see where we could make a small adjustment that might bring big returns in student cooperation. For example, "I don't get it" might show us that we haven't been clear enough about a routine, or we haven't practiced it enough with students.

Listen for relationship. Does this student feel seen and known? Does he see you as an ally or as an enemy? Does he lack the capacity to calm himself, so when he gets agitated, he can't help escalating? These are valuable insights, and they can come from watching and listening carefully as we talk to students.

Your sincerity in the conversation is hugely important. There are times when the overall success of the conference depends on the teacher's openly accepting part of the responsibility for the problem. It requires strength and humility to do so, and may be unpalatable, especially when the student's argument is dubious, but if you figure out a way to agree to change a bit, chances are greater that he will, too.

Neil, I didn't think I was giving redirections only to boys, but now that you've said that, I'm going to pay more attention and keep track of the people I direct to the Break chair, to make sure I'm not unfair.

In the story below, quick conferences provided the insight that a student needed more help than could be provided during class time.

Neela was having a hard spring, and I was surprised. She had willingly participated in the rule-making process in the fall. She had big hopes of having a much better year socially, making good friends, and getting along with everyone. She learned the routines and complied with them most of the time without balking. She did well academically, and handled herself in a friendly manner in school. Sometimes she needed reminders and redirections, but generally that was all it took.

Suddenly her work became sloppy, she didn't get it in on time, and she didn't seem to care anymore. Her appearance went from neat to sloppy, seemingly overnight: she showed up with untied shoes, ill-matching clothes, unkempt hair. Her disposition went from pleasant to grumpy, and she needed more and more redirections from me to stay on course. I had a couple of quick conferences with her about her behavior, but she continued to be disruptive. On the day when I had to have her take a break three times during the first half hour of class, I decided to schedule a longer social conference with her to see if we could get to the cause of the changes. We met during my prep time the next day, and as I listened carefully I began to see that Neela was struggling with questions about her sexual orientation. Thus began a project of rebuilding her confidence and feelings of safety among her peers. It was a challenge, but our talking was the beginning of the end of the misery—for both of us.

—7th and 8th grade teacher, Minneapolis MN

Speak carefully

Adolescents long for independence and competence. They watch for the least nuance that might be construed as unfair. They catch exaggerations and will quickly split the hair of a time or quantity estimate. Avoid generalizations! Adolescents can always come up with exceptions, and someone will use the exception to prove you wrong. Stick to the facts, using specific, descriptive language.

When I talk with students, I make sure that I'm specific about behavior and stay away from words like "always," "never," and "every time." I talk about specific moments and what I observe. I'm very clear with my language. Yesterday I said to a student, "I saw you stand up and throw a piece of paper at Jane. That's what I saw." He denied it. I said, "If I saw something else, you have to let me know." Then he looked at me and said, "That's what I did." So telling exactly what I saw was helpful. I could have said, "You did this," but that's an accusation, and it puts the student on the defensive. Staying away from those aggressive words makes it easier for students to hear what I observed.

Similarly, I give students language to use when they are in partners and need to catch each other's mistakes. They say, "I heard five mistakes" versus "You made five mistakes." We talked about why we use that phrasing. I don't hide this from kids; I tell them why I use the phrasing I use. We use careful language to make corrections, then we move on.

—Middle level teacher, Woodbury MN

Gather the evidence

To be sure you are correctly describing a student's behavior, take time to observe carefully before speaking with her. Ideally, both you and the student pay particular attention to what's actually happening before you confer, then you will both have evidence for what you say.

Sean was considered an outsider by the time he came to our 6th grade. My team worked with him on some of his habits that seemed to push others away. One October morning he asked to see us during our team meeting. He began by walking over to our Social Contract and slapping the "Respect others" rule saying, "The problem in this school is people *always* disrespect me all the time." The adults saw the problem more as an issue of how he spoke to his classmates, not how they spoke to him. We tried to help him see it our way, and modeled and practiced with him ways to respond to those who were disrespecting him, but because he did not see himself as the problem, he was not interested in changing his ways.

To help him with his perception problem, we asked him to begin recording in a private "Journal of Disrespect" any disrespectful treatment of him through the day. We agreed that each day before he went home, we would check in and take a look at them together. The first day Sean wrote down two items: "Summer told everybody to quiet down in art class," and "My spot was taken at lunch."

We discussed each incident, probing for the disrespectful actions of others. On occasion, we asked the students involved, and most times they cleared it up for him by stating their intentions. When we could not clear them up, we practiced how to respond to a disrespectful action. Each day we noticed fewer and fewer items, and by week's end there were none. Throughout the rest of the quarter, he only occasionally would share an incident with our team. He saw that students mostly were not disrespectful, but may have had a reasonable request for him or may have done something not intending any disrespect.

Collecting the information gave Sean a clearer picture of what was happening, which I could never have coaxed him into seeing without the data. He saw that his classmates did not always disrespect him and actually respected him most of the time. At the end of the quarter, students wrote a reflection on the rules, and Sean's comment about the "Respect others" rule was, "Me and my classmates live by that rule most days."

—Middle level teacher, LaCrosse WI

Don't rescue the rule-breaker!

As tempting as it may be to take over a social conference, we must make sure that the student remains responsible for part of the problem-solving. If we do all the work for him—name the problem, present all the possible fixes we can think of, choose the one that we think will work best, and tell him how and when we'll monitor his progress —we've taken all the responsibility from him. If we do this, he has had no input, hasn't had to think, and remains too passive, possibly drowning in a sea of our words and ideas. We haven't helped him to grow; we've taken away his chance to grow in this situation.

Don't talk on and on!

With adolescents, brevity works best. Curb the tendency to lecture, and avoid the student's glazed pretense of attention we all have experienced. After more than three sentences in a row, we've probably lost them! (See reflection story on page 204.)

The Work before the Work: Examining the Root Causes of Misbehavior

Before the conference begins, think about the pattern of the misbehavior, the circumstances that tend to surround it, the character, personality, and possible motivations and needs of the student, and how much effort he typically puts into correcting his mistakes. Sometimes we do a quick conference in the moment when we see that our redirections aren't working with a student, and on the spot we have to use whatever we know about her. However, the conversation is more likely to lead to behavioral improvement if we have some ideas in mind about what's going on. When you see a student beginning to repeatedly break rules, reflect on that student's behavior—the possible causes and potential solutions—so you have some ideas about the direction you'd like to take if and when you need to confer.

Watch students carefully

Thinking about the root causes of misbehavior can be difficult, but there are some standard avenues to explore. They all have to do with figuring out what the student is really up to, what needs are causing him or her to consistently grab onto a counterproductive way of behaving. We want students not only to change their behavior, but also to strengthen their capacity to meet their needs in a socially-skilled way.

What characterizes the misbehavior? What needs are not being met?

By watching the misbehavior, we may perceive that the student may be trying to meet some need by not cooperating. Most rule-breaking behaviors are meant to meet needs, even though from a mature point of view they are ill-fated. By figuring out what need a behavior is aimed at meeting, you may be able to offer solutions in the problem-solving conference that help the student meet that need in appropriate, positive ways.

- If the student is clowning, blurting out, or showing off in general, she may be trying to meet her need for relationship.
- If the student is contrary, defiant, stubborn, and argumentative, he may be trying to meet his need for autonomy. He may want more choices, and might welcome constructive opportunities for leadership.
- If the student does mean things, tries to get even for perceived inju-

ries, and seems to feel sorry for herself, she may be longing to feel more competent and to learn how to better manage her relationships. She may need to be listened to, to have her feelings acknowledged, and to get some help in being more successful socially and academically.

- If the student fools around, jokes, and makes fun of people to get a laugh, he may be longing for opportunities to laugh and play. He might need cooperative games in class, or more fun learning through the arts, or chances just to move around.

- If a student avoids tasks, is discouraged and unmotivated, and gives up easily, perhaps he doubts his competence. He might respond positively to assignments that match his skill level better, and to acknowledgments for the work he does well. He might feel better about school if he were encouraged to set small, incremental goals, and could experience more success.

On the other hand, if a student is off task, she may be under-challenged and hungry for growth. Here again, the need is to match the learning to the learner. See page 124 for more about differentiation to address varying cognitive development and learning styles among students.

See the Appendix F for more about addressing each of the four basic adolescent social-emotional needs (relationship, competence, autonomy, and fun) through conferencing.

How does the student handle redirections?

We can learn a lot about a student by watching his response to our redirections. Knowing his patterns may help us coach him in changing his behavior when he's been corrected.

- Watch his reaction when we redirect him.

How does he take it? What's his initial reaction to getting caught? Can he control his impulse to protest and to express exasperation? Does he appear truly puzzled about why he's being redirected? If he shows exasperation, does it appear to be directed toward himself? Toward another student? Toward me?

Perhaps he perceives any redirect as punishment: shameful, embarrassing, or hurtful. A conversation with him to make clear the non-punitive, transparent intention of our approach may help reassure him. Perhaps he's simply not used to the higher level of scrutiny and integrity of our approach, and usually gets away with his negative behavior. In that case, he needs to hear again his teacher's commitment to uphold the Social Contract at all times and with everyone.

The student may need several quick conversations over a few days or weeks before he really understands what being accountable will feel like for him. If after observing a student during the redirecting process you determine that he's choosing to not cooperate, you can use that information to focus on why—what is the fundamental problem? Go back to the basic needs and the mistaken ways students may try to meet them.

If the student readily accepts redirection, but then persists in breaking the same rules, perhaps her behavior results from lack of clarity about the protocols of the classroom; then she needs a quick tutorial, so she becomes clear about the expectations and has a chance to practice.

- Watch as he works on shifting his behavior, for example in Take a Break.

Does he sit still? Does he appear to be making an effort to center himself? Does he appear to be thinking? Does he appear to be trying to sort things out in his head? How long does he take to get himself back on track?

- Watch as he rejoins the group

When he returns to the regular flow of the classroom, does he get back to work, or does he look around and make off-task eye contact with his buddies, or does he shut down and refuse to do anything? Most important, does he put effort into following the rules, at least for a while? If he's been redirected for talking to a neighbor during quiet independent work time, does he work quietly or does he return to his chat?

Get outside help if you need it

Perhaps there's a physical reason why a student is nonresponsive: maybe he has an undetected hearing loss, or needs glasses but doesn't wear them, which causes him to frequently ask a neighbor to read the board to him. If he doesn't get it—if it's a cognitive issue—or if she can't control herself (if, for example, she suffers from depression or emotional behavioral disorder), a conversation with her may begin to reveal the problem, and can help you lead the student to the help she'll need outside your classroom.

Our skills for understanding the thinking and feeling of our students—especially their underlying causes—have limitations. We may confer with counselors, social workers, and psychologists, or refer our students when appropriate, and we should not hesitate to do so.

We hope to contribute substantially to students' well-being and success by using our power of observation. Contact with families can be a big help in guiding students towards good choices. A mindset of belief in all students' capacity to grow and in the urgency of supporting their growth propels you to guide rule-breakers towards responsibility; your keen awareness and observation help guide you.

Challenges of Problem-solving Social Conferences

Q. *How do I know if a conference is right for a student?*

Before deciding whether it's necessary to talk things over with a student, you may wish to try a variety of redirects, looking for one that seems to work best for the student. Ask yourself, "Is this redirection working? If not, is there another redirection that may work better, or do I need to do the redirection differently?" For example, some students do better with subtle, quiet, or nonverbal cues that allow them to be in control and minimize their peers' awareness of their being redirected. Others may need a more explicit naming of the unacceptable behavior in order to get into action to change it.

Still others do best if they receive a redirect that requires them to move to another part of the room, take a new seat away from the action, and problem-solve there. And some may need to leave the room altogether and get back on track. See page 183 for more about choosing the right redirection.

When you feel your redirections are right and you're still not getting the needed change, a conference with the student might tell you what's wrong, so the two of you can begin to turn things around.

Q. *It's hard to talk with students who are highly resistant. How do I break through so a productive conversation is possible?*

One of the most important steps to take to earn a student's endorsement of anything you're trying to get her to do is to *be in relationship* with her. Consider the strength of your connection with the student who is struggling; reflect on your relationship:

- Do I greet her at the door by name when she arrives? Does she greet me?
- In general, are we pleasant toward one another?
- How much do I know about her?
- What beliefs have I formed about her?
- Am I able to see her as objectively as possible, including her strengths, or has her seeming inability to behave right caused an imbalance in my opinion of her?
- Does she know what I know about her? Have I discussed with her some of what I know about her? If, for example, I know she plays soccer, does she know I know that? Have I expressed interest in her interests?
- Do I acknowledge her strengths as well as responding to her negative behavior?
- Have we discussed the problem?

Before a conversation about her behavior, perhaps shoring up the relationship will help. Invite her to lunch with you. Chat about her interests outside of school. Go to one of her games.

At the conference, restate your goals and responsibilities regarding student behavior. Ask her to say what she remembers her job to be. Let her know you realize following the rules isn't always easy, but you'll never give up on her or the rules. If you feel that a deeper conversation is needed, be prepared to talk about your relationship, and to take some responsibility for working to improve it.

See pages 51 and 234-235 for more about how to assess student relationships on an ongoing basis, before things go wrong.

Q. *What if the student refuses to acknowledge the problem?*

The rest of the meeting is not likely to be productive unless you are able to help the student take responsibility for his actions. If the student rejects responsibility, you could adjourn the meeting, and tell him you're willing to try again soon.

We'll stop now, and go back to class. I'll observe carefully, and I invite you to do the same. We'll meet again tomorrow with any evidence we each have gathered.

Sometimes this clears up the problem; at least it usually provides a starting place for an honest discussion. If it doesn't accomplish that, give him some time to think.

Take a moment and think about the situation. It's clear to me we have a problem, and I'm also sure we can solve it. I'll be right back.

Move ahead with the process, but appeal to his need for power. If after more time to think he still refuses to accept responsibility, tell him that the behavior must stop.

Al, part of my job is to protect the Social Contract, and you're breaking our rules frequently, so you'll have to change. Do you understand that? If you refuse to work with me on this—if you continue to leave your seat to talk to your friends instead of learning—I'll have to put limitations on you. If that happens, you'll lose some freedom and control over your school life. Think about it.

Then walk away. Give him more time, then try once more—he may come around. You might ask him to describe what's happening from his perspective. You can appeal to his desire to be a competent person: mention that admitting mistakes is the first step to getting good at something.

There's no reason why you can't be successful when it comes to staying in your seat during class. A good place to start is seeing the problem.

Q. *What if the student wants to include a solution that I think is problematic?*

Only solutions that fit within the Social Contract and that you judge to be productive for him are allowed on the list. Both you and the student have to agree on the final choice, and it's your job to steer him toward good possibilities for the list.

Owen, I think at this point that solution wouldn't work for you. Let's only include solutions that you have more experience with.

If the student is invested in adding an idea that is workable but not the best, allow it. If he's motivated enough, he might succeed with his plan.

Q. *What if the student is agreeable to our plan during the conference but doesn't follow through when she returns to class?*

With a good relationship with the student, the successful implementation of most problem-solving conferences will hinge upon the actions you take. Reinforce her success when she successfully implements the plan and redirect her when she slips, so you express your level of commitment to her and to the plan that emerged from the conference. Following your plan for checking in also shows your commitment, as does providing both proactive and reactive assistance to the student as she struggles to change the behavior. If necessary, schedule another conference to reinforce what's working and redirect what isn't.

Keep motivation high by noticing and commenting on successes. If a student conferences with you about her inconsistent completion of homework, notice when she successfully gets it in, and discreetly let her know that you noticed.

Elena, I saw you put your homework in the homework box a few minutes ago, and it looks complete. You're on your way to fixing your habit. Keep it up!

Keeping the tone positive and maintaining the relationship adds integrity to redirects when we need to use them.

Q. *How can I find the time to conference in the busy flow of my class hours?*

You may find that by laying the groundwork for student routines, you have more time for a quick conference. Much class time is used for correction of behaviors that a clear routine can obviate.

Because I use modeling and remodeling at the beginning of the year to establish procedures, I am freed from having to be constantly in motion in front of the class keeping everything together. My students get to the point where they can function well without me—they know our procedures and can do them effectively. If I have a situation in class where I need to have a short conference, I can step out of the room to do that.

—Middle level teacher, LaCrosse WI

You get better results conferencing with adolescents if you keep them brief and avoid lectures. You need a quick exchange in which you and the student come to an understanding and create a plan for success. It takes more time to lecture a student on his behavior than to describe it briefly and plan for a change!

Story for Reflection: Brevity

This is a story to help us keep in mind the value of brevity. It could also encourage students' confidence in their teacher if it were told as a promise to try to guide behavior without long lectures.

It was a warm day in early spring. A boy walking by the bank of a river could not resist the temptation to remove his clothes and plunge in for the first swim of the year. But the water proved to be much colder and deeper than it had appeared from the shore. The boy was on the point of sinking when he caught sight of a wayfarer strolling along the shore.

"Help! Help!" screamed the boy. "I'm drowning! Save me!"

Instead of plunging in at once to the lad's rescue, the traveler called out: "You foolish young man, don't you realize that this is not the season to go swimming? What would your mother say if she knew you were in the river at this time of the year? I have a good mind to report this matter to the authorities. Whatever were you thinking of...."

"Oh, save me now, sir," interrupted the struggling boy, "and give me the lecture afterward!"

— Aesop, "The Boy Bathing," *Aesop's Fables*

PROBLEM-SOLVING MEETINGS

In my homeroom, conflicts are seen as opportunities to deepen relationships, increase social skills, and engage in cognitive rigor. To make these moments successful, I rely on our group agreements and the consensus process, both of which we model and practice. For example, when the students have problems at recess, I use a quick problem-solving meeting to clear the air.

Teacher: *We need to have a quick problem-solving meeting about following our Social Contract when you are at recess today. Can someone remind the group of our school agreements?*

Student: *Respect yourself, others, and property. Be positive and have fun.*

T: *OK, so this week many of you have been having a tough time at recess. I need two of you to tell me what you think the problem is.*

S1: *When we're at recess we tend to stop following our rules.*

S2: *We sometimes get mad at someone, and then it comes out when we're outside.*

I then ask a student to paraphrase what their classmates have said.

T: *If people are bringing hurt feelings outside to recess, then we need strategies to use while we're outside to lessen the hurt feelings and follow our agreements. Who can suggest a strategy that we can use to help us during recess time?*

S3: *We can talk it out one-to-one.*

S4: *We could try not to take things so hard when someone disses us.*

T: *Let's decide if you are willing to use those strategies. I need to see:*

Thumbs up if you fully support the solution

Thumbs sideways if you have a few questions about the solution, but will fully support it

Thumbs down if you do not support the solution and will block it

They agreed to try both of the strategies. At recess that day, students had an opportunity to practice problem-solving their issues as they arose using conflict resolution and trying to shrug things off. The next time we were together I asked them to reflect on their experience.

T: *Did anyone use a strategy that we agreed on?*

S1: *I almost got upset when Jamal fouled me when we were playing basketball, but I didn't take it personally.*

S2: *Emilia and I were almost ready to start at each other, but we decided to walk away from the group and talk privately to work out our issues.*

S3: *Before going outside, I asked Tracy if she wanted to solve an issue before recess.*

T: *Great! So it seems as if you can better handle your conflicts when they come up. That's a skill adults need. Turn to a partner and give him or her a high five and a "Good job!"*

—Middle level teacher, St. Paul MN

Students gather for a quick problem-solving meeting

In addition to having one-to-one conferences with students who are having difficulty problem-solving on their own, there are times when we need to stop the regular flow of learning and problem-solve with the group. Most groups who work together (teams, sections, units, crews, shifts, etc.) gather periodically and trouble-shoot; it's a way to keep the group healthy. Coaches blow their whistles and call a quick, on-the-spot team meeting when they see something they don't like during practice. Orchestral conductors call for a section of musicians to work out a problem as a group, providing any assistance necessary.

Using teachable moments can work, too. Stopping the action when things are breaking down allows students to reflect and problem-solve right after something goes wrong, while it is still fresh. Sometimes problem-solving meetings are held when a problem has become chronic and widespread throughout the group—you can plan ahead for those. When your students are introduced to an on-the-spot huddle, and they practice it, they will know what to do. During a problem-solving meeting, the rule-breakers aren't identified. Everyone in the class is in it together: we share the problem, and we share the responsibility of solving it. You model for all a commitment to actively resolving problems, belief in everyone's capacity for growth, and remaining cool in the face of difficulty.

[T]he problem-solving discussion approach not only teaches them fairness, it also teaches them to consider the alternatives of various issues and situations. (Dreikurs 1998, 85)

The basic process of class problem-solving meetings is very similar to other problem-solving approaches. After calling for everyone's attention and settling students into a meeting circle, the problem is identified; potential solutions are generated; a decision is made about which solution to try; and the selected idea is tested, with everyone involved putting effort into making the solution work.

When to use problem-solving meetings

Here are some scenarios for which neither redirections nor social conferences would likely work well, and a group problem-solving process would be more effective:

- When it's difficult to figure out which student or students are misbehaving: if we can't separate the rule-breakers from the rest, and we have to do something to restore the integrity of our rules and expectations

- When several members of the class are breaking the rules at the same time, for example not following established routines such as the signal for silence in spite of modeling and review, or avoiding their responsibilities when redirected

These moments occur at some point in most classrooms, and there are times when they happen even when we've provided just the right type of assistance before and after rule-breaking. We need a structure to stop the action, gather students together, problem-solve, and get back on track with as little disruption and time lost as possible.

When most or all of my students are messing up a procedure that we've practiced a lot and I expect everyone to know, I stop the action to quickly meet with the whole group and get things going right again. We don't have time to waste, so instead of nagging at them with a speech or punishing the ones I catch, I get everyone together in an organized opportunity to name the problem, acknowledge feelings involved, and work to get everything back on track so we can achieve our goals.

I ask two questions:

What do you need from the community to move through this moment or this crisis?

What do you intend to do to repair the damage done?

The first question gives students a voice, the chance to say how they see things. The second helps us create a plan to set things right. I've actually done these huddles right in the hallway during passing time. I say, "If you know what hall behavior should look like, go to the left. If you need some help getting it right, go to the right." I'm not confrontational: "You're not in trouble. I'm just proactive on the small stuff that goes wrong so we can prevent the big stuff." Then I meet with the ones on the right, we figure out what needs to happen, practice a little, and I expect better performance during the next passing time.

—High school teacher, Harrisburg PA

Steps of a Problem-solving Meeting

Let's say that during work time students are not putting forth enough effort to be successful in the short amount of time remaining in class. Use the signal for silence to get everyone's attention, hold a quick huddle, name the problem, and work to solve it.

I notice many of you are drifting from the task at times; several of you are not putting enough effort into your work. What do we need to keep in mind to get back to behaving according to our Social Contract?

Gather everyone into a tight circle, huddle, or equivalent. Proximity is important. If students must remain at desks or tables, make sure they turn their attention—including their bodies—toward you, and make sure there isn't anyone noticeably more distant from the others. You may wish to call "Circle up!" or "Huddle up!" to mark the initiation of a quick group problem-solving meeting.

1. Identify the problem

State exactly what's happening, stressing the behaviors you are witnessing. Include what you see or hear and what you do not see or hear. Remain neutral. The goal is to bring students to an awareness of the problem, and then to quickly get them to collectively think their way to a solution. Avoid manipulative content, both verbal and nonverbal. Focus on what the behavior is costing the group.

We're doing too much irrelevant conversing as we discuss the chapter in our book groups. This is the place to learn to read for meaning, a skill that can make a big difference in your work in life.

Or, instead of your naming the problem, invite students to do so. Consider creating a "problem-finding book" in which students record issues they see as problems in class. If you see a few mentions of the same problem, you can call a meeting. It's often better to allow students the chance to identify the problem. It helps build relationship, autonomy, and competence: they made the rules, they break them sometimes, and they can identify their mistakes and craft a plan to fix the situation.

I don't have to be the only person in our room who watches for rough spots. If you see a problem we're having, do us all a favor and name it. Here's a notebook I'll leave on the windowsill. If you see that we might benefit from getting together to discuss something that's going wrong, something that's keeping us from achieving our goals for the year, write it down, and we might take up the topic in a problem-solving meeting.

2. Brainstorm solutions

The goal is to figure out why the problem is happening and what might solve it. Take comments without discussion, and write them down quickly.

What's happening? What causes students to get off task during group discussions?

Then brainstorm to come up with some solutions. Take and make suggestions, recording them in a list. You may have a chart posted about the relevant routine(s) and can refer students to them as a source for ideas.

Now that we know the problems, we can come up with some solutions. Who has a suggestion?

3. Select a solution (if a new solution is needed)

Choose one idea to implement. Use the consensus process (see page 74) to ensure that everyone is on board.

We've agreed to use Oliver's plan: when we get going again, if you notice one of your group members is starting to get off task, give her a gentle reminder to help bring her back.

4. Take action

Check for understanding

Make sure everyone is clear about the re-established expectation. Instead of telling them the expectation, ask, "What are we going to do when we get back to work?" When they hear it from one of their own, they're more likely to endorse the idea. Don't ask, "Any questions?" Even if someone isn't clear, chances are he'll keep mum at this point, but interrupt later by asking you or another student for clarification. By having a student remind us what we just agreed to do, everyone gets to listen one more time to our new agreement.

Acknowledge and close

Close the planning process with group acknowledgment of the teamwork. If you've huddled up, clap your hands in unison or ask everyone to put a hand in the center of the huddle and raise them together saying a word like "Teamwork!"

Get back to the work at hand, and continue to monitor all student behavior. When students improve their behavior, acknowledge it to everyone, so it's reinforced.

Take note of the way things are running right now. Everyone's paying attention to whoever is speaking, no one is standing up or moving around, there's only one person talking at a time. Keep it up! I knew we could do it.

Redirect individual students who deviate from the model. Reinforcing, reminding, and redirecting supports all students for success.

Terry, we just revisited our expectations. You still aren't following them. Fix that. Take a break to recenter.

5. Check in

After a few days, think with the students about what is happening in your plan.

We had a problem and we came up with some good ideas by problem-solving. We decided to use Oliver's plan. How are we doing? What worked? What didn't? Should we make any changes to the plan or stick to it as is?

Follow through

The most important part of the process is that you act on the plan to shift the behavior. You bring it up again and check to measure progress. Following through on the solution, and continuing to seek a solution when an attempt doesn't work, are proof that you say what you mean and mean what you say.

Preparing for a Problem-solving Meeting

Notice potential trouble before it becomes serious, and be ready to call a meeting if a negative attitude or issue arises again. You may decide to huddle up on the spot, but you will have given thought to the problem and how you might address it. If possible, give the class notice of your intention:

Tomorrow we're going to take some time in class to get to the bottom of why our book groups are not going very well, and what we can do to make them more successful.

The next day, announce that it's time to huddle up, and have students move furniture to allow for a circle. State the problem and your determination that by the end of this meeting the class will have a plan for helping everyone stay focused during book discussions.

You all have goals for doing well in reading this year, but many of you are not using book group time productively. Working together helps everyone think more deeply about the ideas in a book. Show with a thumb up that you're willing to work to follow our book group protocol, sideways if you have serious questions but will go along with it, and thumb down if you cannot agree to this.

If there is or are thumb(s) down, say that those people are surrendering a privilege, a chance to forward their own lives.

Those who aren't willing to fix a problem are either stuck with it or have to accept the solutions others come up with. If you don't work on problems in life, you lose your power to control things. Now I'll ask again, who's willing to try to fix this?

Focus the first problem-solving meeting on something enjoyable

It is effective, if possible, to call your first meeting of the class to plan something that everyone will enjoy. That way they get the experience of setting up and participating in a whole-group circle meeting before having to use it to address a problem. For example, meet to discuss things that *might* go wrong on a fieldtrip.

Our first problem-solving meeting is focused on things that might go wrong when we visit the Science Museum on Friday to see the planetarium show. I know you are looking forward to going. Let's meet in the last 15 minutes of today's class to discuss how we can head off potential problems and get the most out of the day.

Challenges of Problem-solving Meetings

Q. *It takes too long for students to get their groups organized, and so much time is wasted that they don't finish their work. Would a problem-solving meeting be a good way to address this?*

It might, but first consider the possibility that part of the problem might be that you haven't adequately prepared them for the learning process. Before you decide to call a meeting, ask yourself:

- Have I adequately modeled for students the behavioral expectations?
- Did I give them a chance to practice and then reflect on the practice?
- Did I write up guidelines for how the process should look, sound, and feel for them to refer to each day?
- Have I consistently and fairly redirected individual students whenever they failed to meet the expectations?
- What have I done to build and maintain relationships with and among my students so they can work well together?

If you think you can do a better job preparing them for success, set your improvements in motion before you call a meeting. If you've done most or all of these things to create the optimal chance for procedures to be followed and still students are stumbling, then call a meeting to talk about what you can do as a class to improve the process.

Q. *A clique of students gossip and exclude. Should I gather them together and do a problem-solving meeting?*

Problem-solving meetings for a set of rule-breakers usually aren't effective, as opposed to a class-wide issue. If they refuse to accept responsibility, they have the strength of their numbers to blame someone who is not present, or to support a claim that the meeting is inappropriate, invalid, and/or unnecessary. Instead, meet with individuals, one at a time, in problem-solving social conferences to begin chipping away at the problem.

Q. *What if my class starts talking about a problem, but we don't have time to brainstorm solutions and pick one?*

Splitting the conversation into two parts can be very effective. The first day you name the problem, talk about what it costs people, and ask students to think about how to solve it. The next day you brainstorm plans to improve, and decide to move ahead on one or more of the plans. Several days later, check in to assess how things are going. Have a concrete way to keep track of the efficacy of your solution – for example, you could tally the number of times in a week the class employed the plan to successfully change the pattern of behavior. Whatever the behavior is that you're trying to change, you can keep track of the wins or the losses or both, and celebrate when things start to significantly improve.

ROLE PLAY

After I introduced them to the role-play format, students in my homeroom would sometimes request that we do role plays as a way to help them problem-solve potential sticky situations or dilemmas. In one instance, students expressed frustration in dealing with what they felt was disrespect from a teacher. We spent a few minutes problem-solving, using a role play.

Teacher: *Before you leave for science, let's consider how you can respond to any adult if you think he or she is dissing you, and still stay true to our rule of respecting others. Let's say that I'm a student and the teacher gave me a direction that I thought was too blunt and disrespectful. I'll play the student, and we need a student to play the teacher. The teacher will give me a direction in a short and stern way. Let's clap hands to signify action.*

Student (playing the role of the teacher): *Hurry up, Ross, I need you to stop playing around and do your work. Working and finishing your project is your job, so do it!*

T: *Look at my expression on my face. How do you think I'm feeling after her comments?*

S1: *Angry and embarrassed.*

S2: *Frustrated, dissed, and wanting to snap back.*

T: *But I can't snap back or I'll get in trouble, so how can I respond to her in a respectful way even though I'm feeling angry, embarrassed, frustrated, and dissed? I need a few suggestions.*

S3: *You can just do what the teacher asked and not sweat it. Or if you get too mad you can take a break before you do or say something stupid.*

S4: *Take a few deep breaths, finish your work, and find a good time to ask the teacher if she can talk to you in private.*

T: *Let's rewind the role play and I'll try one of your suggestions.*

We chose one of their suggestions, and a student switched roles with me to try it out. After the role play, they went to their next class with a few alternatives in mind to help them succeed in the class. The next day we talked briefly about what happened.

T: *By a show of hands, how many of you were able to use the strategies we came up with yesterday? Jamal, what did you do?*

Jamal: *When the teacher started to talk to me, I didn't get mad, even though I thought her directions were stupid. I just nodded and finished doing my work.*

S2: *When she told me to get on task and do my work, I took her directions, but after class I told her that I was not playing around, only asking Michelle for a pencil.*

T: *It seems that you are learning some new skills about how to manage your relationships with adults even though you might want to snap. Great! On a scale of 1-10, 10 being the most, how often do you think you'll use these strategies with adults this week? [Show of fingers] I believe you are ready to meet the challenge!*

—Middle level teacher, St. Paul MN

Adolescents and young adults struggle with impulse control, risk-taking, and making thoughtful decisions. Many tend to live in the moment, using an "act now, think later" approach to the daily choices with which they are confronted. Brain research has revealed that teens' amygdales (a middle area of the brain) are extremely active, creating craving for excitement, newness, adventure, risk—all the elements that get adolescents into trouble. At the same time, the pre-frontal lobes, the source of judgment and reasoning, are still forming, and are far less efficient and active. In other words, the adolescent is all action and little judgment, not an auspicious combination for prudent behavior. (Weinberger et al. 2005)

Role play helps young people figure out and somewhat experience in advance how to handle social dilemmas so they get at least some of what they want but avoid breaking rules. Learning the habit of "stop and think" in school could make all the difference when a teen is faced with a decision that could lead to trouble and danger. In the process of thinking, discussing, and selecting a morally justifiable, positive, reasonably satisfying course of action, they learn how to get some satisfaction safely and fairly.

When to use role play

Earlier in this book, you encountered role play in our discussion of modeling as a tool for helping students handle the "what ifs" of classroom routines. "What if you forget something, go back to your locker, and get to class late?" Students can dramatize the problem, and the concreteness of the drama helps them visualize themselves working out potential solutions. Role plays can also be very effective in addressing the social dilemmas that arise in the classroom. For example, students are excluding someone:

Let's say Margaret wants to work with your group, but you have enough people already and don't want more. How can the group and Margaret handle this situation fairly? Let's role play it.

Take care to match the topic to the climate of your classroom. Take on topics as you think students are ready for them. After a while, the students may begin suggesting topics of their own. With your guidance regarding appropriateness, they can examine issues important to them in and outside of school. Here are some dilemmas that would make good role-play topics to explore in the classroom:

- Getting help when you need it
- Ignoring distractions
- Staying on task even when you're not interested in the subject or topic
- Responding to a mistake or a failure
- Noticing and commenting on the work of others
- Being honest when you've made a mistake
- Refusing to side-talk when someone talks to you
- Working with a substitute teacher
- Remaining quiet during transitions
- Helping a student who is being bullied

Role play can be used during a problem-solving meeting to help students think about how a solution might work, or in a social conference to get the feel of the newly adopted behavior, or as an advisory activity to address a social issue outside of school. These quick dramatizations help students picture themselves making good choices.

Preparing for a Role Play

Your objective is to teach students how to stop and think before acting, so they can make good choices. Begin by describing a scenario, stopping just before the point when one of the actors will have to make a decision about what to do next. Don't embellish the story with unnecessary details. The first few times you use role play, you may want to write the scenario and read it to the class.

Establish your goal

Remember where you're going with the drama. In the example below, we want to equip students with the skill to respectfully accept or decline a request from a student to join already established working partners.

Recruit students to act out the role play

Initially, you'll play the role of the person who must decide what to do. Role plays typically require two or three actors, so you'll need student actors as well. Some teachers choose as actors students they know they can depend upon to do a good job, but others use the role play as an opportunity to have those who have the *most* difficulty in the kind of situation being examined, so that they can learn as directly as possible, under the direction of the teacher and with the advice of their classmates, some ways to handle sticky situations with social grace. In either case, actors need to play out the scenario as planned, and then act out a solution suggested by the audience. Once you have the actor(s), explain the scenario and tell them how you want them to act it. Tell them precisely where you'll stop (cut) the action. This whole set-up should take only a couple of minutes.

Steps of Role Play (with example)

1. Identify the problem (Scenario)

You want to work with a friend on a History Day project, but another classmate asks if she can join you. How can you respond in a way that stays true to our rule that we treat each other kindly and still get to work on your project the way you want to?

Let's say Megan and Delores have already begun to plan their project, and Katherine asks to join them. I'll take Megan's role, and I need two volunteers to play Delores and Katherine.

Identify the problem (Action)

Clap hands and/or use words or another sound to signify that you are beginning the role play, e.g., "Action!" Act out the scene and stop *at the moment* after Katherine asks to join, before she gets an answer. Show on the faces of the other two girls that they are reluctant to let Katherine join them.

2. Brainstorm solutions (Cut)

Stop the action *before any negative behavior is shown*. Ask the class to think about what Megan and Delores might do and say in response to Katherine's request. Possible responses:

- *Say no, politely.*
- *Ask her if she's willing to go along with their choice of topic and the plan so far.*
- *Tell her that you've already decided some things, but she could help with the remaining decisions.*

3. Select the solution

In a quick conference among players, a solution is chosen.

4. Take action

"Rewind" and act out the scene again, this time adding the solution chosen for solving the dilemma.

5. Check in

Reflect on the effectiveness and rightness of the solution, and then act out some of the other solutions if there's time.

Challenges of Role Play

Q. *Can I use role play quickly, to address a problem on the spot?*

Yes. When you become comfortable with the technique, you can stop and work things out through a quick role play. In your content area, you can increase engagement and extend understanding by having students role play, for example, what might have happened if a historical figure had made a different decision, or create a scene between two characters from two different stories.

Q. *I'm an advisory teacher. Would role plays be a good way for me to help kids handle some of the social issues they deal with outside of school?*

Definitely. There are many social situations that present dilemmas for adolescents. Role playing to the moment of decision, then brainstorming what to do to balance needs and desires with concerns for safety, well-being, and fairness is a good way to solve problems and instill the life-long habit of stopping and thinking. Role playing these situations in advisory with peers helps students develop respectful habits and prudent decision-making.

Example topics

- How to say 'no' to someone without hurting their feelings
- How to say 'no' to a friend who wants you do something bad: smoke, drink, cheat, steal, etc.
- How to say 'no' to unwelcome friendship advances

- How to say 'yes' to someone who asks you to do something you know would be very worthwhile when you really don't want to
- How to ask someone you don't know well to do something with you
- How to go out of your way to make sure a new student feels welcome
- What to do when a friend says something racist, sexist, homophobic, xenophobic, etc.
- What to do when you hear gossip
- What to do when you learn that something bad is going on around your school or community
- What to do when you find someone else's valuables
- What to do when the easiest path to assignment completion involves plagiarism

Keep role plays short, to the point, and positive, and emphasize the problem-solving part. Someday the capacity to stop and think, learned through role plays in a middle grades classroom, could save someone's life!

A sixth grader complained to a classmate that he didn't think the grade he got on a paper was fair. "Don't complain to me," his friend responded. "Don't you remember how we worked that out in a role play last week? Ask the teacher to explain why she gave you that grade, and how you could make it better."

Q. *Why do I have to stop before the negative behavior is shown? Kids are interested in seeing their teachers breaking rules.*

We're trying to create a memory of the way to best behave, not a vivid (and probably more entertaining) picture of poor choices. After a role play with the teacher acting out negative behavior, students will be more likely to remember how the teacher broke the rules than the lessons of the role play.

STUDENT CONFLICT RESOLUTION

It was independent work time in social studies, and I was moving from table to table assessing student work and answering questions. When I got to Zach, he asked if he could talk with me privately about a problem. We took chairs to the front of the classroom where I normally conferred with students.

It's about another student, he said

Have you talked with the person you're having problems with yet? I asked.

No, I wanted to talk with you about it first.

OK, tell me about it.

Erin said some mean things about me being a Jew, and I got really mad. She can't say those things about Jews—that's attacking me and my dad and my whole family, Zach said.

If Erin did that she isn't following our class rules about respect, I replied. *Are you still upset? Are you calm enough to do a HELPS OUT?*

I'm ready for the HELPS OUT.

(HELPS OUT is the acronym for our conflict resolution process. Students are able to use the process largely without adult help because it has been practiced and, for many, instituted in kindergarten.)

Zach approached Erin, tapped her on the shoulder, and said quietly, "I need a HELPS OUT about what you said at lunch." Erin got up and followed Zach to the bench right outside the classroom door. Both students were familiar with the conflict-resolution process; they'd been using it in our school for 3 years. I noted the time and continued my rounds with my students.

I kept my eye on them as I worked with students on their small-group assignments. Everything seemed calm. About eight minutes later, Erin and Zach shook hands and walked back to their work areas.

— 7th and 8th grade teacher, Minneapolis MN

When a conflict arises between two students, they need a structure to guide them step by step to resolution. Face-to-face, nonjudgmental, structured meetings for two students, moderated if necessary by a teacher or other skilled adult, provide adolescents with a safe format for win-win problem-solving.

Like problem-solving meetings or conferences, the conflict-resolution process is all about relationship-building and respectful steps for sorting things out so everyone can get her or his needs met and learn self-management at the same time. The basic process is the same as for our other problem-solving structures: identify the problem, think up ways to fix it, make a decision, carry it out, and check in later to see how things are going.

Stick to the structure and steer away from, not back towards, the hurt and anger that occasioned the meeting in the first place. Before the process of resolution begins, the students involved take time to calm down. Trying to settle a difference in the heat of emotion will not work. They may even need to wait a day or two.

An adult guides the process until students learn it well and can implement it successfully on their own. Much depends on whether they both want to resolve the conflict. The adult can help them assess that, and proceed accordingly, ready to intervene should tempers flare.

Are you ready to talk quietly about this problem? Let's go over here—it's quiet and private.

Steps of Conflict Resolution

Here are the same five steps for problem-solving, applied to a conversation between two aggrieved parties. Students with conflict are gathered together and calm, along with their teacher to offer help as needed.

1. Identify the problem

Each person takes a turn to tell the story from his point of view, talking about how he feels without blaming the other person.

Teacher: *Mario, let's begin with you.*

Mario: *I was messing around with Devon at lunch. I grabbed his bag of chips and sort of swung it away from him, just to bug him, and when I swung back, I accidentally knocked into John's lunch tray, and his food went flying. Then he got mad at me and started calling me an idiot, swearing, and said he was going to get me back.*

Teacher: *John, you've listened quietly. Now it's your turn to tell the story.*

John: *I was minding my business, heading to my spot at the lunch table, and all of a sudden, wham! My food was all over my clothes and the floor. I looked around, and there's Mario, with his arm right in my space, and he's looking at me, and then he started laughing! That's when I lost it and yelled at him.*

Listen to each other

As each person talks, the other listens without interrupting to correct or complain. In some versions of the process, the listener is asked to paraphrase what he heard to ensure careful listening and to give the speaker the satisfaction of feeling heard.

2. Brainstorm solutions

The students try to come up with something that will give each of them some of the satisfaction he wants, but is balanced with what the other needs and wants.

Teacher: *We're ready for some ideas now. Who has a suggestion? What do you need to settle this?*

Mario: *I need John to understand that it was an accident. I didn't mess up his lunch like that on purpose. It was an accident, man. You need to chill out when it's an accident.*

John: *I need an apology—with no laughing—and I need a clean shirt: I got soup all over my jersey. You need to clean my shirt. And if you hadn't laughed, I wouldn't have lost it. So you need to check yourself.*

3. Select a solution

The students make an agreement they both can live with.

Teacher: *What is each of you willing to do in the future?*

Mario: *If I ever do something that makes you mad again, I'll take it seriously and not laugh it off. I can see how that would bug you.*

John: *And I'll try to stay calmer and not blow up when I know it's an accident and you didn't do it on purpose.*

They shake on the deal.

4. Take action

The parties agree to check back with their teacher in a week to see if things are harmonious between them, and to discuss any issues that might have resurfaced. The evidence of the effectiveness of a conflict-resolution process is what happens afterward. Do the adversaries carry the grudge forward? Do they work and play together harmoniously? If a similar situation arises, do they use the behaviors they agreed to? The teacher keeps an eye on them to see if more problem-solving is necessary.

5. Check in

The check-in is the safety net under the conflict-resolution process. The parties return at a prearranged time to report to their teacher whether more incidents like the one they processed have occurred, and whether they are getting along well.

There are other conflict-resolution formats that include some extra steps that are very useful, such as Paraphrase, State Your Needs, Own Your Responsibility for the Problem, and Thank the Person, but the basics are covered in our five-step process. If you want more detail, there are many conflict resolution resources available.

When students are willing to use the conflict-resolution process, things almost always improve between them. Even if they're still somewhat angry or suspicious after the talk, they have heard the other side, and it dilutes their resentment so healing can occur more quickly. Learning a conflict-resolution process and using it often enough to make it familiar creates a valuable life-long skill.

Introducing the conflict-resolution process to students

The best way to introduce conflict resolution to students is to do a sample one, noting the steps beforehand, afterward, and/or as you go. The process is best taught in an advisory setting where there is time to both model and discuss it. An ideal project for an advisory might be to carry the process further and train students to become peer mediators, who help others in disagreement come to a win-win solution. Mediators may be able to help in classroom situations by stepping to the side or into the hall with the disputants and guiding them to a resolution. Mediation skills, and conflict resolution experience in general, are valuable life skills. They not only provide a way to handle troubling peer problems with a five-to-ten-minute conversation during class, but they push young people in general to de-escalate and look for positive solutions in any disagreements.

Challenges of Conflict Resolution

Q. *What if the students can't come to an agreement about how to fix the conflict?*

Perhaps a mediator can help. The adult may see a potential fix that the disputants, because of their anger and hurt, or because of sheer habit, cannot.

The parties may need a longer cooling-off time. If that doesn't help, they might remain alienated, at least for now. The talking may at least have averted a physical fight. If entrenched resentments are involved, such as in gang disputes, a quick conflict resolution process in a classroom is not going to do the job.

Q. *This process takes time I don't have. I can't just stop teaching and mediate a dispute, and I could spend every prep and lunch time helping kids deal with their issues. Does there have to be an adult mediator there every time?*

Many schools that have a comprehensive conflict-resolution program train students to be skillful mediators. These youngsters not only serve their peers in this important way, but they themselves internalize a life-long skill of helping people move from discord to understanding and satisfaction.

ACT OF APOLOGY

An act of apology is a student-initiated and -managed form of problem-solving. Sometimes it is used when "I'm sorry" does not feel like enough of an apology to a person who has been hurt, or even to the person who did the wrong. Sometimes it is used when the first attempt at apologizing verbally wasn't done sincerely and the person wants to make it up. At these times, action to demonstrate the regret you feel can speak louder and more convincingly than words. When an apology is made by means of a sincere act, relationships are strengthened, lingering resentments are mitigated, and often the whole community benefits.

To support the act of apology process, students proactively brainstorm a list of actions someone could take to fix damage to a relationship caused by misbehavior. The list of actions is kept on hand throughout the school year for use when words of apology do not suffice. Similar to the conflict-resolution model, a person who causes damage is empowered to decide what she will do to repair her mistake and the relationship(s) she has harmed. Even in cases where both parties involved have caused harm, acts of apology may be used by each to repair the damage they have done.

We were playing a game during CPR, when a girl felt that the boys were unfairly favoring boys. She blew up. I told her to use Take a Break Out and Back. When she returned, we had a short social conference, and the student chose as an act of apology to address the class. During the afternoon, we took a few minutes for her to do so. She spoke to the class with sincerity about exactly how she had violated the Social Contract. She apologized and finished on a positive note. With this voluntary action, she strengthened the integrity of the classroom community. Most students responded with acknowledgment and encouragement, demonstrating growing mutual respect and social responsibility.

—Middle level teacher, LaCrosse WI

Steps of Act of Apology

1. Identify the problem

When a conflict arises for which a verbal apology is insufficient, the person who wants to sincerely apologize approaches the person he or she has hurt, admits the wrongdoing, and offers to make an act of apology.

2. Brainstorm solutions

The offender can make up a suggestion or ask the hurt person what she would like, and/or they can refer to the list the class has already brainstormed for ideas (see below for more about creating this list).

3. Select a solution

In a successful act of apology process, the rule-breaker is empowered to decide what she will do to fix the problem, and the student hurt by the rule-breaker's behavior has a say in the matter, too. The offender (Jan) may choose a solution and make an offer:

Ormay, I am sorry, and I understand that an apology isn't enough. Will it make it right if I make a card for you?

Ormay may accept or refuse the offer. If she accepts, Jan makes the card and presents it to Ormay in the near future. If Ormay declines the offer, Jan makes another offer:

How about if I bake you a cake? I really am sorry.

Ormay decides whether she will accept a cake as a sign that Jan wants to repair the relationship. If she declines again, Jan moves to her next idea.

Options for closure

There is a potential catch in the process: if Ormay continues to reject Jan's offers, Jan will run out of ideas, and the possibility of success is undermined. In these cases, here are some possibilities for closure:

- Your group may decide to create a rule that makes accepting one from a list of three mandatory. The student who has been harmed must accept one of the offers.

- The offender could invite the hurt person to look over the list and make her own choice.

- If the injured party is unwilling to accept any of the offers, the perpetrator will have to simply give a verbal apology and leave it at that.

It's one of the unhappy facts of life that we may not always be able to fix an injury we have inflicted on someone else, at least not until a longer time passes. These possibilities make for rich conversations with students. If you process the possibilities with them, their capacity to take on the perspective of another may grow, a valuable life skill for resolving conflicts.

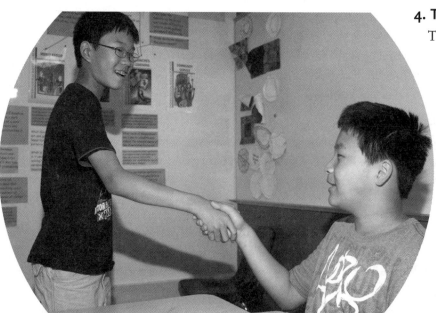

4. Take action

The apologizing student completes the apology by taking the action agreed upon by both parties.

5. Check in

The two parties check with each other within a day or two that things are OK between them now. Sometimes this happens with smiles; sometimes it is verbalized. But the most important measure of the result is the quality of their relationship afterwards. There may be some lingering cautiousness, but if the act of apology has worked, their relationship is recovering. Teachers may observe how things seem to be going between the two parties, but basically the act of apology process is a private matter, and succeeds because the young people can own it and use it autonomously.

Introducing Act of Apology

Connect to personal experience

To introduce making an act of apology in advisory or class hours, the group first talks about ways a person could try to make it up to someone he or she has hurt.

Gather the group in a circle. Ask the students to recall a time when they witnessed a dispute, and although one person ultimately said, sincerely, "I'm sorry," it didn't feel like enough to right the wrong, and have them share their stories. You may offer an example, or invite students to pair up and share a story about a time like this. One or two may share their stories with the larger group.

Explain the system

Explain that you want to have a system in place for them to use whenever they need to make an apology with their actions as well as their words.

Brainstorm ideas

Have a student scribe on chart paper as people share their ideas about actions that might help them feel better when they are hurt or angry.

What are some things we can do to show someone that we are truly sorry for something we've done, and want to make it right? We can add to the list as the year goes on.

Sample student answers:

- Bake a cake or cookies
- Walk home together or sit together at lunch
- Clean her locker
- Organize his backpack
- Shoot baskets together
- Write a sincere letter or card of apology
- Work on homework together
- Make an original work of art—a drawing, painting, poem, etc
- Fix, replace, or pay for repair of ruined items
- Call the student's mother, explain what happened, and apologize to her

Check for clarity

After explaining how the process works and perhaps doing a role play, check to be sure the students understand how to make an act of apology.

Are we clear? Who can summarize for us how making an act of apology is going to work? What are some ways that apologies can be offered and accepted?

Follow up

After the list has been posted for a while, ask students to assess the amount it's being used and its effectiveness:

What's working? What's not? How often are we using it? What should we do to keep it going? What changes might we make to improve its use? Does anyone have a new idea we could add to our list?

Acts of apology will be made more often if you actively promote its use at first. If a student is sent out to Take a Break in another room and she returns with a reflection form that calls for an apology, you could suggest an act of apology. During a conflict-resolution meeting, if a student agrees to apologize verbally and you feel an act of apology might be more appropriate, bring up the possibility. You'll know it's working when students head to the list without your involvement.

Challenges of an Act of Apology

Q. *What if a student wants to apologize by doing something that's not on the list?*

Use your discretion. If the student has a good idea that might benefit others in the future, add it to the list. If you feel the idea is not a good one, refer the student back to the list.

Q. *Where is the limit for using this? Should two students who scream at each other or physically fight be allowed to refer to the act of apology list?*

Not right away. They should go straight to the office for disrupting the class. Our first responsibility is to establish order in the classroom. After there have been consequences, and if and when the disagreement is resolved, one of the students may initiate an act of apology later as a way to repair some of the damage.

Q. *I tried this in my classroom, but it never seemed to get going. How can I bring it to life again?*

The sooner someone tries it after your introduction, the better. And then there is the possibility that you yourself will need to make use of the list to make an apology. That would get things started in a hurry!

After our brainstorming session on ideas for making an act of apology, one of the students created a beautiful poster that had our apology ideas on it. The list hung there, and after a while everyone seemed to forget about it.

One day, as we were discussing a writing assignment, I made a comment about women and men writers to which one of my students objected. We argued our points of view for a short time, then, with the entire class observing with keen interest, I apologized to the student for my statement. She said, "Sorry isn't enough." She may not even have realized it at the time, but she had opened the door to an act of apology from me.

I walked over to the long-neglected chart and silently read several of the ideas. Then, returning to the student, I asked her if I could prove that I cared about making things right by baking cookies for her. "Sure," she said. I told her I'd have some for her the following day. Instantly, other girls declared that my comment had been objectionable them, too.

The next morning, I apologized to each student involved, presenting cookies as an act of apology. They accepted the cookies and my apology, and the restoration of our relationships was complete. That sparked a renaissance of the act of apology process, and it became a common way for students to demonstrate to each other that they were truly sorry for something.

—7th and 8th grade teacher, Minneapolis MN

Stay in the Loop to Achieve Responsible Independence

Many times in this book, we have referred to the Reflective Loop as a tool to help students become accustomed to thinking before and after they do something. The problem-solving structures introduced in this chapter could be thought of as taking time to reflect on what happened, and to plan a path to improvement. Any problem-solving process basically falls into the pattern of the Reflective Loop in that it requires a thoughtful plan, action on the plan, and reflection on the success of the plan as a way to make an even better plan next time.

The motto of this approach to classroom discipline might be, "The unexamined life is not worth living." (Plato's *The Apology of Socrates*) We are trying to develop in our students the habit of thinking before and after they take action in life, to head off trouble and to deal with it effectively when it occurs. When they stay in the loop, they are on the pathway to responsible independence.

PROBLEM-SOLVING: Getting in Gear for Responsible Independence

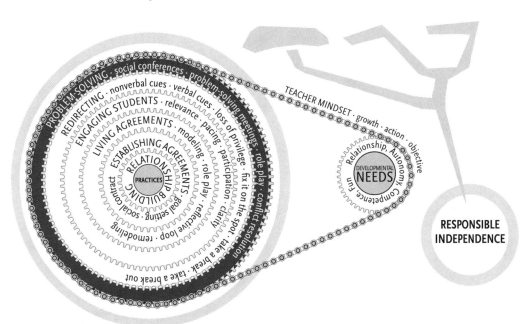

Adolescent Development

The main sources for the following information about adolescent development are *Yardsticks: Children in the Classroom Ages 4-14*, by Chip Wood; *This We Believe*, from the National Middle School Association; and *Teaching Ten to Fourteen Year Olds*, by Chris Stevenson.

PHYSICAL DEVELOPMENT

What are the physical strengths and weaknesses of young adolescents as a group and individually? What are the physical profiles of the students with whom you work?

5th graders: emerging strength and control

Fifth graders are often pretty good at physical activities, and they enjoy a great deal of movement. Without it, they become restless, even boisterous, in the classroom, and concentration suffers. They have strong legs, but still have not developed much upper-body strength. Fine motor skills are good, and fifth graders are capable of assignments that require a good deal of attention to detail, although handwriting may still be loose. They generally have increasing confidence in their abilities, and with practice will develop the skills necessary for hand tools such as compasses.

6th graders: constant movement

There is a huge range in the physical development of sixth graders. Although most have large-muscle development, some are still getting there. There's a constant appetite for movement, which manifests itself in outdoor games and sports, but also in indoor fidgeting and restlessness. Sometimes physicality turns into disorder in which someone can be hurt, or even into aggression. Sixth graders are always hungry, always talking, and they often stay up too late to get the sleep their bodies need. They tend to catch colds and flu and the secondary infections that can accompany them. Their fine-motor skills are well developed, although many still have the sloppy handwriting of younger children. Many of the girls are well into puberty by sixth grade, and just about all sixth graders are experiencing hormonal changes.

7th graders: widespread puberty

High energy is maintained, especially if seventh graders get the large amounts of rest their bodies want. Lots of physical activity, especially group games and sports, and lots of opportunity to refuel with food, are needed. Boys show early signs of puberty—growth spurts, muscle mass, genital changes—and most of the girls have begun menstruation.

8th graders: body self-consciousness

High energy and need for lots of physical movement are still strong, and horseplay among the boys is still common. The girls have pretty much grown to their adult height and are beginning to achieve grace and agility, but the boys, although physically strong, are still awkward. Neither yet has much upper-body strength. Boys' voice changes make them even more self-consciousness, as do complexion problems for both. Body odor, now much stronger, presents new hygiene demands, and neatness can be a preoccupation. Girls and boys both spend increasing amounts of time in front of mirrors, often with increasing anxiety about the acceptability of their appearance. Self-consciousness reigns!

9th graders: loudness and sexual activity increase

The high energy continues (at a higher decibel level), as does the need for lots of physical exercise and frequent food. Boys are still growing, and their upper bodies are beginning to develop. Girls are mostly physically mature, and sexual activity is becoming more common.

Inadequate sleep is still a big issue, but they are less likely to get sick and more likely to keep going even when they aren't feeling well in order to be with friends. Increased drug and alcohol use can do major damage.

SOCIAL-EMOTIONAL DEVELOPMENT

What are the patterns of emotional behavior of your students? Are they worried? Depressed? Anxious? Afraid? Silly? Do they have big mood swings? How much emotional support do they need, want, and get from adults? How does each child navigate the complexities of peer relationships in the middle grades? How well does each get along with family? With adults at school? Is this a popular child? A loner?

5th graders: balance

Ten is sometimes referred to as the last year of childhood, because at this age there is growth, but typically no huge body transitions creating internal uproar, and few criticisms of self and others for not measuring up to real or imagined standards of excellence. Fifth graders, for most of the year, can be pretty satisfied with themselves and life. They enjoy their growing strengths and increasing independence. They tend to remain receptive to adult suggestions, and they get along with most of their peers. They have issues, of course, especially when home life is troubled, but fifth graders have not generally internalized those issues to the point where they give up or freeze into resistance. In the spring, fifth grade girls, who begin puberty earlier than boys, often show signs of interest in cliques and gossip, which can darken the classroom atmosphere.

6th graders: moody

The general feeling of content and sociability of the fifth grader transforms into the highly sensitive, moody, self-absorbed sixth grader who is often either in a funk or angry because something isn't fair, and loves to argue about it. Sixth graders experience wide emotional swings, which are often stronger than they know how to manage. Sometimes this leads to greater interest in hanging out with peers, but also in excluding (cliques), putdowns, and sarcasm. With the adults in their lives it often takes the form of arguments and pushing against limits.

7ᵗʰ graders: peer-orientation

Lots of enthusiasm and uninhibited behavior mixed with growing self-consciousness and identity-seeking are typical seventh grade behaviors. Seventh graders greatly desire peer approval and are empathetic with their friends, while the quest for independence manifests as opposition to the adults around them. Experimenting with sarcasm and language in general can foment skirmishes with adults, as does the search for identity, especially at times when their identity is defined as anything their parents are *not*. Healthy seventh graders basically stay within the parameters adults maintain for them while spending most of their time complaining about those limits and criticizing the people who set them. If the parameters buckle, however, anxiety sets in for the young adolescents.

8ᵗʰ graders: self-consciousness

Self-consciousness and embarrassment peak for many around this time. Eighth graders are frequently scared, touchy, or angry, and some become loners. Dissatisfaction with themselves can become self-destructive. The craving to know who they are can lead them to grab on to associations like cliques or gangs that seem to offer identity definition, or make self-definition seem unnecessary in the face of strong identification with a group. Girls seek close friendships; boys hang out more in groups. Girls are drawn to older boys, rather than the more awkward, less-defined boys their own age. Relationships with parents often hit bottom, and eighth graders will go long periods of time without connecting to family. They critique their teachers harshly and use sarcasm in class. They often don't want to talk to or be seen with parents, or even be at home when their parents are. Instead, they turn to music, T.V., computers, video, or cell phones for constant connection to their world. This is how they gather information about what it means to be cool, popular, good-looking, and desirable.

9ᵗʰ graders: identity emerging

Ninth graders are busy folks, cramming as much into a day as they can. They are beginning to feel that they know something about who they are. They push back against lectures or any other form of domination from adults. They often feel that they already know much of what an adult is saying to them. They are harder on their parents than they are on their teachers, but they often criticize teachers as boring, too easy, or irrelevant. With their strengthened self-concept, they can and do step out into the larger world, and some even begin to negotiate a place in the adult community while they maintain their peer relationships, which are of primary importance in their lives.

INTELLECTUAL DEVELOPMENT

How conceptual can I get in my teaching? What levels of thinking can I expect from my students? How can I teach them to become good problem-solvers, using what they know to figure out what they don't know?

5th graders: knowledge seekers

By ages ten and eleven, cognitive skills have developed to the point where fifth graders generally can organize, classify, and remember information very well. This is an ideal time for accumulating knowledge about the world, science, history, spelling, math facts, and committing poems, scripts, songs, historic addresses, and geographical facts to memory. They have improved concentration skills, and are able to edit work to improve details. Fifth graders are often very curious about the world. They listen, they read with appetite, they notice things and often like to collect and classify them. They like to solve problems. This is a fine age for becoming a peer mediator or joining interest clubs.

6th graders: arguers

Conceptual thinking is now possible, and students can deal with abstractions, but they need practical experiences to construct clear understandings. Ideas interest them, and they are capable of developing hypotheses, making generalizations, and deducing consequences and corollaries from the generalizations. They can quickly get positional, like to argue, and tend to see black and white, but not gray, especially when they uncover a flaw in an adult's statement. Although they tend to grab onto its opposite or the next possibility, they can begin to de-center—with help, they can see from more than one perspective. They tend to go for new projects or experiences instead of working to improve older ones. This makes them somewhat resistant to reflection and revision, the very processes they need to grow socially and academically. They are interested in problem-solving challenges, inventing, novels and biographies that tell of identity-formation, and are up for reasonably challenging tasks, especially ones associated with adult work, like doing research or interviews.

7th graders: sustained work

Seventh grade students show further development of the ability to think conceptually and abstractly, and further growth in being able to see something from more than one point of view. Seventh graders have better organizational skills, more patience for complicated visual-motor tasks, and have the confidence and stamina to plan, organize, and sustain work for a longer time than younger students. Their interest in the wider world expands, especially when they can see the connection to themselves and their peers. They also have the patience to polish their work, and find revision easier and reflection interesting.

8th graders: private workers

Although their abstract-reasoning abilities are strengthening and they are capable of understanding concepts like number or historical patterns and universal social themes, eighth graders' self-conscious inwardness inhibits willingness to reveal their ideas and feelings in public, or to take on challenging intellectual tasks. They are very interested in language, eager to acquire new vocabulary, and readily and easily pick up street-wise ways of speaking, but adults are likely to get one-word answers from them. Parents especially are the targets of rude, loud, and sometimes extreme language at times of opposition to their authority. Eighth graders don't resist revision; in fact, they may take pride in their attention to detail.

9th graders: broad interests

Increased development of abstract thinking means that ninth graders can deal easily with concepts like cause and effect, relationship, or prediction of likely outcomes. They are more interested in nuance and will work to correct errors, try again, or revise a written piece. They like to determine how things work and are interested in technology, math, science, and manual skills, as well as a variety of intellectual challenges such as music, art, psychology, or the problems of the larger world. As they develop beyond the self-conscious inwardness of eighth grade, they begin to work well in groups. Frequent complaints of boredom may have more to do with the continuing distraction of emotions or with social demands to maintain an anti-academics stance, than with actual disinterest.

Assessment

TEACHER SELF-ASSESSMENT

Written Self-assessments

In a journal, we can describe what we do well professionally and what could be improved, and then add possible short- and long-term solutions. Here are some examples:

Sample teacher self-assessment #1

I deliver content very well, and I have very few behavior problems. I don't tolerate any monkey business, and kids don't dare cross the line with me: they know where they stand.

Some students aren't succeeding, though, and there's tension in the room...some seem depressed, and a few are failing. I've tried group work, but haven't been successful: many kids can't handle it. The chaos is too much to bear....I don't know if it's me or what...

Solution, short-term: *I'll shorten my lessons some so I can visit more individual students during work time and try to keep them on track. And I'll start a mandatory after-school study hall for the students who are struggling, so I can give them the help they need. I'm going to stay away from group work, though, for now.*

Solution, long-term: *I'll work some community-building activities into the curriculum and talk casually with the kids more. And I'll teach them HOW to be successful during group work time. I'll need to find some strategies.*

Sample teacher self-assessment #2

Things fall apart in my class behaviorally when I try to give one-to-one or small-group assistance. When I do, the rest of the class' behavior tends to get worse.

But I'm very good at checking in briefly with everyone at the beginning of each period, while we're all still seated in a circle.

Short-term solution: *I'll spend 5-10 minutes each day continuing to check in, reducing the amount of time I offer individual help during work time.*

Long-term solution: *I can problem-solve with students about what we could do to keep them on task even when I'm not watching, and work on implementing the ideas we come up with together.*

Self-assessment Inventory

To create a baseline assessment of your behavior-management capacities, you can begin with a professional-skills inventory like the one below. It addresses what you know, whether you know how to use a particular skill, whether you use it, and if so, how successful you are. To try it out, you can rank yourself on a scale of 1-5, five being the most successful:

I know what makes for a safe, stable, positive professional relationship with my students

I know how to cultivate safe, stable, positive, professional relationships with my students

I have safe, stable, positive, professional relationships with my students

I know what content to teach

I know how to teach content in ways that maximize student learning

I teach content in ways that maximize student learning

Students maximize their learning with me

I know which social skills to teach

I know how to teach social skills

I teach social skills

Students learn the social skills they need

I know which student behaviors are unacceptable

I know how to intervene when I see unacceptable behaviors

I intervene when I see unacceptable behaviors

My interventions are usually successful in getting students back on track

Assessing Student-teacher Relationships

In Donald Graves' book *The Energy to Teach,* he suggests ways to measure the quality and equity of a teacher's relationships with her students. Here is the gist of Graves' process for each class:

1. On paper, create three vertical columns

2. In the left column, write the name of each student in your class

3. In the middle column, write something you know about each student

4. In the right column, write 'yes' if the student *knows* that you know what you wrote about her in the middle column; write 'no' if she *doesn't know* that you know what you wrote or if you are not sure.

Graves' exercise tests the degree to which you are consciously or subconsciously in relationship. You can ask yourself reflection questions and look for patterns:

With which students am I most familiar?

With which students am I least familiar?

What qualities do these groups of students share, if any?

Am I more or less familiar with students I am concerned about?

With whom do I have the most trouble remembering to connect and why?

What types of things did I write in the middle column?

About whom did I write school-related information?

About whom did I write non school-related information?

How many "yes"es do I have in the right column? What does that indicate to me?

Graves would argue that your relationships are strongest with those students for whom you wrote a "yes" in the right column. You were able to write something about them in the middle column, and they know you know it. You must have discussed whatever it was with them, which indicates you have chatted with them at least once.

You can use the results you get from the Graves exercise to identify students who could benefit from some additional conversational attention. Do the exercise for each of your classes. Then, over the next few days, try to hold casual conversations with each of the students for whom you didn't write "yes" in the right column. You might start with those whose middle-column space you left blank, or those you couldn't remember.

Assessing Students' Growth in Social Skills

Here are some assessment approaches used by teachers to assess their strategies for improving social competencies and building a community climate of trust.

Observation, anecdotal note-taking, and tallies of behaviors

The most readily available assessment tool teachers have is observation: you know your students are showing self-control because you see it; you know Carl has been losing his self-control because he has needed several breaks in class every day this week. The more we pay attention, the more we see. That is the quality of "withitness" that makes for attentive teaching.

When we notice the behavior we are tracking, or the lack of it, we can take note. Some carry a clipboard with sticky notes for quick jottings and then attachment to a student's file. Others keep a sheet for each day or each week so they can summarize their notes at the end of the week, and then have weekly summaries to compare to evaluate progress.

A simple tally of the frequency of redirections provides clear information about disruptions. We can focus just on Take a Break, since it requires an explicit response to the redirection and is thus more noticeable. When we are introducing Take a Break, we likely will need to use it frequently until students realize that we mean what we say about small rule-breaking. After a rhythm has been established, however, when the frequency of TAB is up, so is the level of disruption. We don't have to guess about it—the tallies tell us.

A colleague may agree to sit in a class and tally for us or make observational notes. Then we have more than our own perception of the degree of orderliness of the class, and we may also gather detailed information about how some disruptions occur—what happened first, then what followed. None of us, no matter how "with it," can notice every little detail, and the key to understanding is often in the details.

Video and audio recordings

Video and/or audio recording of processes in the classroom allow us to see details we might otherwise miss. Although the camera and microphones can't be directed every-where, they catch a lot where they are focused, and the tapes give us the advantage of seeing both ourselves and our students in action, plus the ability to rewind and review a moment to analyze exactly what went wrong.

Communication requires close scrutiny to catch all the nuance. We can see and/or hear who said and did what and when, and, with video, what the facial expressions and tone tell us about the students' intentions and feelings at the time.

And as for ourselves, no one will ever be as critical of us as we will be of ourselves when we watch and/or hear ourselves. Teachers who have used this process for self-reflection say it is one of the most beneficial things they have ever done, especially when they had practical structures to help them move from what they saw to what they wanted to see. This book describes many of those structures, and the video and audio tapes can help us apply them as needed.

Student surveys

One way we can assess the quality of the climate in our classes is to ask the students. When they are allowed to respond anonymously, we are likely to gain insight into how the students experience the classroom—the degree of order and safety, friendliness and inclusivity, and the quality of social skills exhibited by themselves and others.

Social-climate assessment

There are many formal assessments of student climate. They tend to be thorough, and therefore lengthy. You can make up your own questions and an answer scale to get a snapshot of students' perspectives. Answers can be on a continuum or simply designated as:

Never—Rarely—Sometimes—Most of the time—Always.

Example questions from teachers

Do students in this class listen respectfully?

Do you?

Do students in this class feel safe?

   Do you?

Do students in this class generally follow the rules?

   Do you?

Are most people in this class friendly?

   Are you?

Do you feel accepted by other students in this class?

   Do you show acceptance?

Do you sometimes have fun in this class?

Do you feel comfortable making a comment, sharing, or doing activities in class?

Do you trust your classmates?

   Do they trust you?

Is our classroom free of sarcasm and putdowns?

Can you work with anyone in this class?

Do you feel your voice is heard?

Do you think your teacher respects you?

Do you think your teacher believes you can do the work?

Do you feel comfortable talking with the teacher?

Do you think the teacher wants you to do well?

Do you think your teacher does all s/he can to keep your class safe?

After compiling the results of the surveys, we have source material for a good conversation about how we are with each other and what we might do to make our class a more successful and enjoyable experience for everybody.

Social-skill assessment

Social-skills assessments by teachers and/or students are another survey form that sparks reflection and provides data to monitor social growth. A list of social skills can each have a few criteria for students to self-assess their skill level or for teachers to assess alongside the student evaluation or separately. The Social Skills Rating Scale introduced by Steven Elliot and Frank Gresham (1990) identifies five social skills important to school success: cooperation, assertion, responsibility, empathy, and self-control. These are referred to with the acronym CARES, and can serve as a useful checklist. Responders can indicate how the student behaves in each category: Never—Rarely—Sometimes—Most of the time—Always.

Example describers for CARES skills

Cooperation:

   Finish assignments on time

   Follow directions

Pay attention

Get along with others

Show leadership in groups

Follow well when others lead

Assertion

Introduce myself and others

Start a conversation

Join in

Invite others to join

Volunteer to help

Speak up against unfairness or wrongdoing

Tell an adult when help is needed

Responsibility

Pay attention in classroom, on field trips, in assemblies, and to speakers

Resist peer pressure to break rules

Ask permission to use property

Take care of property

Report wrongdoing

Be on time

Come to class with needed materials

Complete homework and other assignments

Empathy

Give a compliment

Express appreciation for kindness or help

Give sympathy

Offer help

Greet acquaintances, not just friends

Help a younger child

Help an older person

Self-Control

Receive respectful criticism thoughtfully

Show restraint when provoked

Use respectful language

Avoid physical violence

Use cool-down methods to control temper

Example questions from teachers

Consider the following questions from teachers that survey social-skill development more generally.

Do you care about what others have to say?

Do you take an active role working within a group or with the whole class?

Do you offer your opinion in a respectful manner?

Do you offer help when you see someone who needs assistance?

Are you willing to compromise when a conflict arises in a group?

Do you take responsibility for your behavior?

Do you follow the Social Contract?

Interviews with students

For more detailed information, we can use interviews with students. We can choose a handful to follow, and speak with them early in the semester, perhaps mid-semester, and as the semester draws to a close, to see if we have achieved our goals for classroom climate and social behaviors or engagement of students in learning. The interviewees may be selected at random, or we may select some students who generally follow the rules and have good social skills, some who have average skills, and some who seem below average in their social skills.

In the interview, unlike with the surveys, we can ask follow-up questions to get to motivations, explanations of feelings, and clarifications. We may choose to interview students independently or gather them together in a focus group. The advantage of the former is that they do not influence each other's answers; the advantage of the focus group is that they converse a bit among themselves, which may give us greater insight.

What we are looking for in these interviews and surveys is a reality check. What is the experience of students in our classes? What are their perceptions and feelings about the subject, the other students, how things are managed, etc.? The interview does not have the anonymity of the survey, but if we approach our interviewees in a friendly way, making sure they know we can handle negative perceptions and appreciate honest feedback, they will likely rise to the opportunity of having an adult seek, listen to, and respect their opinions. It takes a certain amount of courage to request student feedback, but getting it can provide the information we need to shift our classes into a better climate for learning.

STUDENT SELF-ASSESSMENT

Competency Charts

Middle school teacher Jon Bennet of Paul Cuffey Middle School, Providence RI, uses chart graphics to invite students to identify a set of competencies they possess and convert them to a pie-chart graphic that assigns each competency a percentage of their overall "smartness." When the charts are displayed, classmates can learn about each other's strengths and interests.

Students brainstorm a class list of activities at which they excel while the leader(s) record(s) them. Individual students use the group's brainstormed list to help them create their own list of between five and ten activities they are good at, ranking them in order of the amount of time they spend engaged in each. Students assign a percentage of time they spend engaged in each item on their list in comparison to the other items on their list (not in terms of total time during the day). Using this information, students make large (full page), colorful pie graphs and share them.

After all have viewed the charts, ask students reflection questions. For example:
Based on our observations of these charts, what can we say about our group?
What do you notice about our group's interests and skills?
What connections among us can you see?

Example: Brandon Rowan's chart

40% piano

20% math and science

10% reading and writing

10% soccer

5% communicating with people

5% taking care of pets

4% drawing

2% puzzles

2% solving problems for others

2% fixing technology

Learning Inventories

Academic and social learning inventories help students assess their progress across a variety of specific learning areas. They provide students, teachers, and parents with profiles of student interests, strengths, and weaknesses, and provide a natural segue to formal goal-setting exercises.

Academic learning inventories can be conducted for subject areas, such as reading, math, and writing. Consider the following sample questions.

Reading Inventory

    1. Do you like to read? If so, what do you like to read? If not, why not?

    2. Do you have favorite books? What are they?

    3. Do you have one or more favorite author(s)? If so, who?

    4. What genres of books are you most likely to read these days?

Math Inventory

    1. Do you like math? Why, or why not?

    2. If you were talking to a teacher about your experiences with math so far, what would you say?

    3. What units of math study have you found interesting?

    4. Which math topics have given you the most trouble?

Writing Inventory

    1. Which form of writing do you prefer, creative or expository (fiction or non-fiction)? Why?

    2. Do you write for fun? If so, what do you write?

    3. What do you like about writing? What bothers you about it?

Social learning inventories

You can lead a discussion about social skills such as cooperation, assertion, responsibility, empathy, and self-control, paying particular attention to self-control.

Self-control involves much more than basic impulse control; it includes performance traits like hard work, talent development, excellence, inquiry, flexible thinking, determination, creativity, time management, and organization. Inform students of this broad definition of self-control so they can begin to identify occasions in their daily school lives in which they consistently use or need to develop self-control.

This is one of the first conversations teachers will have with students about their working relationship. Take advantage of the opportunity to emphasize the importance of self-control. In your conversation, you could discuss this quote from Dewey: "The ideal aim of education is the creation of the power of self-control. But the mere removal of external control is no guarantee for the production of self-control." (Dewey 1938, 75)

Alternately, you could tell a story about someone who used self-control to her advantage and/or another about someone who struggled because she lacked it. Be clear that you'll be spending considerable time during the year helping students increase their self-control.

This year, in addition to math, science, reading, writing, art, and all the other areas of learning you'll experience, you'll also be asked to develop five social skills that are critical to success in life: cooperation, assertion, responsibility, empathy, and self-control. The development of self-control in particular will help you direct your best learning self to our daily routines and learning.

Create a working definition of each skill with students; write definitions on the board so all reach an initial understanding of the skills. You may want to provide extra guidance for discussions about the more complex skills of assertion and empathy.

Assertion: getting one's needs met through appropriate actions or speech; the balance point between aggression and passivity

Empathy: the capacity to recognize or understand another person's state of mind or emotion

As in traditional academic subjects, everyone starts this school year with his own set of strengths and weaknesses in these social skills. For example, some of you may already be responsible and have strong feelings of empathy towards others, but may need to work on becoming more assertive. Others may need a lot of work in the area of self-control, but may be pretty cooperative and assertive. When it comes to discipline, you'll be asked to exercise considerable amounts of self-control as we learn the routines of daily life in school and create goals and rules together.

Once these social skills are understood, students use the definition of each to assess the current status of their social-skills development. A simple way of doing this is to ask students to rate themselves by labeling each social skill 'strength,' 'weakness,' or 'not sure,' and tell why.

Example: Brenna's social skill self-assessment

Social Skill	Assessment	Evidence
Cooperation	Strength	I'm good at sharing supplies and working in groups.
Assertion	Weakness	I'm too passive. I let others take the lead, and if I don't agree I stay quiet.
Responsibility	Strength	I always do my homework.
Empathy	Not sure	I feel for others, but if they're being treated unfairly, I stay too quiet.
Self-control	Not sure	I never scream, fidget, or fight, but I need to work on managing time and being determined.

Goals and Declarations

The Transition Back to School: Preparing for goal setting

By Dexter Yee Yick, middle level teacher, Minneapolis MN

Before I ask students to develop their goals and declarations at the beginning of the school year, I engage them in a conversation about the abrupt transition they're being asked to make—from summer time off to school. Regardless of how they've spent their vacation, chances are school life will be a dramatic change for most.

Anticipating this transitional phase, I use our meeting time on our first day to brainstorm with students and create lists of the ways they spent time in the summer. After reflecting on this list, we discuss how they'll be expected to spend their days at school. We look for the differences, name them, and talk about how we can go about getting used to the rigors of school life again. Here is our process:

Summer vs. school year

After forming a circle, we acknowledge as a group that the routines and expectations we live by at home are very different from those at school. I ask students to share reasons why we are governed by different expectations in these two settings. I remind them that our classroom community will become their second home and that we each play a role in shaping it into a healthy and safe one.

To ensure that I reach each student, I let them know that even teachers have to make a transition—from "summer-minded" people with no schedules and no routines to "school-minded" teachers who are responsible for educating young minds. I let them know that they have the power to govern their own actions, but when they are being unsafe, it is my job to guide them back toward responsibility, which, in turn, allows them the opportunity to achieve their goals.

We draw images that represent transformation to further interest students in the idea of change itself: a tea cup morphs into a car; a hammock becomes a school chair; an ice cream cone turns into a pencil. The playful acknowledgment of the demands of life in school really helps set the stage for them to declare specific, attainable goals for the year.

School year routines made real

Finally, we create charts around what school routines might look, sound, and feel like. How will we begin each day? How will we circle up for meetings? What protocols will we use for participating in discussions (hand-raising, calling out, calling on each other)? The more specific I can be with them about appropriate school behaviors, the easier it is to hold them to those behaviors.

This procedure helps my students shift into a school-oriented mindset on a positive, relationship-building note. They see that I care about and appreciate them, and that I have empathy for them. They also see I expect them to make the leap from summer to fall, and that I will insist they do so. After these discussions, students are better prepared to create meaningful goals and to adhere to our rules, rather than push back against them. Most importantly, they are introduced to a new way of thinking, a way to proactively strategize how to be successful at the beginning of any big transition in their lives.

Goal-setting Conferences with Families

Before the conference

As early in the school year as possible—perhaps even before the first day—send home a welcome letter to families. Include a brief explanation of the goal-setting process and a goal-setting form (see example form on page 250). Families and students can preview the form and pencil in some potential goals. To guide families, you may decide to send along sample goals and a simple formula for goal-making. See a few sample goals on page 248 below.

During the first days of school, students complete the goal-setting form in advisory. If families have contributed, their goals can be added. If families have not participated to this point, send completed goals forms home and ask families to comment on the goals listed and how they could support achieving them.

At the conference

The advisory teacher, who is likely to know the student best, can conduct most of the conference. You can allot time for both a substantive talk with the advisory teacher and at least a few minutes with each content-area teacher in a round-robin format. Schools often hold such events in large common spaces, such as media centers, lunchrooms, or gymnasiums, so students and their families can quickly locate teachers. In schools where goal-setting conferences are not part of the established culture, teachers can separately schedule meetings with families of students from any of their classes.

Whatever your relationship with the student, you can begin each conference with introductions. Then provide the family with a brief overview of your experience with the student to date and invite families to share their experiences and hopes as well. Next, review the goals and declarations statements already created in class and/or at home. Students, families, and teachers provide input about initial progress toward the goals, and may suggest changes in the goals themselves.

Invite students to show family members around classrooms and hallways, especially to view recently posted student work and your goals and declarations display.

Determine the purpose of the conference

If the main point is to establish a starting place for learning, to connect to school and the rules-making process, you can focus the goal-setting conference on declaring a stake in the year. Students and families consider goals made in class, expanding or altering them as a way to examine why school matters to them and what the rules are protecting. You are reinforcing an internal locus of motivation for behavior that supports learning. Tell families that you will reflect on the goals with students to support connection to the rules and to school success in general throughout the year. Be clear that the purpose of these goals is not for detailed, ongoing academic or social assessment.

If you plan to revisit and refine social or academic goals throughout the year, clearly define during conferences what the procedure will be. For example, explain that goals forms will be sent home with progress reports and report cards so movement toward the goals can be assessed and families kept in the loop. If your school is committed to this approach, you may wish to allow time for conversations about goals between families and all the student's teachers. The advisory teacher can focus on social growth and provide a gathering place for all goals—a broad, integrated picture of the student—and content-area teachers can provide a closer look at specific academic goals.

Closing the conference

Check for understanding and clarity. You might make a copy of the goal-setting form for each family to take home. Encourage parents and guardians to remind students of their goals now and then. Monday mornings and Friday evenings are natural times to plan and reflect. Goal-setting forms look good affixed to the family fridge!

Commonly-used Goals

Sample math goals

Gain a solid understanding of each new concept

Show all work

Check all work

Seek help when uncertain

Stay caught up

Do extra-credit problems once per week

Look for multiple ways to solve problems

Sample writing goals

Focus on expository writing

Learn how to write an effective introductory paragraph, including a thesis statement

Provide quality examples that directly support your opinions

Pay attention to mechanics, especially proper comma use

Delve into revisions—don't just proof a rough draft and consider it done

Write neatly and legibly

Sample reading goals

Increase comprehension

Read for deeper understanding

Stay focused while reading

Read a wider variety of books, magazines, etc.

Read "between the lines" –implications, ramifications, etc.

Make connections between text and self, text and world, and text and other text

Read faster

Read for enjoyment

Read for 20 minutes each evening before bed

Sample social-skills goals

Keep old friends while making new ones

Improve public-speaking skills

Improve listening in groups

Cooperate with group members during work time

Assert: get needs met without trampling on others

Be responsible: accept responsibility for my actions

Show empathy when someone is in need

Increase self-control: stay focused; resist the urge to blurt

Sample study-skills goals

Improve note-taking skills

Improve test-preparation skills

Designate specific times and spaces for study

Create and adhere to a "homework before free time" policy

Improve report-writing skills

Sample organization-skills goals

Create a system for keeping materials for each class together and in good condition

Hand in all work when it's due; meet deadlines

Record all assignments in an academic-assignment planner

Keep track of pens, pencils, and other materials; arrive at classes prepared

Sample extracurricular goals

Try out for a sports team

Join a band, strings, or orchestral ensemble

Help produce a publication or play

Run for student council

Join a club (chess, debate, math, green, quiz bowl, history day, physics, etc).

Goal-setting Form

Use this form to set goals with students in advisory. There is space for content-area classes, social skills, and an undefined area, which could be used for an additional subject area or extracurricular goal. This form can be sent home before or after completion by students to solicit family input and support for achieving the goals.

My Goals for the Year

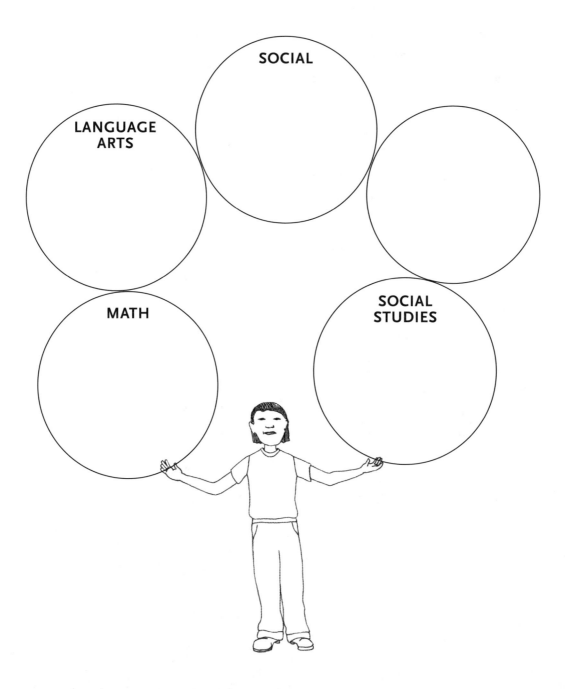

Goal-setting Form for Content-area Classes

Students use this form to write one or two goals and list three steps they will take to achieve the goal(s). Teachers and parents or guardians can also contribute ideas.

Steps to My Goals for the Year

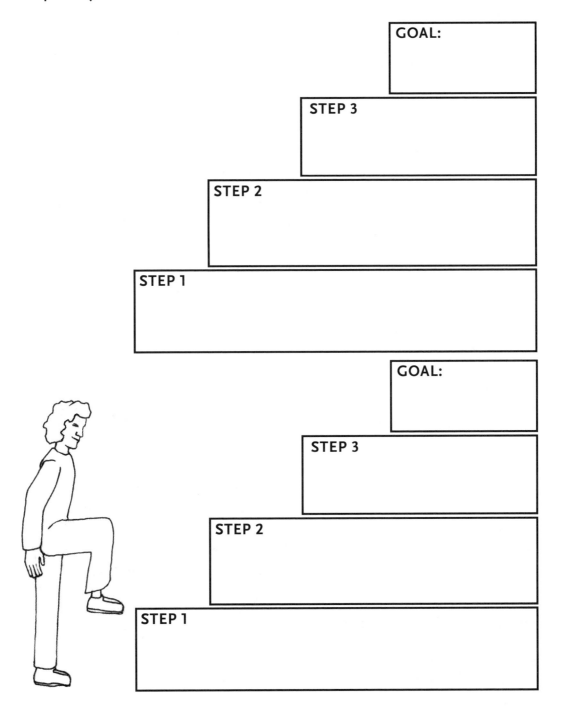

GOAL:

STEP 3

STEP 2

STEP 1

GOAL:

STEP 3

STEP 2

STEP 1

Expanding Student Goals for Academic and Social Growth

Consider the following process to develop student goals into specific goal plans for the purpose of assessing ongoing social and academic growth.

Advisory as the home for students' goals

If possible, all student academic and social goals, wherever they originate, are gathered together in one place. Advisory is the natural place for that gathering. Subject-area teachers or the students themselves can bring subject goals to the student's advisory teacher so the advisor can serve as a knowledgeable supporter for each student's achievement of specific goals. Advisory is also the place to integrate social, organizational, study, and subject-area skills. Pulling everything together in one place assures that at least one adult has his or her eye on the whole student, his goals, and his progress in achieving them. The student's connection with that adult can make a big difference in school success. Using the student-designed goals, teachers can provide steady encouragement to work hard in school all year.

[B]ecause the basic neuronal circuitry of decision-making is still being formed and shaped, parents and other adults who are in touch with and responsible for growing teens are still needed to help guide the process. At a minimum, the data suggest that teens need to be surrounded by adults and institutions that help them learn specific skills and appropriate adult behavior. (Weinberger, Elvevag, and Giedd 2005, 3)

Using goal-setting forms for year-long assessment

From the beginning of the year forward, a goal-setting form is a working document. See pages 250 and 251 for sample goals forms. Hand the students' forms back to them at least once a month to review progress, and update them with revised or new goals at least quarterly. Families can participate in this process: you can send original or revised goals forms home for discussion. They provide families with clear reminders of the goals, and report the progress made toward meeting the goals. Goals and declarations are most useful when they are reviewed and updated at least quarterly, and doing so at home as well as at school is so much the better.

More frequent reflection

Some students benefit from a *daily* reminder of their goals, or may need to set goals for each day. Perhaps a goal is written and posted, or written and kept personal. Perhaps just taking a moment to plan a small step the student can take that day toward a goal is enough. A reminder may involve moving to where the goals are displayed and taking a moment to refresh students' memories, or it may consist of returning completed goal-setting forms to students to remind them of what they hope to accomplish.

If weekly checking in seems realistic, Monday or Friday morning could be goal-checking and reflection time. For example, on Monday morning, ask students to identify a goal and make a specific plan for when and how they will make progress toward the goal within the week. Remind students of their plans during the week. On Friday, ask students to compare their plan with what they did and plan for next time: "What might you do next week to continue making progress toward your goal?"

Some schools include in their regular newsletters to parents an invitation to ask their children about their progress toward a weekly or longer-term goal. The idea is to keep everyone aware of and committed to the goal.

Revising goals

As students fulfill their declarations, new declarations may need to be created. Conversely, if a declaration seems unrealistic, it may need to be altered, or a detailed plan for fulfilling it may be required. If you are an advisory teacher, you can keep tabs on your students and make it your business to find out from colleagues how your advisees are doing with their subject-area goals. And check in with students during your class hours at least every couple of weeks to make sure each one has his or her eye on the goal (and knows that you do, too). You can ask some basic questions:

- *How much progress have you made so far this semester toward your goal? What are some indicators of that progress?*

- *What further progress needs to happen?*

- *Is there anything you need to do that you are not doing, or anything you need to do differently, to improve your chances of success?*

- *How might a teacher help you?*

Remind students occasionally to look at their goals, to review the plans to meet them, make necessary revisions, and then to get back to work, focused on them.

Deepening Connections to School Supports Goal Setting

By Richard Frost, 8th grade history and science teacher, LaCrosse WI, and instructor, Viterbo University, LaCrosse WI

Dr. William Glasser encourages students to ponder what he calls their personal, unique "quality world." For Glasser, examining one's quality world involves thinking about the positive, meaningful connections each of us has made to people, things, ideas, and ideals. "Our quality worlds contain the knowledge that is most important to us.... If what we are talking about is in our quality worlds, we care deeply." (Glasser 1998, 45)

Several years ago, I decided I wanted to help my students put school into their "quality worlds." William Glasser believes, as I do, that if students can be persuaded to do this, they will become more invested in the school community and eventually become life-long learners. He also says we must try to keep students from taking school out of their quality worlds, to persuade them not to divorce themselves from school. Here's one way I've encouraged my advisory students to value school.

Each fall, to begin our discussion of what each of us includes in his/her quality world, I hold a series of three "quality shares" during our daily morning meeting. The three topics are "quality objects," "quality places," and "quality people."

I begin by sharing a quality object, the Tibetan prayer rug I acquired when I lived in India. I lay out the beautifully-colored rug in front of the class and share a short story (1-3 minutes) that includes two important points: why the object matters to me, and how the object has shaped me as a person. I then say, "I am ready for questions and comments." Students are eager to ask questions about the object and its connections. This sets the stage for each student to be assigned a day in which he or she can share a quality object with the class.

Over the next two weeks I introduce a quality place (through pictures and stones from a favorite island) and quality people (through pictures and objects representing a special person) into our sharing. Students again follow with their own shares, conveying why the objects, places, or people are special and how they have been shaped by them. By the third week, students are proficient at engaging, open-ended shares, and my class has built a wonderful sense of community because of the personal thoughts we hear and contribute.

Connecting school to quality worlds

With the stage set, I am ready to aim for my main goal: to encourage students to value school and learning so much that they will include them in their quality worlds. I start by sharing my school-based quality objects. I show students my high-school diploma, my bachelor's-degree diploma, and my master's-degree diploma. Following conversation about and interaction with the object, I hold up my high-school diploma and ask, "Who wants one of these?" They all raise their hands. I remind them that this is why they are here in this school: to learn everything possible, earn a diploma, and be entitled to everything a diploma represents.

I feel that when they raise their hands to indicate they want to earn a high-school diploma, they are endorsing the idea that learning is a worthwhile endeavor, that time at school is to be valued, and that school is indeed a part of their quality world.

Boosting Student Motivation Strengthens Connection to School

In their self-determination theory research, psychologists Richard Ryan and Edward Deci examine intrinsic motivation and the conditions that support its development and growth. For educators, their research considers the critical question: What are the social conditions that create internal motivation in students to learn—to see the social and/or academic learning of school as relevant to them?

Ryan and Deci found that "[P]eople must not only experience competence or efficacy, they must also experience their behavior as self-determined for intrinsic motivation to be in evidence." (Ryan and Deci 2000, 70) Further, the positive address of the need for relationship significantly increases our capacity to invest ourselves in work that is externally driven.

Because extrinsically motivated behaviors are not typically interesting, the primary reason people initially perform such actions is because the behaviors are prompted, modeled, or valued by significant others to whom they feel or want to feel attached or related. This suggests that relatedness, the need to feel belonging and connection with others, is centrally important for internalization. (Ryan and Deci 2000, 73)

Intrinsic motivation is the type most likely to lead to sustained effort, persistence, and growth. (Ryan and Deci 2000, 70) People are intrinsically motivated to do things that bring them pleasure, enjoyment, or internal gratification. Imagine a student who is intrinsically motivated to play the guitar; for him, it is an enjoyable activity. It is performed by choice (autonomy) and he enjoys how he sounds (competence).

All other forms of motivation are extrinsic, and less than ideal; yet teachers well understand that at least some of their students will not walk in the door self-motivated to learn the curriculum. Not all students find math or reading or writing enjoyable activities. However, some external forms of motivation are routinely internalized, which can lead to high levels of positive effort.

From this research, we see that teachers need to draw on positive relationships with students and infuse learning with experiences of autonomy and competence. Ways to apply this understanding to behavior motivation include maintaining student-teacher trust, the trust that we have their best interests in mind and believe in their abilities. From this base of relationship, we can increase choice and independence as students show social-skill growth. We acknowledge their growing competence with increased autonomy. And among many other possible proactive measures, we show students how our management structures encourage the independent resolution of problems with adult assistance as needed.

To understand how to increase academic motivation through addressing these three needs, consider our guitar-playing student: he would rather play guitar than do his math homework. In fact, he seems unmotivated to do almost anything in math class. His math teacher inquires into his interest, and enjoys listening to him describe why he plays, how he got started, and what his goals are for his music-making. In a subsequent conversation, she describes to him the connections between math and music. If she knows music well enough, she shows him how to use math to identify scale and chord intervals, and tells him how important an understanding of music theory is for musician mastery. "The better you get at math, the better guitar player you become, because you're exercising some of the same parts of the brain when you do one or the other."

The teacher showed how the student could extend his feelings of autonomy and competence from guitar playing to math. Seeing the connection, he might choose math to deepen his understanding of music.

Ryan and Deci would call this motivation external: The idea of learning the math came from someone else (the teacher). Although externally sourced, the guitar-playing student's endorsement of the idea encouraged through his teacher's skillful presentation was the key. Once endorsed, the idea begins to be internalized, and the extrinsic motivation moves toward becoming intrinsic.

Stories and Conversations that Inspire Goal Setting

Brainstorming personal purposes of education

During advisory and/or in class hours, ask students to briefly brainstorm reasons for coming to school or for studying specific subjects. Have them write their responses to questions like these in a notebook:

Why are you here? Why come? Why school? Why learn to read for information? Why learn how machines work or plants grow? What's your purpose here? Where are you going with your education? How are school and life connected?

Give students all the information they need to be successful. Sample directions might be:

- you have two minutes
- think and write silently (no talking)
- you'll be sharing your ideas with others after you write
- responses must be stated positively and be school-appropriate
- you may write complete sentences or create a list
- your answers will be used to help set goals later on

Have a pair of students model how pairs should interact, including greeting each other, voice level, listening, body language of speaker and listener, and thanking each other when the sharing session is finished. Then pair all the students, and have them share their responses to the questions

After the sharing, pairs report their ideas to the whole group while you or a student scribe a list of responses on large chart paper.

After a student reads the list aloud, post it. Check for understanding (are there any items on the list that are unclear?), then celebrate.

We have established and discussed what our purposes are. Knowing why we're here will help us as we think about our goals for this year. Let's keep this list in mind as we proceed.

Outside inspiration for goal setting

Discuss an excerpt from a movie or literature or an image you present to inspire hope. Consider the following language, which includes discussion questions designed to be asked after showing the movie "Pride."

We're going to watch an excerpt from the movie "Pride," which is about what it takes to overcome all sorts of obstacles and become successful. Watch carefully: you'll be responsible for knowing what the main characters in the film desired, what got in their way, and how they overcame the barriers to success. I'll ask you for your input, so pay attention.

Check for understanding

What did you notice? What were the characters' goals? What were obstacles they had to overcome? Did they have inner obstacles? What inner qualities did they possess that allowed them to persevere?

Create a link between the spark and students' lives

The movie we just watched included characters who struggled, but once they set meaningful goals and committed to achieving those goals, nothing could stop them. Here we are, at the beginning of a school year. Let's come up with some goals of our own. What are your goals for this school year?

Picture books that inspire courage in goal setting

Let the Celebrations Begin! Margaret Wild and Julie Vivas
As World War II nears its end, women in a concentration camp make toys out of anything they can scrounge, and plan a party to lift children's spirits. Facing post-war hardships, they triumph over them.

Nobody Owns the Sky Reeve Lindbergh
The inspiring story of Bessie Coleman, an African-American woman who overcame daunting obstacles to achieve her dream of flying planes

Knots on a Counting Rope Bill Martin Jr. and John Archambault
As his grandfather counts the many times in the life of a blind Native American boy that he has told the boy's story of growing strength and courage, the boy begins to believe in himself and in the his own courage, despite his handicap.

Zen Shorts Jon J. Muth
In three small stories told to three children, a magical giant panda teaches them to look beneath the surfaces of things for the meaning and rewards we seek.

Salt in His Shoes Delores Jordan with Roslyn M. Jordan
Michael Jordan's parents encourage him to have the hope, patience, and determination to become a basketball player in spite of his short stature as a young boy.

Float Like a Butterfly Ntozake Shange
Young Cassius Clay, later to become Mohammed Ali, decides to become a champion boxer after someone steals his bike. He achieves championship not with brute force but with quickness, bravery, cool, and discipline, ducking and bobbing his way to a gold medal at the 1960 Olympics at age 18. He believes in the possibility of his own excellence.

Harvesting Hope: The Story of César Chávez Kathleen Grull
César Chávez is a shy boy who is often teased at school, but he has the courage to take charge and speak up, and starts a successful movement to organize migrant field workers in California.

Matthew's Dream Leo Lionni
A mouse becomes inspired, which helps him think and behave in extraordinary ways, and he brings beauty to his dreary attic home by creating art.

Display Ideas for Declarations

Peace cranes

By Christopher Hagedorn, former middle level teacher, Minneapolis MN

At Clara Barton Open School in Minneapolis, we decided to use origami peace cranes as the vehicle for our beginning-of-the-year goals and declarations exercise. I was skeptical at first, mostly because I had never taken the time to learn how to make origami art. After learning the various folds and tricky spots, and committing to try the process with my students during the first week of school, I found peace cranes to be a good choice.

Just about every middle level student can fold a beautiful crane if given adequate time to learn—and they really like making them. Students benefit from folding a few practice cranes before making the crane that will be displayed. Thirty minutes to an hour was enough time to teach my class the folds. The students who already knew how to fold or who picked it up quickly taught others in small groups (a good social interaction with a learning goal for the first week). I gave everyone plenty of time to practice.

Before folding the final cranes for display, we gave students the option of making their declarations public or private. If they chose to make them public, they folded their cranes first, and then wrote their goals on them. If they chose to keep them private, they wrote on the back side of the origami paper before beginning the folding, so the goals end up hidden. Each student made two cranes: one for the homeroom advisory class, the other for a school-wide display.

After students had finished making and writing on their cranes, we hung them up. Options for hanging in a classroom included hanging each crane on a thread and hanging it from the ceiling or stringing together several cranes, vertically or horizontally. Our school display was done in a common space that all students use regularly.

The classroom and school-wide sets of cranes remained on display all year, so the time invested in making them look beautiful was worth it. The time we spent practicing and then making the final cranes was very pleasant. We played some background music, chatted quietly while we worked, and experienced a creative, positive mood together—a good beginning for the year.

Goals and declarations process that includes home support

By Lourdes Ramirez, middle level teacher, Hudson MA

For homework on Day 1, I had students ask a family member to share a story about a goal s/he achieved; I began Day 2 with a partner share, in which each partner exchanged information about the story s/he had gathered. In this way, I got families involved with what we were doing, and students learned a little more about family members.

Then I had partners brainstorm a list of things successful students do. "What makes for a good student? What are the characteristics?" Their responses included:

- Study every night
- Ask for help when they need it

- Do homework on time
- Believe in themselves
- Come to class prepared
- Follow directions
- Behave well
- Listen in class
- Be a good sport
- Complete all class work
- Take their time so they do their best work
- Help others
- Stay organized
- Proofread their work
- Show kindness to students and teachers

As we studied the brainstorm list, I asked students to think about areas they struggled with last year. They mentioned things such as homework not done (or it was completed but not turned in), procrastination, test-taking problems, and not bringing to school what they needed.

To help students generate their own set of goals and declarations for this school year, I read the short story "The Back of David's Head" from *Chicken Soup for the Pre-teen Soul.*

Before open house, students wrote and sent home messages containing their goals and declarations, and student-generated suggestions about how parents/guardians could help them accomplish their goals. These ideas included: remind me to check my planner, quiz me, read to me at night (written by a struggling reader), help me get organized, and help me pack a healthy, big lunch each night before school.

We still had to create a set of guidelines within which we would help each other achieve our goals, so I started the process with my advisory group by reading the de Poalo children's book *Swimmy* as a spark. It's about a group of fish who joined together in a school to protect themselves. [More about the *Swimmy* display process is below.] I gave the students pieces of construction paper on which to write their goals. After students left that day, I arranged the pieces in the shape of an arrow on the bulletin board. The funniest thing happened when my students came in the next day: they saw the arrow shape and immediately started telling each other "Look, it's Swimmy! When we swim together we will achieve our goals!" We were now ready to define the rules of our Social Contract to uphold the goals declared!

Swimmy the fish

Use a fish template to create a paper fish for each student (templates are available online). As a spark, read Leo Lionni's picture book *Swimmy*. Each student writes his declarations on a fish. Individual fish are organized to create a big fish. Teacher may choose to write her declarations on a different-colored fish and post it in the eye position.

Gecko tessellations

1. Using several colors of 8 ½" x 11" cardstock, copy a gecko tessellation pattern (see www.originsonline.org Gecko Tessellations). Each student will need only one gecko.

2. Students carefully cut out and tape together one gecko each.

3. Students print their names in large, neat letters in the middle of the gecko's body.

4. They write words that describe their personal assets on the gecko's head, and goals on its forelegs, hind legs, and tail.

5. They decorate the remaining blank spaces on their geckos.

6. Finally, on a large sheet of black bulletin-board paper, students arrange their geckos together to create a tessellation. (Black tends to make the colorful geckos show off better than other colors.)

Begin by affixing a gecko in the middle of the large sheet, then add other geckos around the first one, working from the inside to the outside edge of the paper. The effect is achieved by carefully gluing or taping the geckos together so that arms, legs, heads, and tails fit together tightly.

Rock star

Provide students with templates or stencils for a variety of musical instruments.

1. Students choose an instrument: guitar, bass, drums, keyboard, violin, trumpet, saxophone, microphone, (for vocalist), mixing board (for non-musical "techie")

2. Teachers provide construction paper and stencils or patterns, and students cut out the shapes of their instruments. Sizes can vary; a final shape somewhere between 3" x 6" and 5" x 8" is ideal. There needs to be enough room to write declarations, but the displays are to remain

up all year, so avoid working too large: you'll need the wall space for other things!

3. Students carefully draw essential details of their instruments to make them identifiable (keys, strings, etc), leaving room for their declarations.

4. Students neatly write their declarations on their instruments. Remember to frame it so they include academic, social, and study-skills declarations.

5. Students take a final opportunity to color/add detail to their instruments.

6. Instruments are displayed on the classroom wall. The teacher may choose to surround the instruments with a stage or music store design to give the display context.

Poetry booklet

Students create booklets containing their declarations. To make one without staples, tape, or glue, follow these instructions. Use a large (8 ½" x 14" or 12" x 19") piece of white paper.

1. Fold in half, three times: Orient paper in landscape (hot dog) direction. Fold up (in half). Keep crease at bottom. Fold in half, left to right, and again, left to right.

2. Unfold paper completely. Orient paper in portrait direction. Fold up (in half). No new crease will be made.

3. Starting at closed crease, bottom center, use scissors to cut to center of paper, where creases intersect. (Note: if scissors aren't available, students may carefully tear along fold line to center intersection)

4. Unfold paper completely again. Orient paper in landscape (hot dog) direction. Fold up (in half). Crease at bottom should be open along its middle, but intact along its left and right sides.

5. Grab left and right quadrant. Hold horizontal, with the cut crease facing your torso. Leave center two quadrants untouched. Gently push/guide/manipulate quadrants so middle two (those with cut crease) separate at top and bottom, forming a diamond shape you can see through. Outside quadrants remain folded, closed, and horizontal.

6. Magic step: Continue to gently push, guide outer two quadrants towards each other, collapsing the diamond shape. Fold book shut. (Note: this final step is a bit awkward the first time you do it.)

You now have a booklet that includes a cover page, six interior pages, and a back cover. Cover page can be used for a title, e.g., *Roger Smith's Declarations for 7th Grade at Lincoln Middle School*. The remaining pages may be used for academic, social, study, organizational, and or extracurricular declarations. Books may be decorated to taste and displayed.

Four-flap

Students write declarations under flaps and post them on a bulletin board.

1. Students create their four-flap displays using a colorful piece of construction paper or tag board. Orient paper in landscape (hot dog) direction. Fold down, but not quite in half: leave approximately one inch of bottom half of paper uncovered by top portion.

2. Use scissors to cut three straight slits in top half (shorter half) of paper. Start cutting at open end of top half. Stop at crease. Slits run perpendicular to crease and should be evenly spaced so they create four flaps out of top portion of paper. When finished, orient paper in landscape position, with crease on top.

3. Along bottom inch of paper not covered by flaps, student writes her name and title (e.g., *Kitty Carlisle's 2008 Declarations*)

4. The four-flap paper construction is now ready to be used to display declarations in a variety of ways. For example:

   Students write a core academic area on each flap top (language arts, math, social studies, science).

   On reverse side of each flap, students write one or two social skills goals for each academic area indicated.

   Underneath each flap, students write one or two academic goals.

Time capsules

Declarations are sealed in individual or class "time capsules," and opened at the end of the year (periodic references to the capsules are necessary to keep the spirit of them alive)

Seeds

Declarations are written on small strips of recycled paper and planted in the ground along with seeds of perennial plants. The resulting plants become surrogate declarations. Visit them frequently for watering and cultivation. Keep weeds and pests (obstacles to success) away!

Fortunes

Declarations are written on small strips of paper and placed inside a hollow-bodied clay figure. The figure is glazed and fired. At the end of the year, it is broken open, revealing the declarations. Discussions follow: the declaration was written long ago, but you have incorporated it into who you are today.

Trees

A large leafless tree, including its roots, is drawn and posted on the wall. Sun and rain are added to the drawing. Students write their goals on small strips of paper and place them along the roots of the tree. Then they write what they'll do to achieve their goals on separate strips and place them near the sun or water. Throughout the year, they add leaves to the tree whenever they take steps toward meeting their goals.

"Recipe for Success"

Students use a basic recipe to organize their declarations into a recipe for success. Consider this example using a banana bread recipe.

Banana Bread	John Jackson's Recipe for Success
2 eggs, beaten	2 years of organizational skills progress
cup buttermilk	cup of determination
½ cup vegetable oil ⅓	½ cup focus ⅓
1 cup mashed bananas	1 cup positive attitude
1 ½ cups white sugar	1 ½ cups participation
1 ¾ cups all-purpose flour	1 ¾ cups assignment completion
1 teaspoon baking soda	1 teaspoon self-control
½ teaspoon salt	½ teaspoon new friends
½ cup chopped pecans (optional)	½ cup extracurricular activities (optional)

John's biggest areas needing growth (organizational skills, assignment completion, participation, and positive attitude) became the largest ingredients. Areas in need of minor tweaking (for John, self-control and creating new friendships) receive the smallest amount of ingredients.

More declarations cooking

Students could expand the exercise (and practice using a variety of verbs!) by writing a paragraph describing how they'll combine, add zest, and cook (grill, mince, chop, mix, whip, stir, knead, blend, broil, separate, sift, freeze, peel, heat, add, dice, blanche, fold, beat, chill, boil, pluck, roll, grease, pinch, scoop, steam, bake, fry, grind, toast, julienne) their ingredients to create a successful school year.

Example:

1. Separate homework assignments and predict how much work time and effort will be required for each.

2. Fold ½ cup of focus into each assignment. Go for deep understanding. Concentrate.

3. Blend in 1 cup of positive attitude before, during, and after homework. Remember how good I'll feel when I'm finished, and have done well.

4. Stir 1 teaspoon of self-control into the work. Don't get up in the middle of working on each assignment

5. Chill with my friends when I'm done!

Recipes are placed on traditional index cards and affixed to a bulletin board entitled, for example, "Cookin' with Room 208," or "Mr. Hemming's Class Bakes Up Success." Students may add photos or drawings of gourmet delicacies and optional baking or cooking steps.

Social Contract

Forming and Using the Social Contract

One teacher's story adapted from Origins' *Developmental Designs* newsletter

Jennifer Gavrin Klein, a middle grades teacher at the Greenfield Hebrew Academy (GHA) in Atlanta, Georgia, uses engaging, relevant activities to link student behavior to GHA's Social Contract. GHA students and teachers first create classroom Social Contracts, then work with the whole school community to refine these contracts into a school-wide contract. Jennifer feels her students need to construct their own understanding of what a Social Contract is before they can be expected to abide by it. To guide them to such an understanding, she leads her students in a free-association word activity in which they write as many words as they can that relate to what "social" and "contract" mean to them.

During one such activity, her students came up with the following list for the word *social*: "our grade, Ms. Seffrin, not in cliques, friends, talking, socialize, hockey, spending time together, social life, socialize, Adam, CPR, lunchtime and recess, swimming, 6th graders, kids/teenagers, adults." Then Jennifer had students produced associations for the word *contract*: "paper you sign, Declaration of Independence, big document, dictionary, mortgage contract, agreement, peace treaty, bill, law, court, music contract, signature, quill pens, important people, tax bills, parcel."

Reflecting on this word-association process, Jennifer said, "It is hard to not feed words and ideas into the students, and let them truly come up with their own genuine thoughts. I try to assign myself the job of a scribe and nothing more during the brainstorming part of the process." When she feels students may be getting off track, she facilitates the discussion more actively, taking care to not reveal her interpretation of the words.

After the class compiles its free-association lists, Jennifer facilitates a conversation about the lists, leading them toward a working definition for *Social Contract*. Finally, she and the class work together to formulate a concluding statement:

We might say, then, that a Social Contract is an <u>agreement,</u> something like a <u>peace treaty, written on paper we all sign</u>, that we'll use like a set of <u>laws</u> that will help us to become independent. We—adults and kids alike—will use it to guide the time we spend together, as we <u>socialize and talk</u>: in <u>our class, our grade, at lunchtime and recess</u>, etc. It will help us all be <u>friends</u>, and will help assure that we <u>not form cliques</u>.

The final rules within Jennifer's school's Social Contract came to be:

- Uphold an appropriate classroom environment
- Be responsible
- Show *Kavod (respect* in Hebrew)

Using the Contract

Jennifer seeks ways of allowing students to assess the degree to which the entire community is living according to the rules laid out in their Social Contract. One strategy is to create and distribute to students a simple survey. It asks students the following questions to assess the degree to which teachers, other students, and they themselves are living by each of the Social Contract's rules:

- To what extent are you being responsible?
- To what extent are your classmates being responsible?
- To what extent are your teachers being responsible?

Direct questions like these allow her to unearth potential challenges in upholding the contract, thus granting Jennifer and her class the opportunity to amend any problems.

When they are completed, Jennifer collects the surveys and tabulates the results. The data she gets for each category provide her and her students with a starting point for conversations about the status of the Social Contract.

On a scale of 1-10, with 10 being the most successful, Jennifer's students produced the following average scores:

- students being responsible 7.14
- classmates being responsible 6.71
- teachers being responsible 9.64

Using the data, it appears that students saw their teachers being very responsible, while they saw themselves as being fairly responsible and their classmates slightly less responsible. With this data, Jennifer and her students were able to engage in conversations about several topics:

- noticing responsible behaviors
- recognizing irresponsible behaviors
- maintaining responsible behavior
- changing irresponsible behavior
- reflecting on why one's own behaviors are assessed more positively than classmates' behaviors
- following responsible, contract-abiding teacher models

Words guide actions

Jennifer now has several ideas about how to help students do better when it comes to following the Social Contract's rule about being responsible. If students have mentioned that they have been wasting time by not responding quickly to the signal for quiet, they (and Jennifer) may choose to remodel and practice how that procedure works. If they notice that their teachers show responsibility by being ready with their lesson when the bell rings, students might brainstorm ways to arrive on time and ready to learn.

Cultivating and Celebrating the Rules

By Tracy Lysne, middle level teacher, Hudson WI and Minneapolis MN

When I was a classroom teacher, the way I approached rules was very similar to the way I garden. Let me explain!

In late winter, as the weather begins to warm, my thoughts turn to planting. I think about what I want to grow this year, and I buy the seeds. When the threat of frost wanes, I carefully till the soil and plant my seeds. I stand over my freshly planted garden and water it as I contemplate the harvest that lies ahead. "So far, so good!" I say to myself.

Then my garden sits. Plants grow slowly. I get busy with other things. I see my garden out of the corner of my eye each day as I rush by. Sometimes I forget to water it, causing the plants to droop and falter. I don't weed as often as I should; when I get around to it, the weeds are sometimes far more plentiful than the vegetables. Pulling them out becomes a real chore.

Although I sometimes forget daily maintenance, like weeding, I still get lots of vegies come harvest time, but they are not as beautiful as they might have been, nor as tasty.

Opportunities for cultivation

At first, my approach to classroom rules was similar. On the first day, my students and I thought about the year ahead. We shared our goals and created rules we felt would help us reach those goals. We looked at our social contract and thought to ourselves, "So far, so good!" before signing our contract and posting it on the wall. And there the rules remained, drooping and sagging, neglected, except when things went *so* wrong that we were forced to turn to the rules to resolve big issues. If I forgot the daily maintenance, weeds grew quickly. Sometimes I missed opportunities to cultivate and celebrate the rules—to make them truly proactive, as they are meant to be.

Growing the students

Why do many students dislike rules? One reason is because we call attention to them only when things go wrong, so they see them as negative—a big drag—and to be discussed only when the teacher is disappointed or mad. This prompted me to think about what I could do to make them a positive part of our classroom, and to lead students to live by them more proactively. I needed to cultivate and celebrate our rules on a daily—even hourly—basis, so they could begin to see them in a positive light. I needed to help my students think about what we were doing well, and how living by the rules helped us succeed. I also wanted to use our Social Contract to set goals for what we needed to do better.

Ideas for cultivating and celebrating classroom rules

Dots: "I Rock, We rock"

At the end of the class period give each student two sticky dots of different colors. Have them place one colored dot on the rule they followed well that day and the other on what they felt the class as a whole did well that day. Have a few students share specific examples.

Dots: "I need to grow; we need to grow"

At the beginning of the class period (or before a work time), give each student two sticky dots. Have them place one dot on the rule they will concentrate on that day and one dot on what they feel the class needs to concentrate on that day. At the end of the period check in and have a few students share about what they noticed.

The box

Provide a box, into which students can anonymously slip written examples of others' behavior whenever they see someone "living the rules." Naming students observed is optional. Place the box near the social contract. From time to time, pull out a slip and share it with the class and celebrate!

Touch someone who

Use the acknowledgment activity Touch Someone Who, but tailor the categories to your class rules/Social Contract. For example, "Touch someone who showed *respect* during advisory meeting," "Touch someone who showed *responsibility* by having their homework done," or "Touch someone who *treated others fairly*," etc. (See www.origin-sonline.org for a description of Touch Someone Who.)

Secret friend

At the beginning of the week or class period, students randomly draw a partner. Tell them to watch their "secret friend" that day or week, noting examples of how they see their friend living the rules. At the end of the day or week students acknowledge their secret friends by sharing what they noticed and how it connects to the class Social Contract.

Partner share

Students pair up and share one rule they are going to work on during class. Partners brainstorm things they need to do to live out that rule. Tell them to watch one another and plan to quickly check in with each other at the end of the period. What did they notice? What were some examples of their partner living the rule?

Personal check-in

At the end of the class period, do quick self-assessments of how well the rules are being honored. Read each rule and have your students think about it before they give themselves a thumbs-up or a thumbs-down. You could do this privately (behind a notebook) or for all to see.

Note to self

Each student receives a Post-it note and writes a quick note to him/herself, naming a rule they are going to live by that period. At the end of the period, they assess themselves and note an example (or evidence), writing both on their Post-it. This note becomes their "ticket out the door." Collect all tickets.

On target

Create a target symbol on paper. Choose a rule for the class to work on (or one gleaned from one of the above activities). Talk about what the rule means and what it looks like to live it. At the end of the period give each student a dot and have them place the dot on the target showing where they felt they were that day. Were they on target or did they miss the mark?

It takes effort to change

At the start of a class period, invite students to read the rules. Have them select the rule they believe will be the most difficult to follow during that period. Then invite them to predict how much *effort* it will take to successfully live by it. On a scale of 1 to 5 (5 representing the most effort), students may write their predictions in their academic planner. At the end of the period, students look at their predictions and assess how much effort was actually required to follow the rule selected.

I noticed

Name it! If your students are doing something well, don't forget to say so. Be specific: let them know what you are seeing, how it reinforces the rules, and the impact the positive behavior is having on your classroom and learning. This can be done spontaneously in the flow of learning, or at specific times such as at the start or close of class. *I'm seeing a lot of peer-to-peer support during our work today. People are helping each other with ideas and encouraging each other.*

Spontaneous celebrations

Have a party! If your students have been living the rules, why not have a party to celebrate? However, don't dangle the carrot ("If you behave according to the rules for the next two weeks, we'll have a pizza party."); this is a recipe for resentment. Students don't want to be manipulated, but they love surprises and celebrations.

Reap what you sow

I wish I'd known about all these strategies (and the importance of making positive connections to the rules on a daily basis) earlier in my teaching career. After years of teaching students and adults, and observing classrooms in which students feel the rules are only brought up when they're broken, I have become convinced that you'll have a more bountiful harvest—a more successful school year—if you do daily rules maintenance. The key is getting into the habit of making proactive, positive connections to your social contract. Teach students to see the rules positively, as desirable, as guideposts; to "live the rules" and reap the benefits of knowing that good rules help everyone learn and grow. Happy cultivating!

Modeling

Routines to Model

Responding to the signal for quiet

Entering the classroom

Reading and responding to the daily news message board

Listening

Heading papers

Greeting a classmate

Shaking hands

Moving chairs, desks, or tables

Being ready to learn

Sharpening pencils

Tagging a member of the other team

Moving around the room during activities

Paying attention during large-group lessons

Taking notes

Raising hands and waiting to speak

Asking for help or clarification

Asking a probing question

Obtaining a bathroom/hallway pass

Getting a drink

Getting materials

Handing in papers

Recycling paper or scraps of paper

Working independently

Working in pairs

Working in a small group

Positively asserting oneself in a small group

Reminding a classmate to pay attention

Seeking help from a classmate

Sharing an idea

Reflecting on learning

Collecting and storing learning materials

Asking for input from a classmate

Acknowledging a classmate

Thanking a member of the community

Leaving the classroom

Hallway behavior

Eating in the lunchroom

Modeling safe tagging

Begin by modeling and practicing forming a circle in large spaces as well as in the classroom. Stand a few yards from students and call "Circle up!" Give the signal for quiet, and time the students to see how quickly they form a circle as described above. After practicing it once or twice, students should be able to quietly circle up in ten seconds or less.

Gather in a circle where the tag game will be played. Students and teacher should stand evenly apart around the circle, facing the center.

1. Elicit ideas from students

We'll be playing lots of tag games during the year. Why is it important to develop a method for tagging—to come up with some tagging rules?

Sample student answers:

So no one gets hurt while we play.

So we know how and where to tag each other.

So we agree on one-hand or two-hand tag.

So we don't argue about whether someone was tagged or not.

2. Demonstrate the right way

Select one or two student to demonstrate tagging with you. Walk through the process with the student(s), staying inside the circle so all can see clearly. Make sure everyone involved in the demonstration models tagging (and getting tagged) correctly. The modelers need to know where to tag, how to tag, how hard to tag, and what to do after getting tagged.

Watch carefully as Sharon and Stephen demonstrate the fine art of tagging. They're going to show how we need to tag each other safely and fairly, which I'll insist on. I'll be asking you what you noticed in a moment, so have an answer ready. Any questions? OK. Here we go.

3. Notice the details: how behavior fits rules

Thank you, Sharon and Steve. Raise your hands and wait until I call on you if you have an answer to these questions: What just happened? What did you notice about how Sharon tagged Steve? Think about our Social Contract: how does tagging the way Sharon and Steve just demonstrated support our school-wide rules?

Sample student answers:

Sharon tagged him with one hand.

Her tag was firm enough for him to feel, but not too hard.

She tagged him on his upper back, by his shoulder blades.

She was in control of the rest of her body; no other contact occurred.

Steve stopped and froze after Sharon tagged him.

They didn't argue about whether she tagged him; they were quiet.

4. Practice

Pair up students and have them practice the tagging and freezing technique they just saw. Make sure they move slowly; they aren't playing yet, so catching up to someone shouldn't be necessary. No running, dodging, or feigning in this practice.

Now let's all try. I'll number you; remember your number. Find the person who has the same number as you, then take turns tagging each other, and freezing when you get tagged, exactly the way you saw Sharon and Steve model it. We're just practicing how to tag right now, so when you're not the tagger, don't try to avoid it: just freeze when you feel it.

5. What-if's

Address potential obstacles to successful, rule-following play. For example: *What if you're not sure whether you've been tagged?*

We're going to institute a rule called 'Tagger's Choice.' With this rule, the tagger's word is final. We're trusting the tagger to make the call, and expect him to be honest. If the taggee isn't sure whether she's been tagged, and therefore doesn't freeze, the tagger simply shouts out "I gotcha!" if she did tag her, and the taggee must freeze. Remember, no arguing over a tag. If you argue, you'll have to sit out a round.

Let's play. Remember the Tagger's Choice rule. We'll talk about how well we did when we finish.

During play, teacher carefully monitors tagging, making sure students tag and freeze according to the model. If she sees rule-breakers, she may ask them to sit out for the duration of the game or interrupt the game and remodel, or, if things are not going well at all, end the game.

Follow-up to reinforce and check in

Circle up and reflect on the degree to which players followed the tagging model. Students can offer individual, verbal responses, or the teacher can elicit nonverbal assessments (thumbs up, thumbs sideways, thumbs down; fist of five, etc.)

How did we do? How well did we follow the model Sharon and Steve gave us for tagging?

What can we do next time to make our tagging go more smoothly?

Sample student answers:

We can add more taggers so it isn't as hard to catch up to the taggees.

We can remind the taggers to yell 'I gotcha!' loudly enough to make it extra clear to the taggees that they were caught.

Taggees need to freeze more quickly, and not take a few extra steps before stopping.

Modeling the signal for silence

The signal for silence needs both a visual and an auditory component. The two can be modeled, discussed, practiced, and implemented in the first days of the year. By raising a hand and watching her students as they respond, a teacher establishes a clear guideline about what's to come next: a time when everyone must pay careful, silent attention. Also use an auditory signal for silence—a certain word or phrase, bell, rhythmic clap, or chime—for times when students are likely not to notice the visual signal alone.

1. Elicit ideas from students

Ask the class to generate a list of reasons why responding quickly to a signal is a good idea.

In class this year, why will it be important to respond quickly to our signal for silence?

Sample student answers:

So we can get more done.

So we won't miss any important information.

So we use our time well; it's important because everyone has a right to hear the teacher and you can't hear very well when people are talking.

2. Demonstrate the right way

The teacher demonstrates the signal (e.g., hand up, eyes on students, body and feet still, positioned in a place where most students are likely to see her). Then teacher demonstrates responding to the signal. Student playing the teacher raises his hand, and teacher looks at him, keeps her body still, puts down what she has in her hands, and waits silently.

Watch me carefully as I respond to the signal Anthony will give me; in a moment, I'm going to ask you what you saw.

3. Notice the details: how behavior follows rules

What did you notice about the way I responded to the signal?

Take a look at our Social Contract for a moment. How does responding to the signal the way I did support our agreements?

Sample student answers

You stopped talking.

You looked at the person giving the signal.

Your body was still.

You remained quiet.

You responded quickly.

Our contract says we need to respect each other, and it's respectful to be quiet when someone needs to talk to the class.

4. Practice

Practice the signal with the class. Have students strike up a conversation with a neighbor. After a few seconds, raise your hand and keep it raised until all students are quiet, still, and looking at you. Time them. Tell them how long they took. Repeat the process.

That took eight seconds. Let's try it again. How quickly can we respond? Let's find out.

Now that we know we can do this in a few seconds, I'll be expecting a quick response each time the signal is given, whether it's by me or another person.

5. What-if's

Discuss with students the potential problems with the signal, such as when the visual signal isn't enough, or when a student is speaking with someone.

When your backs are turned, for example, or when you're working around a table in small groups, or concentrating so hard that you don't see a signal, I'll use an auditory signal—something you can hear—to let you know it's time to sit up and pay attention.

Follow up

Check in with students later in the class and in the next few days to measure the level of implementation and provide reminders.

How well did we respond to the signal during the meeting? On a scale of one to five, five being the best score, what do you think?

What can we do to respond even more quickly next time?

What might we do to politely remind someone to respond if we notice a classmate isn't paying attention?

Redirecting and Problem-solving

Addressing Needs through Problem-solving Social Conferences

Meeting the need for relationship

When a student fails to use the opportunity to fix her own mistakes and you notice her seeking the attention and approval of one or more classmates at the same time, perhaps her real need is relational: she may be looking to improve her relationships but hasn't learned how to do so in appropriate ways. You may be able to provide her with better ways to build relationships with her classmates, including

- assigning her to work in small groups with people you think would be positive influences for her

- putting her in the spotlight in positive academic or social situations, so her need for attention is met

- allowing her to show what she's learned through use of drama

- calling on her at random more frequently during large-group discussions, to keep her attentive and make sure she gets small but regular moments of attention

- giving her chances to sit with whom she chooses, but only if she follows the rules

It looks like friendships are very important to you, Gretchen. I love being with my friends, too. If you can handle the privilege of choosing where to sit and follow our Social Contract while you're with your friends, great! But if and when I redirect you, you have to show me that you can change your behavior, or I'll have to move you someplace else. Let's see how things go tomorrow. I know you can do this.

We're using her powerful need for relationship as leverage as we move her toward responsible independence. The choice is hers.

Meeting the need for autonomy

A second needs-based reason why a student might be wasting her chances to fix her own mistakes may be power-related. By requiring her to do something—even if what she's directed to do is clearly good for her—you are taking some of her power, which may cause her to resist. To fix this, try giving her some constructive power.

Think of a fun, challenging, unique thing to turn over to a student in need of power, and consider framing it so the power she's granted is in some way helping you to improve your teaching. This models a desire to improve, by sharing your growth mindset with your students. Make sure that you coach the student so she doesn't over-power others or become bossy, and alienate them.

- Put her in daily classroom leadership situations she can handle. These could be academic or social. Think of ways she could become a "teaching assistant" for you or for a teacher of younger students. Put her in charge of attendance, collecting homework, distributing papers or materials, leading a class meeting, leading a quick stretching exercise mid-class, leading the signal for silence, writing assignment reminders on the board, etc.

- Get into the habit of asking for her opinion during class discussion time.

- Get her interested in Student Council.

- Invite her to think about careers that require leadership, and introduce books, articles, or Web sites that explore qualities or frames of mind good leaders need. Then invite her to try using some of these at school.

- Encourage her to join community-based clubs, extracurricular activities, and then to become a captain or officer within the activity she chooses.

I once put a power-struggler in charge of monitoring my speech for verbal tics, which she was then to report back to the class; she started listening carefully, and I quickly became motivated to clean up my speech patterns! When I had reduced my "likes" and "okays" down to near zero, we celebrated my improvement and the student's vigilance.

—Middle level teacher, Minneapolis MN

Another tack to take with a power-seeker is to circle back to comments you made when you introduced reactive strategies to students in the first days of school. You will have said something about how empowering it is to be able to have regular opportunities to fix one's own behavior, about how when students work closely with their teacher to fix student mistakes, the resulting increased self-control, problem-solving ability, and resilience will launch students to responsible independence. Remind the whole class of these thoughts. Power-seekers might hear you better the second time; if not, at least you'll have paved the way for a one-to-one conference with the student which you may need in the future.

Meeting the need for fun

A third need she might be seeking to fill by refusing to be cooperative is *fun*. It might seem like fun to refuse, watch the teacher get upset, and see what happens.

During a conference, point out to the student that his fun is in defiance of the Social Contract, and, therefore, the entire class. He needs to find ways to have fun that do not interfere with learning. You can help him think of possibilities. And you can even try lightening up your redirections of smaller offenses a little playful. Some teachers are able to use a light, cheerful touch when they catch rule-breakers, but still manage to insist that all students fix their mistakes.

One thing that might come from such a problem-solving conference is your agreement to try to provide him—perhaps everyone else—more opportunities to have fun in class in the form of games or jokes or student performances, either as a part of a lesson or during brief breaks. (See *The Advisory Book* and originsonline.org for many ways to build fun into the academic day.)

Meeting the need for competence

Another important need that may be involved when students repeatedly resist is competence. Some students experience redirects as a sign of failure, so when they receive one they withdraw, and have trouble getting back on track. The student digs herself into a deeper hole with each failure. We need to help her get out of her rut, to help her begin to feel that she's capable, even though she makes mistakes.

Students who lack a sense of competence need small successes, with lots of reinforcement and encouragement from you. This is best accomplished when one specific behavior is selected for attention. For example, if your redirects aren't working for a student who consistently blurts out, focus on that behavior and choose a redirect for it. Confer with the student about your plan. Whenever a significant amount of class time passes without the mistake, let the student know you notice she's succeeding, and have her acknowledge the success she's having.

Redirect her as you said you would when she forgets. Redirects can be subtle and positive, as can acknowledging her successes: quick eye contact, an unobtrusive thumbs down or up in her direction, or jotting a quick note to her: "In the last ten minutes, your comments have been relevant to the subject, and you've raised your hand and waited to be called upon. Do you notice this?"

Meeting Student Needs

The message is: *I accept you and your needs, but not the behavior you are using to satisfy your needs.*

When students are...	and you feel...	try this
Clowning, blurting, showing off, pestering, people-pleasing	Annoyed Irritated Pestered Burdened Guilty	BUILD RELATIONSHIP: Give student special jobs in classroom (e.g., paper-passer, attendance-taker). Give student time to share, tell a joke. Let student teach part of a lesson or demonstrate. Let student scribe notes on overhead or board. Assign a special desk. Set up nonverbal cues between you and student. Notice changes in his/her appearance or behavior. Ask questions about personal life; sports, hobbies, etc.
Oppositional, contrary, stubborn, disobedient, argumentative, untruthful	Provoked Threatened Dominated Defeated Angry	BUILD AUTONOMY: Give choices about where to work, what materials to use, how to represent what has been learned. Have student share an interest or hobby. Ask student to lead the class in a game. Let student be the one to demonstrate. Ask student for his/her opinion.
Stealing, lying, getting even, feeling sorry for self	Hurt Disappointed Nervous Victimized Angry	BUILD RELATIONSHIP AND COMPETENCE: Listen to expressions of feelings without judging. Acknowledge student's feelings. Get to know students better. Provide scaffolds to academic success. Have student practice asking for what s/he wants. Discuss options other than getting even; mediate conflicts. Teach centering/calming practices.
Using sarcasm, making fun of people, pranks, fidgeting, inappropriate joking	Annoyed Irritated Pestered Angry Frustrated	INCREASE FUN: Offer interesting choices for student work. Offer choices for where and with whom to work. Play both academic and silly, zany games. Sing, dance, move, and stretch. Tell jokes, riddles, and puns. Dramatize history, literature, science, math. Draw while you teach.
Giving up, avoiding work, setting unrealistic goals, putting self down, discouragement and wanting to be left alone	Frustrated Discouraged Inadequate Self-pitying A desire to rescue	BUILD COMPETENCE: Treat student as if s/he is capable and growing. Notice small improvements. Set small hourly goals. Teach in small blocks. Give easy assignments to practice skill of completion. Have student reflect on progress made. Encourage and walk away. Check in often to note progress.

Student Reflection Form for Take a Break Out and Back

What did you do that broke our agreements?

_____

_____

Put a check by the rule that you did not follow:

School Rules:

_____Respect ourselves and each other

_____Work hard to do your best

_____Take care of our school and supplies

What need do you have that you were trying to meet when you broke the rule(s)?

_____I wanted to have some fun and relax.

_____I was trying to be noticed.

_____I wanted to be in control.

_____It's not fair—I wanted to get even.

_____I needed help.

_____I wanted people to like me.

_____Other: _____

What will you do to meet your needs in a more appropriate way?

_____

_____

_____

_____

_____

Do you need help from anyone else? ☐ Yes   ☐ No

 If yes, what support do you need, and from whom?

_____

_____

What action(s) might you take to repair any hurt or damage?

_____

_____

Sign: (Student)   Date:

_____

Sign: (TAB Out monitor or Behavior Room Teacher)

_____

Sign: (Class Hour Teacher)

_____

More Stories that Reflect on Behavior

Tell real-life stories of struggle and growth to seek student endorsement of the work of building self-control.

Wherever you are in life you're going to need self-control to be successful. There will be times when you'll have to summon strength from within to face something difficult, to do something that doesn't interest you, to put in extra time and effort necessary to make something extra wonderful for someone you care about, to work on something you don't want to work on because you're not good at it, but you understand that the skill is important.

Story: Learning to drive

When I was learning to drive, I had trouble with parallel parking. I knew that I would have to parallel-park the car during my driving test, so I practiced it many times. I used my powers of self-control to focus on parallel parking, even though I felt it wasn't the most important part of driving. I drove my mom crazy and wore the tires down by scraping them against the curb. I passed the test, though! I used my self-control to make it happen.

Scenario: Applying self-knowledge

Let's say you know enough about yourself to know that you need to get up and do something physical every 20 minutes or so to be successful at school. Knowing that about yourself, and coming up with a plan between you and your teacher that will accommodate that need, is an example of using self-control. The benefits of having that type of self-control are huge: you'll concentrate and learn better during the time you dedicate to school work. The plan may ultimately help you get into the college of your choice in a few years.

Story: "Pride"

Showing movie clips in which characters bounce back from difficult events and persevere is another way to build resilience in the face of redirections. For example, from the movie "Pride," show the approximately 12-minute segment in which the inner-city swim team from Philadelphia goes to its first meet in the suburbs, expecting to breeze to victory, but gets crushed instead. On the way back to the city, rather than showing disappointment or caring, they fool around and laugh, as if the swim meet didn't matter to them. Their coach comes down hard on them, telling them not to come to practice the next day unless they take it seriously.

The coach expects most of the swimmers will quit the team, but instead, they all show up early for practice the next day. When the coach walks into the pool area, his team is waiting for him on the starting blocks; they're quiet, serious, intensely awaiting his orders. They're even wearing the uniform swim trunks he hadn't been able to talk them into wearing before!

The swimmers didn't quit. They thought about it and made a decision to refocus, redouble their efforts, and try harder. Highlight this moment. Talk with students about:
- the importance of listening to adults who have your best interests in mind

- the importance of not giving up
- the importance of bouncing back after an embarrassing moment
- the importance of being serious when it's time to be serious

It's OK to stay strong and not crumble when someone (a caring adult in your life, like a teacher, para, or administrator) wants to help you improve your behavior. Controlling your language has important benefits. Hang in there, stand tall, accept the wisdom your teachers have for you about academic learning and social skill-building.

Sometimes you say you won't sit by this boy or that girl, that you won't shake hands with X or greet Y, that you can't be in a group with this person or that person. These are not the ways we want to be, according to our Social Contract. We made our rules, and they demand that we try harder to be respectful. The rules aren't just for when it's easy to abide by them; they are for everyone, all the time. When we feel like living smaller than our rules, that's when we have to rise to our own expectations.

Behavior Management beyond the Classroom

Middle schools, junior highs, and high schools thrive when the adults who staff them work well together. It takes high-level teamwork to keep a community of adolescents learning and functioning smoothly, and teamwork depends on three basic school-wide elements:

Establishing and maintaining good relationships

Establishing and maintaining purposes and agreements

Responding to rule-breaking consistently and respectfully

These elements are important to the well-being of every school; in schools where students move from room to room all day, they are essential to the success of the school. If students experience positive relationships with peers and teachers in some classrooms and not in others; if routines are practiced in some rooms and not in others; if standards for behavior differ from room to room, the pathway through the school day is strewn with misunderstandings, episodes of alienation, confusion, and misbehavior. This is partly because adolescents explore and sometimes push against the status quo, and partly because in an environment of inconsistency, students must make frequent shifts to align with changing expectations.

Because student experience is school-wide and incidents occur that require adult response beyond the classroom, the adult community needs to make school-wide expectations, climate, routines, and responses to rule-breaking as clear and consistent as possible. *Classroom Discipline* is about the management practices necessary to create an orderly, productive, engaged learning experience for adolescents in the classroom. School-wide issues are largely outside the scope of this book, but the following provides a quick look at strategies for creating consistency in discipline throughout the building and for use when interventions are necessary by behavior staff, administrators, or security personnel. All of these practices depend on the adults in the school working with each other and with students harmoniously, consistently, and with trust.

Establishing and Maintaining Good Relationships

Collaborating with colleagues

The adult community constitutes the framework within which everything happens in school. The way adults communicate with each other verbally and nonverbally sets the tone for the school environment. The degree to which we come to know our co-workers and the ways we communicate with them shape the context and set the example for the entire culture of the school.

Healthy adult communities in schools rarely occur spontaneously. Schools purposely form teams, hold team and staff meetings, and create learning communities as ways to establish and nurture connections. When a student knows that every teacher is committed to her success, both when things are going well and when they are not, and when she experiences a rigorous and consistent response to rule-breaking, then she can confidently settle into responsible behavior. Team meetings are important forums for discussing individual student needs. They are opportunities to share what's working and seek help with what's not.

Like student bodies, staffs are diverse in life histories, lifestyles, politics, religions, class, ethnic backgrounds, primary languages, and affinities. We must make our adult community the foundation of a positive environment for teaching and learning.

Creating guidelines for the adult community

The adult community's expectations for itself need to be clear. Every year, we need to express our goals for our work with young people and our goals for our work together. We need to declare our individual intentions to help our goals live in our school, and we need to establish guidelines for our adult community that will guide us toward our professional goals.

Once the guidelines have been created and agreed upon, we need to plan how living them will look, sound, and feel as we work together day after day. The more concrete the plans, the more real and valuable the guidelines will become. Our guidelines and plans become the framework of our professional community—what we are collectively up to and how we have agreed to treat one another. We agree that when our actions fail to live up to our guidelines we will nudge each other back on track with honest, non-judgmental communications that do not reflect or create resentment. Then we can welcome students into the clear, fresh air of our school community and reasonably expect them to participate positively.

Creating positive student-teacher relationships school-wide

Students are much more likely to participate positively in the school community if they experience good relationships with adults. Adolescents are constantly watching for whether they are liked and respected, and when they sense that they are, their minds and hearts are more likely to be open to our guidance. The challenge for each of us is finding time and opportunity for relationship-building interactions with individual students. When can I have interactions with students that will increase my knowledge of who they are, help me to become a real person in their eyes, and let them know that

I truly care about their welfare? When can we talk?

Advisory is one of the richest opportunities for relationship-building. When schools provide a time each day or several times a week for students to meet with adults to talk about their lives, address problems, and play and laugh together, everyone gets to know everyone else better. Our advisory students frequently become the students we manage best in other settings, simply because we guide from the base of our strong relationships with them. Coaches and adults who direct after-school clubs have a similar opportunity to establish relationships with students. And eating lunch with individuals or groups of students can be the beginning of the end of loneliness or alienation.

Other opportunities such as one-to-one social conferences, even brief ones, can establish connection, share information, and nurture trust. Social conferences to problem-solve rule-breaking behavior can strengthen relationships between adults and students, and a good conflict-resolution process can repair damaged relationships among students. All-team and all-school meetings, although they lack person-to-person intimacy, allow everyone to get to know each other better, especially when they are centered on student work and projects, and led at least partly by students.

Frequent opportunities for building community with our students occur in small moments of interaction—as students enter or leave our rooms, encounters in the hallways and other shared spaces, crossing paths before or after school, or at after-school events. Each little moment provides time for a smile, a high-five, a "how's it going?" Knowing the names of our students, and using names often, strengthens connection. Let no student in our community have a whole day pass with no one saying his name in a casual, friendly way!

An effective teaching mindset

None of this is easy. The developmental stance of adolescents is full of impulsivity, lacking in the judgment to monitor those impulses, and fueled by a constant urge toward autonomy and the various, often inappropriate versions of what they call fun. A steady, consistent stand among adults requires a mindset that refuses to take things personally, steps up to all opportunities for guiding students on the right path, and continues to believe in students' desire and capacity to succeed, regardless of evidence that suggests the contrary. The stronger the positive mindset of adults who interact with adolescents, the more likely the adults can help them succeed.

Establishing and Maintaining Purposes and Agreements

Just as the adults in the school need agreements about their goals and plans, students need to name and invest in their personal reasons for being in school. They also need to create guidelines that will give everyone the best chance to succeed with their goals. None of this happens simply by wishing; creating school-wide guidelines shows that as a community, we promise ourselves order and safety.

Creating group agreements school-wide for students

Individual goal-setting can happen in advisories and subject-area classes, as can the establishment of a few broad rules for everyone. To bring those multiple sets of rules together into a set of school-wide rules is a step toward a consistent, clear framework for everyone, everywhere in the building, all day long. Since an important portion of each day occurs between classes and in shared spaces, having one set of guidelines that everyone knows, understands, and can remember is extremely helpful, especially when that one set is created by the students themselves, with the guidance of adults.

The Constitutional Convention is the name we give to the collaborative process of merging the rules from separate advisories into one school-wide set. See page 76 for more information.

School-wide definition of living the agreements

After school-wide rules are established for students, staff can come to a collaborative decision on how those rules will look in daily school life in classrooms and common areas such as the lunchroom and playground. They can decide together the protocols and routines important to moving through the day smoothly, design just what those routines should look like, and agree that every teacher will introduce and consistently reinforce the rules and routines by having students model and practice. This way, teachers create a clear process that everyone can learn, eliminating confusion and the wasted student effort of having to learn different protocols for different classes.

Example: Signal for silence

Once the staff has agreed on a signal to call for silence and focus on the speaker, everyone can introduce, practice, and consistently use that signal in classrooms and in shared spaces. The signal will take on an automatic quality, as it, along with the other routines, is reinforced all day, every day, by everyone.

Responding to Rule-Breaking Consistently and Respectfully

Respect and consistency from classroom to classroom

The staff can agree on how they will re-direct students when they stray from the rules, and on the processes they will all use to help students problem-solve when they fall into patterns of repeated rule-breaking. They can design a protocol for responding to students for whom taking a break in the classroom is not enough of a change of pace to move them from disruptive behavior back to learning within the community. They may, for example, support each other with a system that uses a change of scene from one classroom to another as a way to redirect a rule-breaking student (in our approach, this supporting structure is called Take a Break Out and Back). They may design a way of recording incidents of disruption or of having students do written reflections to focus themselves and create the right mood for a return to class.

A staff may collaboratively establish methods for responding to misbehavior to help a student change direction, including guidelines for welcoming the student back into the classroom so it's clear that the teacher cares about her and believes that she can grow. Teacher language can be defined to use certain phrases consistently, avoiding sweeping praise or criticism, sarcasm, or judgment, using instead specific, neutral descriptions of student behavior. The adult community can agree to daily seek out opportunities to reinforce positive behavior through acknowledgments, and decide on ways to facilitate students' acknowledging each other for kindnesses and courtesies, peer-to-peer support being a potent motivator and pro-social behavior.

A consistent teacher mindset

All of these things that staff can decide upon and consistently use must be nourished by attitudes that support students: refusal to take things personally, and insistence that all students want to and can succeed in school, and commitment to do everything we can to help that happen. A staff working in common for the good of all is a formidable support for student success.

Respect and consistency beyond classrooms

There are times when despite all the consistent routines practiced and reinforced throughout the school, and all the processes for responding in the classroom to disruptive behavior, some students need help beyond what classroom teachers can provide. When students are a danger to themselves or others, or when they cannot or will not regain self-control by taking a break in their own or another classroom, other interventions are necessary.

A behavior room can be carefully designed to create a non-punitive environment in which students can experience the support they need to restore themselves and return to their classrooms. It can be structured by a process that includes cooling down, honest reflection with the guidance of an adult, and the creation of a plan for changing behavior. In some schools, the office is the designated place to bring students who are out of control.

Out-of-control students always need an adult to accompany them to the designated space, since at that point we cannot rely on them to behave responsibly. The walk to the designated place is an opportunity to support the de-escalation process. A conversation with the upset student about something other than the trouble he is in at the moment, even if that "conversation" feels more like a monologue on the adult's part, can be useful in focusing the student's attention on something more neutral and calming than the mess he is in. Asking, "Did you watch the game last night?" says that all is not lost, life goes on. It says "I don't hold anything against you personally, and I care enough about you to want to ease your mind, or at least distract you a little."

The walk back to the classroom provides time for the accompanying adult to prepare the student for re-entry into the classroom. The conversation can help focus him on his goals and what he must now do to achieve them. It gives the message that the adults in the school believe in his capacity to set things right.

Schools can involve families when patterns of behavior first emerge that require assistance from the office or the behavior room. Teams often identify a need when a student is struggling with behavior before a visit to the office is required, and designate one person to connect with the family. It is easier to invite families into a partnership to assist the student when the problem is smaller. Conversely, families might well be upset by being first contacted after a problem has escalated. The school staff always communicates caring and a belief in the student's capacity for success.

Every school must establish protocols for discipline beyond the classroom that in extreme cases may include security guards, law enforcement, restraints used by trained staff, and removal from school. All such protocols must include a chain of responsibility that makes it clear who is next in line to step in to manage an out-of-control student, and accountability for such actions. The protocols also include informing families and enlisting their support during and after the incident. Re-entry into school includes family support in the return process, which requires honest reflection and planning for future success.

The more we establish and consistently uphold together the rules and routines that are necessary for a healthy school community, the less often incidents of out-of-control behavior will occur. When they do occur, we will do what needs to be done. At such times, it is more important than ever that we are motivated by belief in each young person's capacity to straighten himself or herself out, with help as necessary, and an abiding respect for the great effort it takes to do so.

REFERENCES

Aesop. 1947. The Boy Bathing. In *Aesop's fables*. Kingsport, TN: Grosset & Dunlap.

Anderman, Eric M., and Martin L. Maehr. 1994. Motivation and schooling in the middle grades. *Review of Educational Research* 64 (2): 287-309.

Bandura, Albert. 1997. Self-efficacy. In Vol. 4 of *Encyclopedia of human behavior*. Ed. V.S. Ramachaudran, (4): 71-81. New York: Academic Press.

Berman, Sheldon. 1997. *Children's social consciousness and the development of social responsibility*. New York: State University of New York Press.

Blackwell, Lisa S., Kali H. Trzesniewski, and Carol Sorich Dweck. 2007. Implicit theories of intelligence predict achievement across an adolescent transition: A longitudinal study and intervention. *Child Development* 78 (1): 246-263.

Boyer, Susan, and Penny Bishop. 2004. Young adolescent voices: Students' perceptions of interdisciplinary teaming. Ed. David Hough. *Research in Middle Level Education* 28 (1): 1-19.

Bryk, Anthony S., and Barbara Schneider. 2003. Trust in schools: A core resource for improvement. *Educational Leadership* 60 (6): 40-45.

Bushweller, Kevin. 2006. Student motivation: What works, what doesn't. *Education Week* (August 30). http://www.edweek.org/chat/transcript_08_30_06.html.

Canfield, Jack, Mark Victor Hansen, Patty Hansen, and Irene Dunlap. 2000. *Chicken soup for the preteen soul: 101 stories of changes, choices and growing up for kids, ages 9-13*. Deerfield Beach, FL: Health Communications, Inc.

Charney, Ruth. 2002. *Teaching children to care: Classroom management for ethical and academic growth, k-8*. Turners Falls, MA: Northeast Foundation for Children, Inc.

Collaborative for Academic, Social, and Emotional Learning (CASEL). 2003. *Safe and sound: An educational leader's guide to evidence-based social and emotional learning (SEL) programs*. Chicago: Author.

Comer, James P. 2005. Child and adolescent development: The critical missing focus in school reform. *Phi Delta Kappan* 86: (10): 757-763.

Crawford, Linda. 2004. *Lively learning: Using the arts to teach the k-8 curriculum*. Turners Falls, MA: Northeast Foundation for Children, Inc.

———. 2008. *The advisory book*. Minneapolis: Origins.

Deci, Edward L., with Richard Flaste. 1995. *Why we do what we do*. New York: Penguin.

Dewey, John. 1909. *Moral principles in education*. Boston: Houghton Mifflin.

———. 1938. *Experience and education.* Indianapolis: Kappa Delta Pi.

Dreikurs, Rudolf, Bernice Bronia Grunwald, and Floy C. Pepper. 1998. *Maintaining sanity in the classroom: Classroom management techniques.* New York: Taylor & Francis.

Dweck, Carol S. 2007. The perils and promises of praise. *Educational Leadership* 65 (2): 34-39.

———. 2007. *Mindset: The new psychology of success.* New York: Ballentine Books.

Elliott, Stephen, and Frank Gresham. 1990. *The social skills rating system.* Circle Pines, MN: American Guidance Service.

Fall, Kevin A., Janice Miner Holden, and Andre Marquis. 2003. *Theoretical models of counseling and psychotherapy.* New York: Brunner-Routledge.

Gladwell, Malcolm. 2005. *Blink: The power of thinking without thinking.* New York: Little, Brown and Company.

Glasser, William, M.D. 1969. *Schools without failure.* New York: Harper & Row.

———. 1998. *Choice theory: A new psychology of personal freedom.* New York: Harper-Collins.

Goleman, Daniel. 2006. *Social intelligence: The revolutionary new science of human relationships.* New York: Random House.

Graves, Donald. 2001. *The energy to teach.* Portsmouth, NH: Heinemann.

Jensen, Eric. 2005. *Teaching with the brain in mind.* Alexandria, VA: Association for Supervision and Curriculum Development.

Johnston, Peter. 2004. *Choice words.* Portland, OR: Stenhouse.

Kamii, Constance. 1991. Toward autonomy: The importance of critical thinking and choice making. *School Psychology Review* 20 (3): 382-388.

Kohlberg, Lawrence. 1981. *Essays on moral development.* New York: Harper and Row.

Kohn, Alfie. 1993. *Punished by rewards: The trouble with gold stars, incentive plans, a's, praise, and other bribes.* New York: Houghton Mifflin.

Kounin, Jack. 1970. *Discipline and group management in classrooms.* New York: Holt, Reinhart and Winston.

Libbey, Heather P. 2004. Measuring student relationships to school: Attachment, bonding, connectedness, and engagement. *Journal of School Health* 74 (7): 274-283.

Makkonen, Reino. 2004. Advisory program research and evaluation. *Horace* 20 (14): 11-13.

Malecki, Christine Kerres, and Stephen Elliott. 2002. Children's social behaviors as predictors of academic achievement: A longitudinal analysis. *School Psychology Quarterly* 17 (1): 1-23.

Marlowe, Bruce A., and Marilyn L. Page. 1998. *Creating and sustaining the constructivist classroom.* Thousand Oaks, CA: Corwin Press.

Marzano, R.J. 2003. *Classroom management that works: Research-based strategies for every teacher.* Alexandria, VA: Association for Supervision and Curriculum Development.

Marzano, R.J., D.J. Pickering, D.E. Arredondo, G.J. Blackburn, R.S. Brandt, C.A. Moffett, D.E. Paynter, J.E. Pollock, and J.S. Whisler. 1997. *Dimensions of learning: Teacher's manual.* 2nd ed. Alexandria, VA: Association for Supervision and Curriculum Development.

National Middle School Association. 2003. *This we believe: Successful schools for young adolescents.* Westerville, OH: National Middle School Association.

Nelsen, Jane. 2006. *Positive discipline.* New York: Ballantine.

Oliner, Pearl M. 1988. *The altruistic personality: Rescuers of Jews in Nazi Europe.* New York: Free Press.

Palmer, Parker. 1998. *The courage to teach.* San Francisco: Jossey-Bass.

Payton, J., R.P. Weissberg, J.A. Durlak, A.B. Dymnicki, R.D. Taylor, K.B. Schellinger, and M. Pachan. 2008. *The positive impact of social and emotional learning for kindergarten to eighth-grade students: Findings from three scientific reviews.* Chicago: Collaborative for Academic, Social, and Emotional Learning (CASEL).

Power, F. Clark, Ann Higgins, and Lawrence Kohlberg. 1989. *Lawrence Kohlberg's approach to moral education.* New York: Columbia University Press.

Rogoff, Barbara. 1990. *Apprenticeship in thinking: Cognitive development in social context.* New York: Oxford University Press.

Ryan, Richard M., and Edward L. Deci. 2000. Self-determination theory and the facilitation of intrinsic motivation, social development, and well-being. *American Psychologist* 55 (1): 68-78.

Sheets, Rosa Hernandez and Geneva Gay. 1996. Student perceptions of disciplinary conflict in ethnically diverse classrooms. *NAASSP Bulletin* 80 (580): 84-94.

Sousa, David. 2005. *How the brain learns.* Thousand Oaks, CA: Corwin Press.

Stevenson, Chris. 2002. *Teaching ten to fourteen year olds.* Boston: Allyn & Bacon.

VanDeWeghe, Rick. 2006. What is engaged learning? *English Journal* 95 (3): 88-91.

van Manen, Max. 2003. *The tone of teaching.* Ontario: Althouse.

Vygotsky, L.S. 1934. *Thought and language.* Cambridge, MA: MIT Press.

Wallis, Claudia. 2004. What makes teens tick. *Time* (May 10): 56-64.

Weinberger, Daniel R., M.D., Rita Elvevag, Ph.D, and Jay N. Giedd, M.D. 2005. *The adolescent brain: A work in progress.* Washington, D.C.: The National Campaign to Prevent Teen and Unplanned Pregnancy.

Wolfe, Patricia A. 2001. *Brain matters: Translating research into classroom practice.* Alexandria, VA: Association for Supervision and Curriculum Development.

Wood, Chip. 2007. *Yardsticks: Children in the classroom ages 4-14.* 3rd ed. Turners Falls, MA: Northeast Foundation for Children, Inc.

York-Barr, Jennifer, William A. Sommers, Gail S. Ghere, and Jo Montie. 2001. *Reflective practice to improve schools: An action guide for educators.* Thousand Oaks, CA: Corwin Press.

ABOUT THE AUTHORS

Linda Crawford is the Executive Director of Origins. She has taught at every grade level from kindergarten through graduate school. She was principal of an arts-integrated elementary school for five years, and has led professional-development seminars and workshops for educators for nearly thirty years. She is co-founder of the *Developmental Designs* approach to integrated social and academic learning for adolescents. She is the author of *To Hold Us Together: Seven Conversations for Multicultural Understanding; Lively Learning: Using the Arts to Teach the K-8 Curriculum*; videos on multicultural education through the arts; and numerous articles and books on the integration of social and academic teaching and learning. She has a BS in English Education from the University of Wisconsin and an MA in English Literature from the University of Minnesota.

Christopher Hagedorn is a *Developmental Designs* consultant, workshop facilitator, and writer. He taught middle school English in Indianapolis, Indiana; high school English in Quito, Ecuador; and middle school language arts in Minneapolis, Minnesota. He implemented many of the teaching practices described here. He has led professional-development workshops for educators for nearly ten years. He has authored numerous articles and other teacher-related materials, including guidelines for *Developmental Designs* training. He has consulted in secondary schools in 17 states and the District of Columbia. He has a BA in English from the University of Minnesota and a MS in Secondary Education from Indiana University.

INDEX

DEVELOPMENTAL DESIGNS®

An integrated approach to social and academic learning

This book was developed through the work of Origins, a nonprofit educational organization, and its research-grounded approach to teaching known as *Developmental Designs*. The *Developmental Designs* approach offers practical structures designed to keep young people safe, connected, responsible, and engaged in learning. Because many adolescents struggle to focus on work or to manage assignments or to generally exercise the self-control needed to learn, they are not likely to succeed in school unless someone consciously teaches them social and emotional skills. Teachers use *Developmental Designs* structures to help young people learn how to learn.

DEVELOPMENTAL DESIGNS TEACHING PRACTICES

Community-building Advisory—The Circle of Power and Respect (CPR) and Activity Plus (A+) are meeting structures for building community, social skills, and readiness for learning.

Goals and Declarations—Students declare a personal stake in school to anchor their learning in a meaningful commitment to growth.

Social Contract—Based on their personal goals, students design and sign an agreement that binds the community to common rules. Its principles are modeled and practiced every day.

Modeling and Practicing—Social competencies are learned by seeing and doing. Nothing is assumed; all routines are practiced.

Reflective Loop—Ongoing, varied reflective planning and assessments ensure continuous, conscious growth.

Empowering Teacher Language—Gesture, voice, and words combine to create a rigorous, respectful climate for building responsible independence.

Pathways to Self-control—When the Social Contract is broken, teachers have an array of strategies, such as redirections, fix-its, loss of privilege, and Take a Break. Social skills grow without loss of dignity.

Collaborative Problem-solving—Students and teachers use social conferencing, problem-solving meetings, conflict resolution, and other problem-solving structures to find positive solutions to chronic problems.

Engaged Learning Strategies (including Power Learning)—Social interaction, experiential learning, choice, exhibition, reflection, and other practices help connect young adolescent needs and the school curriculum, so students are deeply engaged in learning.

Power of Play—Play is designed to build community, enliven students, and restore their focus, ensuring more time on task.

LEARN MORE ABOUT
THE DEVELOPMENTAL DESIGNS APPROACH

Professional Development Opportunities

- One-day, half-day, and 90-minute overviews
- One-day follow up workshop
- Week-long workshops: *Developmental Designs* 1, 2, 3, and Building Academic Communities Through the Arts
- Classroom and school-wide consultation providing on-site training, implementation coaching, and support for school-wide sustainability

Publications and Resources for Middle Level Educators

- Other books from Origins supporting the *Developmental Designs* approach: *The Advisory Book: Building a Community of Learners Grades 5-9* and *Greatest Hits! Tried and True Games, Greetings, Shares, and Tributes.*
- Free newsletter with articles by classroom teachers and *Developmental Designs* consultants
- Free, informative e-notices supporting *Developmental Designs* implementation
- Website with articles, teaching ideas, and other information: www.OriginsOnline.org

For details, contact:

Ӝ ORIGINS

3805 Grand Avenue South
Minneapolis, Minnesota 55409

612-822-3422 / 800-543-8715
Fax: 612-822-3585
www.OriginsOnline.org
Origins@OriginsOnline.org